THE IDEA OF THE CITY IN ROMAN THOUGHT
From Walled City to Spiritual Commonwealth

LIDIA STORONI MAZZOLANI

THE IDEA OF THE CITY
IN ROMAN THOUGHT

FROM WALLED CITY TO
SPIRITUAL COMMONWEALTH

Translated from the Italian by
S. O'DONNELL
with a foreword by
MICHAEL GRANT

Civitas est in civibus non in parietibus
ST. AUGUSTINE
Sermo de urbis excidio, VI, 6

HOLLIS & CARTER
LONDON   SYDNEY
TORONTO

ACKNOWLEDGMENTS

Extracts from the works of Cicero, Livy, Caesar, Plutarch, Sallust, Tacitus and a number of other Latin writers are here reproduced in English by kind permission of The Loeb Classical Library and Harvard University Press. Extracts from the works of St. Augustine are here reproduced in English by kind permission of T. & T. Clark, Edinburgh, publishers of the Rev. Marcus Dods' edition of The Collected Works of St. Augustine.

L'idea di città nel mondo romano
© Riccardo Ricciardi Editore, Milan, 1967
English translation © Hollis & Carter Ltd. and Indiana University Press 1970
Foreword © Michael Grant 1970
ISBN 0 370 00339 x
Printed and bound in Great Britain for
Hollis & Carter Ltd
9 Bow Street, London w c 2
by C. Tinling & Co Ltd, Prescot
Set in Intertype Baskerville
First Published in Great Britain 1970

CONTENTS

List of Abbreviations Used in the Footnotes, vi
Foreword by Michael Grant, 7
Author's preface, 11
Introduction, 16

   I. The Views of the Conservatives, 25
  II. Gradual Advancement of Subject Races and
       Lower Classes, 34
 III. Cultural Factors and the Ecumenical Idea, 49
 IV. Gradual Penetration of New Ideas, 62
   V. Foreign Religions, 68
  VI. The Precedent of Alexander, 82
 VII. From Sulla to Augustus, 99
VIII. Augustus, 125
  IX. The Idea of Rome Gains Precision, 142
       1. Roman Reaction to Greek Disparagement, 142
       2. Roman Reaction to the Religious and
          Social Demands of the East, 152
   X. Rome as the City of Mankind, 173
  XI. 'The World Made Stable', 182
 XII. Social and Economic Disintegration, 201
XIII. Spiritual Factors in the Crisis, 218
XIV. The City of God, 242
       Bibliography, 281
       Index, 283

LIST OF ABBREVIATIONS
used in the footnotes

Am. J. Philol.   *American Journal of Philology*
Cl. M. St.   *Classical and Medieval Studies*
Cl. Rev.   *Classical Review*
Cl. Quart.   *Classical Quarterly*
Cod. Th.   *Codex Theodosianum*
C.I.G.   *Corpus Inscriptionum Graecarum*
C.I.L.   *Corpus Inscriptionum Latinarum*
Diss. Pann.   *Dissertationes Pannonicae*
Harv. Th. Rev.   *Harvard Theological Review*
H.A.   *Historia Augusta*
H.E.   *Historia Ecclesiastica*
J.R.S.   *Journal of Roman Studies*
Mél. Arch. Hist.   *Mélanges d'Archéologie et d'Histoire*
Mél. Cumont   *Mélanges Cumont*
Mél. Glotz   *Mélanges Glotz*
Mem. Am. Ac. R.   *Memoirs of the American Academy in Rome*
M.G.H.A.A.   *Monumenta Germanica Historiae Auctores Antiquissimi*
P.G.   *Migne, Patrologia Graeca*
P.L.   *Migne, Patrologia Latina*
Rend. R. Acc. L.   *Rendiconti della R. Accademia dei Lincei*
Rev. Arch.   *Revue Archéologique*
Rev. Et. Anc.   *Revue des Etudes Anciennes*
Rev. Et. Lat.   *Revue des Etudes Latines*
Rev. Hist. Rel.   *Revue de l'Histoire des Religions*
Rev. Quest. Hist.   *Revue des Questions Historiques*
Trans. Proc. Am. Philol. Ass.   *Transactions and Proceedings of the American Philological Association*
Yale Cl. St.   *Yale Classical Studies*

Foreword by Michael Grant

It is natural, and indeed right and proper, that writers dealing with the Ancient World today should attempt to find suggestive similarities and analogies between its life and our own. And, heaven knows, they are available in rich crops. Thus the whole subject of this book, and particularly of its later chapters, revolves round this theme which seemed pressing to the imperial Romans and is most painfully urgent today: how on earth are we to reconcile the good life with the lives we have to lead?

But it is equally valuable for a modern author to detect the vast and profound differences which yawn between ancient and modern ways of living. Educationalists, erroneously repeating that Vergil was a naturally Christian soul, are apt to steer clear of them, but it is more fascinating and bracing to see that they are there. And conspicuous among these differences is the concept of the city. For one thing, unless we happen to be citizens of San Marino or a few other places, our practical experience will give us no assistance at all towards understanding what it was like to live in an independent, or even an autonomous, city-state. Most of us, as a matter of fact, would find it highly disagreeable; if we feel momentarily carried away by the glory of Periclean Athens let us reflect on the unpardonable interferences and discomforts it inflicted (even if we happened not to be a slave). It remains true, however, that it seemed to Greeks, except the peasantry, the natural way of life, and that the idea was firmly inherited (partly through Etruria) by the Romans. And so you get the peculiar situation which lies at the root of this book: a Roman went on thinking of himself as the citizen of a city-

7

state even after that city-state had become a large national and supra-national state and then a vast international affair.

This was a peculiarly Roman situation, and it is fitting that an Italian, who can see the Renaissance as intermediary between then and now, should write about it; he or she is more likely to be able to comprehend some of the basic points involved than we could, with our alien tradition. Indeed – a point I had the pleasure of discussing with the authoress herself – it is almost impossible even to translate the word *Città* into adequate English. 'City' will obviously have to do, especially as so much has to be said about St Augustine's two Cities, but there are many overtones and undercurrents as well, which is not surprising when one recalls that both *civitas* and *urbs* are involved. However, this we can confidently leave to Lidia Storoni Mazzolani, who stands back and away from continuous narration to give us a broad sweep from the earliest times down to Augustine. It is all part of the same story. I once tried to say as much to a senior theological colleague in my university when I (whose job it then was to teach Latin Literature) rashly announced my desire to give lectures on Augustine. He politely but firmly warned me off – thus setting a bad example of compartmentalised study which the present book admirably avoids.

The thoughts provoked by this great subject, ranging from city-state to world state to city in heaven, are many and far-reaching. But what really brought the whole problem into the open was the unprecedented size of the Roman dominions. It has often been remarked that this was the only time in history that the Mediterranean area, not to speak of its vast hinterlands, has ever been unified; and it does not seem likely to happen again. Unification was in many ways, to use the reassuring terms of elementary history, A Good Thing. And yet the writer of this book, admirably detaching herself from chauvinistic considerations (which often find no difficulty in harking back for a couple of millennia), is perfectly right to see in Roman history, among other things that were better, an appalling series

8

of arrogant cruelties and injustices. Out of the evil, then, came good. And out of the good comes evil. That is why Augustine felt he had to write *The City of God* – to explain why the coming of Christianity had coincided with innumerable disasters: and it had indeed, in some ways, contributed to their occurrence. And the ages that have followed would have caused him horror. Until quite modern times, many of the worst atrocities of the western world have been perpetrated in the name of the gentle Saviour. This abomination has not been so apparent in very recent history, but only for an inglorious reason – because Christianity has no longer been the major driving force influencing the minds of men.

Or, rather – for the word must be repeated – of *western* men. For there is a curious parochialism about the ways in which our Mediterranean spiritual ancestors thought. When Greeks spoke of the Cosmopolis, it was usually, though not always, a Greek cosmos that they had in mind. When Romans spoke of their universal rule, when the coins of their civil war in A.D. 69 proclaimed the 'Health of the Human Race' and the 'Peace of the Whole World', they did not really mean the whole world at all; they meant their own empire, which, though vast, was never seriously thought of as potentially world-wide.

And so it was with Christianity, too. The earth shall be filled with the glory of the Lord, but it was along the roads and waterways of the Roman empire that the Word spread: and it did not spread very far beyond them. Or rather, there were Christians beyond them; the Persian empire, for example, had the same sort of proportion of Christians as the Roman empire: but Persia never had its Constantine, and never went Christian. Nor, therefore, did the vast areas beyond. Such exceptions as occurred were much later, and relatively unimportant: Christianity has still become nothing like a world religion. Ecumenism has to be thought of, somehow, in much wider terms than a union of all Christians, if our civilisation, built up so laboriously through the methods Signora Storoni has described, is to endure; and those wider terms must surely

9

include all the best of the marvellous things that the classically inspired Christian City of God has to offer. 'So much fighting', wrote an archaeologist recently, 'so many peoples destroying themselves and others, yet at the same time such tremendous achievements. What is one to make of it? I don't know – except that it has to stop. Some other pulse must drive us on into the future.'

MICHAEL GRANT

Gattaiola, 1970.

Author's Preface

The people must fight to save its laws, as it
fights to protect the walls of the city.

HERACLITUS, *Fragment*, 44

MY OBJECT has been to trace the course of an idea through the
history of Roman thought – the idea of the City, considered not
as a political or legal institution, but rather as a design for a
society in which men could live together. I have also tried to
depict the inherent contradictions between these two views of the
matter. This book does not claim to give an exhaustive or
systematic account of all the existing literature; it is simply the
fruit of a long and affectionate study of the writers of antiquity.

Ab Urbe Condita (From the Foundation of the City) is the
title of Livy's decades; *Urbem Romam* are the first words of the
Annals of Tacitus. For thinking men in those days, history began
when the unformed mass of humanity was converted into a social
organisation – when the City came into the world. The City is
identified with the State, and also with the home of the national
gods. It represents the only conceivable formula for a civilised
community. It inspires both self-sacrifice and a fertile spirit of
competition. As time goes on, its founders recede into the shades
of legend, and critics of a later day begin to look back with
nostalgia at the small original settlement as they express their
disdain for the contemporary scene. Meanwhile theoreticians and
Utopian thinkers begin to yearn for a City of the future, planned
by reason and ruled by justice, and their speculative projects
express the innovating spirit of new generations.

11

The wind of innovation began to blow through the streets of Rome in the third century B.C. Roman thought began to be affected by doctrines which presupposed the unity of the human race. Religious influences, originating in the eastern Mediterranean, favoured a universal conception of mankind, and on the horizon loomed the legendary figure of Alexander. These factors were foreign to the spirit and the traditions of republican Rome, and brought with them the first insubstantial hint of the Great City, the common homeland of all humanity, whose model was the universe ruled by a single God, and whose laws were to be inspired by Reason and Nature. These embryonic ideas met with prolonged opposition from the guardians of the traditional order. At home, this order was based on respect for republican institutions; abroad, it rested on an exclusive attitude, which was dedicated by economic and social considerations, and inspired by a confident belief in racial superiority. Power, as the Romans wanted to exercise it, could only be applied by indirect means, which would not involve mingling with people of other races; it had to grow naturally from civic institutions, without any delegation of powers to representatives who might abuse them.

With territorial growth and the influx of slaves and immigrants, however, a heterogeneous population installed itself in the City of Rome, bringing with it its own gods, its own customs, and its own social requirements. Under Augustus, the sheer size of the Empire demanded the institution of a census and of a network of military garrisons. Administration became more and more unified, more dependent on the central government. Temples dedicated to the goddess of Rome or to the trinity of Capitoline gods sprang up in many parts of the provinces. And at the same time an ideological transformation could be observed, a change from the view of life appropriate to a single town, rooted in the soil of its territory and the rites of its gods, to a universalist philosophy. Various inevitable historical circumstances and influences urged this transformation forward.

Bringing the institutions of the city-state into line with the

12

magnitude of the City became the task of politicians and jurists; bringing the ideals of the Republic into conformity with the spirit of a world-wide State was a matter for thinkers and writers. Military dictatorship turned into political power deriving not from a legal constitution but from personal moral prestige; it was gradually transformed into an Olympian, paternalistic authority, and finally emerged as a theocracy, deeply tinged with Persian and Egyptian elements.

Like Janus, the Empire faced both ways from its earliest beginnings: on the one hand dutifully preserving the active moral features of the Republic which were so dear to the ruling class of Rome, but on the other accepting the spiritual influences that flowed westward from the eastern half of the Empire. Unable to hold back these religious, cultural and social forces, the Empire assimilated them, and began to find its own moral driving force in them. Augustus paid conspicuous, devout reverence to the spiritual values of the Republic, and decisively rejected the Utopian dreams of the East; yet at the same time he managed to gain control of those dreams, to add them to the mainstream of Roman tradition, to convert them into an instrument of power. They were cosmopolitan ideals, foreign to the ancient spirit of the City; and yet their union with the older tradition was the source of the new legend of Rome.

In the first two centuries of the Empire, there were few extensions of its territory, except for Britain (already briefly invaded by Julius Caesar), and Dacia, which was annexed by Trajan. The main activities were the consolidation of the frontier areas and the unification of the administrative system. But on the mental plane, the walls of the City, which the founders had originally made far wider than they needed, 'in the hope of a greater multitude to come',[1] now spread out to enfold all the past enemies of Rome. The Roman metropolis, the City of all mankind, emerged as the archetype of civilised and orderly society. To belong to the City, to obey its laws, was a cause for pride – not so much an act of submission as a spontaneous decision to join the forces of law and civilisation against the powers of evil.

13

In those days the doctrine of *Romanitas* took on the form in which it was later transmitted to the Middle Ages. It derives its main features from ideas evolved hundreds of years earlier, and puts the finishing touches to an historical development which was already almost complete. This development was a progressive acceptance of racial equality, which became so general that the final grant (in A.D. 212) of Roman citizenship to all dwellers in the Roman world earned remarkably little comment from contemporary writers.

But the third century A.D. brought increasing pressure from the barbarians; also internal collapse, which weakened the feeling of belonging to a unified society. To economic and social discontents and to re-emergent local nationalisms was added the philosophical inspirations of Christian preaching. The Christian had inherited the prophetic vision of the Jews, and hoped to see the coming of a City of light, immovable, timeless and outside history, untainted by the atrocities and tyrannies that poisoned the City of the world. The celestial homeland was always represented in strong contrast with the earthly Empire, and all prophecies of the coming of the timeless City presupposed the earlier downfall of Rome.

But when the barbaric flood did sweep over Rome, at the time of its sack by the Visigoths, the faithful suffered a cruel disappointment. The hope that had helped them to survive was spent; Rome had fallen and the heavenly City had still not opened its adamantine gates to all believers. At the same moment, the Empire which for centuries had been the homeland of every thinking being had practically ceased to exist. Spiritual confusion reached the point where the leaders of the Church had to hasten to the rescue, explaining what had happened, and giving new heart to the faithful. They also had to minister encouragement to unbelievers, who, even more than Christians, had lost the very reason for their existence. For though the sack of Rome by the Visigoths in A.D. 410 did no irreparable damage to the buildings which bore witness to the ancient greatness of the City, it saw the dissolution of the political, military and economic forces from which the capital drew its strength, and above all the dissipation of the moral basis of its prestige.

Only memories were left. St Augustine's *The City of God*, that lengthy oration to the reader, is indeed directed against the past. Deeply affected by the burning nostalgia which he knew had been rekindled in the hearts of the refugees who fled before the Goths after the fall of Rome, the saint put forward a new ideal plan for a City, a fresh nucleus of solidarity to which they could cling. Though continually pointing the contrast between his City and the City of the past, he often made use of the same concepts and the same words which had been valid for Rome, the only imaginable earthly City in the period just ended.

He incorporated all the visionary philosophy of the biblical tradition into his City, all the sublime thoughts of his master, Plato. But while urging the faithful to place their hopes in the life to come, he also encouraged them to attempt the building of the City of God in this world, amid all the distress and horrors of the age – though the citizens might be isolated, few in number and frustrated in their aims, and might indeed even be non-Christians, so long as they believed in the overriding necessity of obedience to the City's laws.

NOTE TO CHAPTER

1. *In spem magis futurae multitudinis.* Livy, I, viii, 4.

Introduction

Auctoritas is inalienable for ever in dealings with strangers.

> *Twelve Tables*, III, 7[1]

Alexander desired to render all upon earth subject to one law of reason and one form of government, and to reveal all men as one people.

> PLUTARCH, *On the Fortune of Alexander*, I, 8, D

Nature produced us related to one another, since she created us from the same source and to the same end.

> SENECA, *Letters*, XCV, 52[2]

We long to have you enrolled as a citizen in the service of a higher and nobler country.

> ST. AUGUSTINE, *Letters*, XCI, 1[3]

In THE political thought of the ancient world there is no systematic legal basis for coexistence between nations. The rights and duties of citizens, both towards each other and towards the State, were exactly and strictly regulated; but relationships between one people and another interested neither the theoretician nor the legislator. The outer world was only significant if it threatened invasion or promised plunder.

The Greeks never produced a political formula which was not deeply rooted in the concept of the *Polis*, the politically autonomous city. The moral superiority of the political institutions of Athens is quoted by Thucydides as the reason for her supremacy, and by Aeschylus as the reason for her victories. The devotion of Socrates to his City and her laws led him to accept even the most unjust of them – the law that condemned him to death. Many books were written about human brotherhood, but they contained sublime philosophical pronouncements, not practical plans for its realisation. When they turned to politics, the very thinkers whose minds were full of theories about union between the elements of the physical universe were unable to look beyond the boundaries of the *Polis*. Like Plato, they drew up constitutions for imaginary republics; or like Xenophon in the *Cyropaedia* they dreamed of the rule of some idealised monarch. Associations between states, whether they went by the name of alliances or federations, were transitory affairs, dictated by necessity rather than elaborated by theoretical study. Political interest was focused on the internal structure of the City, which was regarded as a miniature version of the rational plan imposed on the universe by divine wisdom. For this reason, the task of building the City of Justice in the world of reality became an imperative moral duty, an attempt to carry out the work of God on earth. We find thoughts about man in general, about mankind as a homogeneous group, in Greek poetry and philosophy from the very beginning. But similar statements referring specifically to foreigners only appear in a later period, when Sophists, Cynics and Stoics begin to speak of them as limbs of the same body, sailors on the same ship.[4] For the earlier Greeks, foreigners were, basically, mere *barbaroi*.

Even before the word *barbaros* came into common use, the Greeks seem to have possessed the certainty that they belonged to a culturally superior society, and had the right to impose their culture on others. In the *Iliad*, the Achaeans march in an orderly manner, obeying their leaders, while confused cries are heard from the Trojan camp, the hideous gabble of mercenary troops of different races (*Iliad*, IV, 438). In Euripides' *Iphigenia in Aulis* (1400-1), the heroine, awaiting the sacrificial knife, says to her mother : 'It is right for Greeks to rule barbarians, not for barbarians to rule Greeks. They are slaves, we are free.'

Sophocles indeed shows us Antigone setting individual conscience before the edicts of the City, and exalts the wonders of which man is capable. But the humanity of which he speaks is the Greek humanity he knows best – a race which can respond to unwritten laws precisely because of the ethical level which it has reached.

The Greeks' confidence in their own superiority was based on the concept of spontaneous obedience by the individual to an internal code of conduct, which had more of moral than of civil law about it, and flowed from the common will of various classes of men, whose lot was to share the task of government. The main characteristic of *barbaroi,* on the other hand – even more striking than their brutality – is their inability to achieve a regular system of social coexistence, which inevitably leads them to an abject state of servitude. 'They fall on their knees before a mortal man,' says Isocrates of the Persians, 'addressing him as a divinity' (*Panegyric,* 151). 'Greek is it not to wish to override the laws' (Euripides, *Orestes,* 487). And Plato is said to have given thanks to the gods, just before his death, 'first, that he was born a human being, then that he was a Greek, and neither a barbarian nor an irrational animal'. The association of ideas is worth noting.[5]

But times changed and the *Polis* of the fifth century, for all its pride in the repulse of the Persians and the invention of a model society, went into a decline, which caused a profound unease in the hearts of men. Greek literature and philosophy began to reflect violent disagreements between the various schools of thought that put forward different solutions for the problems that tormented the Hellenic world.

During the Peloponnesian wars, from 431–404 B.C., the Sophists began to question all the values which, for the restricted world of the City-State, were sacred – laws, local religions, traditions, and social classes. But this subtle process of depreciation was not accompanied by constructive proposals for a different form of human society. The thinkers of the following century, however, though still devoting themselves to enquiries into the

18

origins of the universe and of natural law, were inspired by the wish to construct a code of conduct applicable to humanity on those vast foundations; they wanted to bring the government of the earthly City into line with the principles laid down by God in the days of Creation, to equate political laws with the law of the universe.[6] This led to a completely abstract political theory, a yearning toward better things which could not be translated into reality. The ideal ruler, inspired by Reason, must keep his eyes for ever turned up to heaven; 'towards things fixed and immutable', in the words of Plato, 'all in order moving according to reason; these he imitates, and to these he will, as far as he can, conform himself' (*Republic*, VI, 500, C5).

The instability of a period in which every certainty seemed to be shaken led the rulers of the *Poleis* to make some attempts at federation between their states – though only on the understanding that each of them would be allowed to keep its own laws. But these aspirations came to nothing, precisely because of the powerful hold which the concept of the City maintained on the minds of the citizens of each state. Some of them were impelled to lay aside their traditional hatred of monarchy and invoke the intervention of a prince, who must be capable of reconciling the opposing interests of the states without interfering with their individual constitutions – preferably remaining invisible all the time, like a tutelary deity. They put their trust first in Philip of Macedon, and then in Alexander, hoping each time that they had found the regal benefactor who would compose the quarrels of the Greeks and give expression to their aspiration towards world leadership. But the brief glory of Alexander's career disappointed those hopes, and his empire broke up into a number of monarchical succession states, each of which contained several Cities. Then the need of a common bond became apparent, and the hearts of men instinctively turned toward the hope of a single God, the expectation of a supreme and far-seeing King. Such was the historical basis of the concept of the brotherhood of mankind, of the idea that man's real country can only be the wide world, and that the tattered concepts of City, race and class must be cast aside like worn-out garments.

The above is a brief sketch of the phases of Greek thought which the Romans found in the Hellenistic world. Their first contacts with it – through the settlements of Magna Graecia, and then more directly after the capture of Tarentum (272 B.C.) and the Macedonian wars (212–168) – led to the transplantation of the potent seeds of the ancient cultural heritage of the Aegean into the Republic situated on the Tiber.

The most active sections of cultivated society in Rome gave an enthusiastic welcome to the ideas of equal laws for all humanity and of the brotherhood of man; but they were outnumbered by citizens who detested those doctrines. Individual morality began to bear the mark of the new ideas, but even those who embraced them as truly noble theories were content to leave them on an abstract plane, and did not deduce from them any rules for the conduct of political affairs. The Republic had long been exposed by its geographical position and by the accidents of history to the hazards of contact with other peoples. She had concluded pacts and alliances with them; she had often ignored racial and religious differences and adopted measures which tended toward the gradual assimilation of the conquered. But these were isolated actions, dictated by temporary necessities, not by theory – unconnected operations whose motives were strictly practical and had nothing to do with the new doctrines which, admittedly, were increasing their hold on many members of the intellectual class. During her centuries of growth, Rome often granted the conquered terms suggesting assimilation rather than domination; but it would be hard to maintain that she did so out of equalitarian principle.

Gradually, the transplanted Greek ideas began to bear fruit, aided by the solid qualities of the Roman mind. From this process emerged a fully conscious theory of universal brotherhood. The idea of Rome as an ecumenical organism spread from the thought of Poseidonius, as well as from that of Polybius in the previous century, and ultimately took root in the time of Augustus. Roman thinkers began to formulate the doctrine of a universal Empire, and this led them to realise that the practice of racial assimilation, which had been intermittently followed in the past, coincided quite closely with the basic ideas of Greek thought. Then the Empire began to be seen as coterminous with the *Orbis Terrarum*; the Senate as an august council, legislating not merely for the benefit of the original tribes of citizens but for all humanity; and Rome as the Great City of the Utopian dreamers, the queen of her sister nations. The insignia of globe and sceptre began to appear on the coinage.

From the second century B.C. onward, the new direction of Roman thought is determined by Greek ideas – ideas which sometimes contradict each other. So when Rome, after a period of letting policy be dictated by events, became aware of the original and fruitful nature of the process of racial levelling which she had for various reasons been fitfully following – when she wanted to elevate it to be the guiding principle of her new, world-wide domain – she found the justificatory doctrines in the works of the masters of Greek thought.

But in the initial stages, when the seeds were being sown, the clash between the welcomers of this message of racial and social equality and the guardians of the old exclusive policy became very obvious.

The first group held the new, enlightened views, and had at least an inkling of the opportunity to create a world-wide society which was implicit in the Empire's territorial expansion. The second group had no thoughts of accepting foreigners on an equal basis, and could imagine no constitution for a City of Justice for mankind that differed from the constitution of their own Republic. This clash of views continued for centuries, and was reflected in political groupings, in the thinking of Roman authors, in sculpture, and in the language of the visual. It was a clash between the idea of supremacy and the idea of assimilation, between Senate and Emperor, between democratic custom and theocracy, between realism and Utopian idealism.

The vast territorial expansion of the Empire began to demand

21

a doctrinal basis on which it could proceed; and then the policy of assimilation, already well on the way to completion in practice, became the theoretical inspiration of the Roman system. In their effort to make this policy their own, the Romans sought out precedents that went right back to Romulus. The Roman nation was one of mixed origins, because it had been created by the assembly of various tribes at a natural cross-road; and its quiet annexation of populations and gods was presented as a deliberate policy, practised by the mythical founder and carefully followed by successive rulers down to the time of Augustus – a gradual progress towards the ecumenical concept of Rome.[7]

Converted in this way into a theoretical basis for imperialism, the system of racial levelling could be represented as a regular, steady process; but this was to simplify the matter in retrospect. In reality, during the centuries of imperial growth, the system of domination practised by the Romans was built up out of a vast number of separate decisions on the relationship to be observed with different subject peoples. The basis of the treaty that bound a community to Rome might be either alliance or conquest, implying different degrees of subjection, different obligations, and different rights. Some states had to pay tribute in grain, others in cash, others in recruits. Some had the right to trade with the Romans, others the right of intermarriage, others the right of voting in Roman elections.

These inconsistencies may have helped the Romans to maintain their dominant position; they certainly had nothing to do with any unifying theoretical principle. It was the urgent wish of their new subjects, first of all in Latium, then in the rest of Italy, and finally all over the known world, that led the ruling nation to widen the scope of the assimilating process, and to introduce more and more uniformity into the administrative systems used for various subject peoples.

With all its variations and unevenness of application, Roman practice did, on the whole amount to a happy mean between the isolationism of the conservatives and the universalism of the intellectuals – a fair outcome of the long see-saw struggle between city-state and ecumenical system. Thus a spiritual stirring was gradually converted into an act of moral will and a conscious political policy. The holders of political and economic power, who had been the first to believe in the idea of racial levelling, began to oppose it when they became aware that it brought with it not only the achievement of an ideal, but also the dissolution of their class, their moral code, and their faith.

Assimilation was a slow process, lasting hundreds of years, and was brought about by the most various means, including promotion for valour in the field and carefully phased demagogic concessions.[8]

The patricians regarded themselves as guardians of the structure of the State. Having a monopoly of priestly office, they claimed that their will was identical with the will of the gods. Their power was not merely that of an oligarchy – it was an *auctoritas,* a paternal authority enlightened by divine inspiration, a prestige handed down traditionally from father to son, and jealously maintained.

Faithful to the original idea of a City strictly divided into classes, they hated social upheavals and trespassing across social frontiers. But it was not long before men arose who were inspired either by political calculation or by theoretical idealism to undertake the building of a vaster City, inhabited by a wider brotherhood, for future generations.

First of all we shall examine the views of the conservatives. Then we shall go on to consider the progressive spreading of the cosmopolitan idea, which is made up of a number of ideological elements. They can however be summarised into three basic factors – Greek philosophy, Eastern religions, and the precedent of Alexander.

NOTES TO CHAPTER

1. *Adversus hostes aeterna auctoritas esto.*
2. *Natura nos cognatos edidit, cum ex isdem et in eadem gigneret.*

3. *Supernae cuiusdam patriae etiam te ipsum civem habere vellemus.*
4. H. C. Baldry, *The Unity of Mankind in Greek Thought*, Cambridge 1965.
5. Plutarch, *Marius*, 46, 1. Lactantius, *Divine Institutes*, III, 19, *P.L.*, VI, 413.
6. A. J. Festugière, *La révélation d'Hermès Trismégiste*, Paris 1949, II, pp. 270–4.
7. In the words of Ennius, quoted by Cicero, *De Orat.*, III, 168, *Nos sumu' Romani qui fuimus ante Rudini.* See also *Pro Archia*, IX, xxii.
8. Roman citizenship was granted to other peoples as follows: to the Latins in 640–616 B.C. (Livy, I, xxxiii, 5 and IV, iii, 4); to the Tusculans in 381 B.C. (Livy, VI, xxvi, 8); to Veii, Capenae and Fidenae in 389 (Livy, VI, iv, 5); to Lanuvium, Aricia, Nomentum, Antium and Pedum in 338 (Livy, VIII, xiv, 3, 4); and to Acerrae in 332 (Livy, VIII, xvii, 12).

I

The Views of the Conservatives

> It seemed to the gods an affront that honours
> should be prostituted, and the distinctions of
> birth confounded.
>
> LIVY, V, xiv, 4[1]

In THE earliest days of the City, the Romans' attitude toward
expansionism was highly unfavourable. Their ideas exemplified
the prudent mentality of a tiny state with very modest means,
very modest territory, and no enthusiasm for adventure. Never
abandoned by the conservatives, this view is echoed in the pages
of the historians of the imperial epoch, who indeed attach special
importance to it as the most typical characteristic of the Roman
spirit. Appian, writing in the second century A.D. speaks of 'tribes
of barbarians, some of whom I have seen at Rome offering
themselves, by their ambassadors, as its subjects; but the emperor
would not accept them' (*History*, preface, 7).

Individual Romans might be privately receptive to broadly
humanitarian theories, but they regarded the Republic as a
complete world on its own, autonomous and unchanging. This
unwavering certainty made it impossible for them to accept plans
for the future improvement of society. It was oriented toward
the past – the legendary period[2] when the City had been
governed by institutions directly inspired by the gods.

Then there had been no lack of human relationships, in a
small society with close links between families. The will of the
gods had been identified with the will of the ruling classes, and
the gods extended their benevolence only to citizens – to men

25

who had been born within the precincts of Rome, and who satisfied certain ritual obligations. The government of the City was then the only source of moral and legal standards. All the citizens were poor, and consequently abstemious. If there was no legitimate heir, the property of a family went back to the state (*Twelve Tables*, V, 5). Every *gens* had gods of its own, which were added to the communal Olympus when it moved into Rome from the country. Sometimes, indeed, these rural deities were identified with the gods already established in the City. 'No man sought to bring in strange gods,' says Propertius.[3]

This was the City toward which thinkers of later centuries looked back with admiration and regret. Its discipline, abstemiousness and soldierly valour – virtues which could hardly be avoided by a people surrounded by enemy tribes and barren malarial territory – were regarded as the result of a moral code. The sparing habits of ancient Latium were represented as a deliberately chosen ascetic way of life. Manly courage, feminine chastity and frugality are the virtues praised in the few epitaphs that have come down to us from the republican era. They exemplify the moral criteria of a closed society, shut in by the walls of a city.

Conservative Romans were bewildered to find themselves living in a city whose walls, metaphorically speaking, embraced the whole world; and their dismay led them to seek the spiritual meaning of life in the traditional past. The historical writings of Sallust and Livy were composed in the twilight of republican liberty, those of Tacitus in the midday splendour of the Empire under Trajan, and those of Ammianus Marcellinus not long before the end – but all alike show how potent an influence nostalgia for the past can exercise on a nation, by imprinting an unchanging stamp on its ideals. They also show how completely these historians took it for granted that the Empire owed its political supremacy and its permanence solely to the ethical merits of its founders.

This moral excellence of republican Rome retained such immense prestige that even in imperial times politicians drew their inspiration from this source, and panegyrists found in it flattering examples of virtuous conduct at which they could hint when addressing emperors. When it came to foreign policy, even expansionists always paid lip service to certain principles which typified the republican moral heritage : first, never to attack without provocation; and secondly, to respect local autonomy as far as was advantageous.

Roman domination of the world was not, in fact, the result of a clearly expressed or consciously followed policy. Sallust's *Letter of Mithridates*,[4] a moralising statement of the king's case against the Romans, reproaches them with a 'profound lust for dominion and wealth'; but this was never a clear-cut political aim, nor was the Empire the result of a premeditated design. According to the sincere belief of the ruling patrician class, relations with other countries should be regulated by strictly legalistic principles; the process of subjugation, moreover, was discontinuous. A scholar[5] has remarked that the relative scarcity in Latin of legal terms referring to relations with subject peoples is a clear sign of the poverty of the Romans' contribution to international law. There is far more clarity and detail about their ideas on civil law. The individual rather than the State was the centre of interest for Roman legislators.

The republican authorities, while leaving a nominal autonomy to vassal-states and client-states, aimed at exercising a real supremacy over them, both as proof of the racial superiority of Rome and as a security precaution. But they tried, as far as possible, to avoid expansion in areas difficult to defend, and to escape the burdens of direct administration – which would involve the despatch of governors to distant areas, where their authority would be very difficult to control from the capital.

This prudent attitude was dictated by various considerations.

First, it was all too easy, in the early years, for new subjects of the Empire to become citizens of Rome. They had only to take up residence in the City in order to be counted among the tribes and entitled to vote.[6] A progressive increase in the number and membership of the tribes meant a widening of the

27

base of the electoral system which would involve a change in its character.

Secondly, the magistrates sent into the provinces under a system of direct rule would have an opportunity to accumulate wealth and form alliances which would enable them, on return to Rome, to exercise a dangerous influence in the political life of the City.

A third brake on the process of expansion was the very real difficulty of finding the men and materials necessary to conquer, garrison and administer new territories.

These were practical reasons for following a policy of caution, whose main prop was the fear that new customs might replace the old way of life, foreign religions supplant the religion of Rome, and newcomers deprive the privileged classes of political office.

The legal safeguards demanded by these apprehensions were personified for the Romans by the Fetials. This venerable priesthood regulated relations with foreigners, and invested even the act of aggression with an aura of religion. It was the task of the Fetials to ensure that no infractions of international law were committed. The earliest treaty of which the Romans had any record – the pact which preceded the trial of strength between the Horatii and the Curiatii – was concluded in the presence of a Fetial (Livy, I, xxiv, 6), and so was the peace between Rome and Carthage in 201 B.C. (Livy, XXX, xliii, 9). The order comprised twenty priests, who supervised all international transactions, and its founder was traditionally King Ancus Marcius. He had fixed the wording of the formula to be pronounced by the *pater patratus,* or leader of a delegation, when he went abroad to present the demands of Rome to a foreign power; and also the wording of the invocation to Jupiter, calling him to witness that the demands were just.[7] If the enemy refused to accept the rightful claims of the envoy, he would invoke the help of Jupiter, Juno, Quirinus, and all the gods of Heaven and the Underworld. On his return from this preliminary notification, the leader of the embassy would authorise the actual declaration of war. This,

28

however, could only follow after long discussion by the Senate, and after the lapse of thirty-three days from the moment when the offender had been asked to abandon his evil course and surrender his ill-gotten gains. The bearer of the declaration of war always added a clause which concerned him personally – a prayer that the gods might never let him see his native land again, if his demands were dictated by impious or unjust motives. Finally he hurled a spear into the territory of the enemy, to signify the opening of hostilities. Cicero describes this legalistic aspect of the act of aggression as a most holy thing, inspired by justice.[8]

The same view is expressed even more strongly by Livy, who tends to attribute to the creators of the Empire sentiments which really belong to his own contemporaries, concerned solely with its preservation; he also invests the heroes of antiquity with all the virtues that can be read into the history of their times.[9] Reluctance to make war is far from uncommon – the military campaign against Veii is said to have aroused the opposition of the lower classes, who were stirred up by the tribunes of the people (Livy, IV, lviii, 9–10). In 202 B.C., the consul had to speak at great length in support of intervention against Macedonia, and he was only able to persuade the restive citizens of its necessity by showing that the choice was not between war and peace, but between campaigning overseas and being invaded at home (Livy, XXXI, vii, 3). On this occasion too the Fetials were consulted, after three days of prayer. The Roman people seemed unwilling to move on to the conquest of the world.

Cicero considers war to be legitimate only if it is declared in a regular manner, and undertaken with the object of living 'in peace and without harm' (De Officiis, I, xi, 35). The wording of the law makes no provision for an openly aggressive policy – though the principle of undeniable Roman superiority remains axiomatic in all dealings with foreigners. 'Eternal authority', as we have seen, is prescribed by one of the laws of the Twelve Tables (III, 7).

Even on the occasion of the most obviously deliberate acts

29

of aggression, elements of caution and hesitation continue to haunt the Roman mind, disguised as questions of procedure. As Caesar moves on to the conquest of western Europe, he describes how his legionaries trembled at the prospect of attacking Ariovistus, because of the traditional ferocity of the Germans – but later historians say that the soldiers feared the punishment that the Senate was empowered to inflict on them for undertaking a war which was unjust in itself and had never been the subject of a regular vote (Dio Cassius, XXXVIII, 35, 2).

Caesar describes his confrontation with the German chieftain, who justifies his own encroachments on the territory of northern Gaul as having the same objects as the Roman encroachments in Gallia Narbonensis. Caesar replies by drawing a subtle and revealing distinction between the mastery acquired by armed conquest and the very limited authority exercised in practice by the republican government. 'If priority of time was to be the standard', he says, 'then the sovereignty of the Roman people in Gaul had complete justification; if the decision of the Senate was to be observed, Gaul should be free, for after conquest of the country the Senate had willed that it should continue to be autonomous and to observe its own laws' (*Gallic War*, I, xlv, 45). This is a masterly summary of the republican attitude toward foreign affairs – and also a clear indication of the clash between legislative authority and military might.

Even according to the legalistic views of the Senate, there were ample legitimate reasons for the military command obtained by Caesar, first in Cisalpine Gaul and Illyricum, and then in Transalpine Gaul (59 B.C.). A barbarian king had been thrusting his way westwards from Dacia; harassed by Suevian raids, the Helvetii had undertaken a migration which threatened the Aedui and the territory of Gallia Narbonensis. These developments, distant as they were from Italy, justified the prolongation of Caesar's command and the marching and countermarching of the legions, as long as it could be maintained that the sole object of all these campaigns was, as Caesar untiringly claimed, the protection of the territory of Rome from invasion.

Caesar never confessed to openly expansionist intentions; but he did demand the celebration of special religious festivities to mark his victory over the Germans – the victims, some said, of a treacherous attack. Then Cato rose indignantly in the Senate to propose that the conqueror should rather be handed over to those whom he had injured, lest divine retribution for his crime should fall on the whole people of Rome.

Though the times were ripe for a move which would have invested his power with a mystical halo and set it above the need for justification, Caesar never lost sight of the fact that the basic element of military prestige, in the Roman mind, was defence. Later he was to claim a sort of divine right, based on descent from Aeneas and, through Aeneas, from Venus,[10] as the foundation of the power he sought, but he presented himself initially as the political heir of Marius. He set up a memorial to his supposed predecessor in the Capitol, showing him in the act of defeating the Cimbrians and the Teutons.

The threat of enemy attack and the need to give loyal support to allies in times of danger were regarded as the only legitimate reasons for aggression. The legalistic basis of these views was reinforced by an ethical factor – the moralists condemned the enrichment of the individual and the aggrandisement of the State. Sallust blames the decline of standards of conduct on the excessive powers conferred on Rome by her victory over Carthage (*Catilinarian War*, X, 4–6). After describing the arduous life of men of earlier generations, liable to be devoured by the beasts of the forest, Lucretius points out that they were *not* liable to be butchered in their thousands around a military standard.[11] Imperialism was obviously not compatible with the *ataraxia*, or freedom from passion, of the Epicureans, nor with the remote indifference of the Stoics. 'We check manslaughter and isolated murders', wrote Seneca, 'but what of war – that much-vaunted crime of slaughtering whole peoples? . . . Deeds that would be punished by loss of life when committed in secret are praised by us because uniformed generals have carried them out' *Moral Letters*, XCV, xxx).

31

Behind the voices idealising power, we can hear others – quiet, compelling voices – deploring its spread, and continually calling on the Romans to return to the modest scale of earlier days. The dreams of empire are most effectively expressed by the visual arts and by poets. The dark imprecations which the tribune Ateius directed against Crassus, as the triumvir set out to make war against the Parthians in 55 B.C., were always remembered as a dismal omen of the kind that rightly fell to the lot of men who committed the crime of embarking on a war without provocation.[12]

Though hungry for power, then, the Romans were loyal to ancient custom that did not permit aggression without just cause. Sermons on moderation poured from the pulpits of the various sects of philosophers; and a trend of ideas current among the Greeks in Asia led to the spread of a tendentious way of writing history, intended to discredit the power of Rome. 'At one time,' wrote Pompeius Trogus, an author who reflects the anti-Roman view of history, 'the people made it their business rather to defend than to enlarge their dominions' (I, i, 3).

There was accordingly no lack of anti-imperial tendencies. The more rapidly territorial expansion took place, the more strongly the need was felt for a justificatory theory. Rome, it was said, had the right to rule because of the moral excellence of the men who had won her so much glory : Rome must preserve her ancient virtues, if she wanted to keep her Empire. 'If you desire our country to be immortal', wrote Cicero, 'if you desire our Empire to be eternal and our glory everlasting, it is against our own passions that we must be on guard.'[13] And, well aware of the hostility of certain Hellenistic circles, Livy[14] was lavish with the most high-sounding excuses for aggression : 'Surely you are the same Romans,' runs Livy's version of a speech by the ambassador of Rhodes, 'who boast that your wars are successful because they are just; who glory not so much in the issue of them, in that you conquer, as in the commencement of them, because you do not undertake them without a just cause' (Livy XLV, xxii, 5).

32

NOTES TO CHAPTER

1. *Indignum dis visum honores vulgari, discriminaque gentium confundi.*
2. The idealised past is an underlying theme of Latin literature, from Cicero's *De Republica*, V, i and *De Natura Deorum*, II, viii, down to the *Saturnalia* of Macrobius, III, 14 in the fourth century A.D.
3. *Nulli cura fuit externos quaerere divos.* Propertius, IV, i, 17.
4. *Letter of Mithridates*, 5, in Sallust, *Histories*, IV. See also E. Bikerman, *La lettre de Mithridate dans les Histoires de Salluste*, in *Rev. Et. Lat.*, XXIV, 1946, pp. 131 ff; A. La Penna, *Le "Historiae" di Sallustio e l'interpretazione della crisi repubblicana*, in *Athenaeum*, XLI, 1963, pp. 201 ff; S. Mazzarino, *Il pensiero storico classico*, Bari 1966, Vol. III, pp. 373 ff; R. Syme, *Sallust*, Berkeley, California 1964.
5. P. C. Sands, *The Client Princes of the Roman Empire*, Cambridge 1908, p. 8. See also A. N. Sherwin White, *The Roman Citizenship*, Oxford 1939; G. Stevenson, *Roman Provincial Administration*, Oxford 1949; C. E. Goodfellow, *Roman Citizenship*, Bryn Mawr College 1935; E. De Ruggiero, *La patria nel diritto pubblico*, Rome 1921.
6. Of the original twenty tribes, four were from the City and sixteen from the surrounding country. The following additions were made in the fourth century B.C.: four new tribes after the capture of Veii, in 387 B.C. (Livy VI, v, 8); two more after the renewal of the Latin League in 358 (Livy VII, xv, 12); two in 332 (Livy VIII, xvii, 11); two in 318 (Livy IX, xx, 6); and two in 299 (Livy X, ix, 14). See Lily Ross Taylor, *The Voting Districts of the Roman Republic*, Rome 1960.
7. Livy, I, xxxii, 10. See also Polybius, III, 25; Dionysius of Halicarnassus, II, 72; Aulus Gellius, *Noctes Atticae*, XVI, iv, 1.
8. *De Officiis* I, xi, 36 – *Ac belli quidem aequitas sanctissime Fetiali populi Romani iure perscripta est.* See also *De Legibus*, II, ix. Tradition, as represented by Servius, *Ad Aeneidem*, VII, 695, attributes this institution to a period later than the Roman code of laws. But the analogies which it presents with the rites and customs of the other Sabellian and Latin tribes provide grounds for thinking that in fact it goes back to Italian prehistory.
9. R. M. Ogilvie, *An Historical Commentary on Livy I – V*, Oxford 1965; P. G. Walsh, *Livy, His Historical Aims and Methods*, Cambridge 1961, pp. 86 ff.
10. Suetonius, *Life of Julius Caesar*, VI. See also J. Perret, *Les origines de la légende troyenne de Rome*, Paris 1942, p. 529.
11. Lucretius, *De Rerum Natura*, V, 999 – 1000: *At non multa virum sub signis milia ducta, Una dies dabat exitio.*
12. Plutarch, *Crassus*, 16. See also Appian, *Civil War*, II, iii, 18; Annaeus Florus I, xlvi, 3; Lucan, *Pharsalia*, III, 125–7.
13. *Pro Rabirio Perduellionis*, xii, 33. See also *De Republica*, V, i, 2.
14. M. A. Levi, *T. Livio e gli ideali augustei*, in *La parola del Passato*, IV, 1949, pp. 15 ff.

33

c

II

Gradual Advancement of
Subject Races and Lower Classes

> So long as no stock was disdained, no race
> rejected, wherein appeared sparks of virtue,
> the Roman's Empire became mighty, and
> flourished.
>
> LIVY, IV, iii, 13[1]

THE RELUCTANCE of the Roman ruling classes to annex new
territories for direct administration was matched by their unwillingness to grant equality to members of the lower classes or
other races.

But enslavement could only lead, sooner or later, to assimilation. In the first place, other nations accepted the authority of
Rome because they had no choice, or because of common
interests or common defence problems, or because they wanted
to cooperate in a vast policy of world-wide scope. Later, they
achieved a state of relative equality. By a similar development
of internal policy, the plebs had successively acquired the right
to serve in the army, the right to have its own councils and
tribunes, and finally the right to occupy the high offices of the
magistracy – the censorship in 351 B.C., the praetorship in 337,
the priesthoods in 300, and the consulship in 172.

In the opening stages of this slow process, the patricians'
resistance to change was clad in an aura of religious duty. Their
refusals took on the air of divine commandments, their oligar-
chical powers were invested with spiritual significance. Appius

34

Claudius expressed horror at the idea that the plebeians should presume to lay hands on the holy mysteries. 'Wherefore let pontiffs, augurs, kings of the sacrifices be appointed at random. Let us place the tiara of Jupiter's *flamen* on any person, provided he be a man!' (Livy, VI, xli, 19).

When they made themselves sole interpreters of the Divine Will, monopolists of the right to grant religious sanction to any action, whether public or private, the pontiffs took on a certain legal function. They suffused all the actions of civil life with religious significance : a prophetic system of law existed alongside the civil system. The gods, for their part, could be relied on to send down plagues from heaven to manifest their wrath, if at elections when the auspices were solemnly taken, 'honours should be prostituted and the distinction of birth confounded' (Livy V, xiv, 4; 395 B.C.).

In 216 B.C., after the defeat of Cannae, Spurius Carvilius proposed that membership of the Roman Senate should be granted to two citizens from each of the peoples of Latium, to fill the gaps left by that disaster. But Fabius Maximus declared that this was an impious proposal. 'That rash suggestion of one individual ought to be annihilated by the silence of the whole body; and if there ever was a declaration in that Senate which ought to be buried in profound and inviolable silence, surely that above all others was one which deserved to be covered and consigned to darkness and oblivion, and looked upon as if it had never been made' (Livy, XXIII, xxii, 9).

The road to advancement of non-Romans was as long and as stony as that of the plebeians, and it claimed a number of victims. In 92 B.C. Livius Drusus was killed for proposing the concession of Roman citizenship to all Italians – a measure which had to be put into effect two years later, (Lex Julia, 90 B.C.; Lex Plautia Papiria, 89 B.C.).

Newcomers might be accepted into the Roman family with limited rights – and might be prevented from exercising even those – but they still felt proud of their new title of *Civis*

Romanus, of the summons to dedicate their efforts to the service of the Republic.

Cicero describes the feelings of the 'new' men (*homines novi*) in the next decade or so after the passage of the laws just mentioned. 'Surely I think that all natives of Italian towns have two fatherlands, one by nature and the other by citizenship. . . . We consider both the place where we were born our fatherland, and also the City into which we have been adopted. But the fatherland must stand first in our affection which in the name of Republic signifies the common citizenship of us all. For her it is our duty to die.'[2] A man no longer feels himself 'shut in by walls as a resident of some fixed spot, but is a citizen of the whole universe, as it were of a single city.'[3]

From these ideas, carried all over the Mediterranean with the spread of Greek culture, sprang thoughts of cosmic significance. Within the world of Jewry, Philo of Alexandria, writing in the imperial period, gave extra weight to a universalistic tendency which was already present in the Old Testament. The spiritual supremacy of the People of Israel, an ineradicable part of Jewish thought, was now accompanied by the idea of a Great City, ruled by a single God, judged by a single law.[4] 'He who comes to the truly Great City, this world, and beholds hills and plains . . . the rivers, the sea, the air with its happily tempered phases, and the whole firmament revolving in rhythmic order, must he not naturally, or rather necessarily, gain the conception of the Maker and Father and Ruler also?' (Philo, *On the Special Laws,* I, vi, 34).

Twenty years later, Seneca, whose language was Latin but who came from Spain, shows us a vision of the Great City whose scale dwarfs the human race: 'Consider that I am coming to give you advice at your birth: "You are about to enter a City," I should say, "shared by gods and men – a city that embraces the universe, that is bound by fixed and eternal laws" ' (*Ad Marciam,* XVIII, i).[5]

Seneca's conception also includes two Cities; but he does not distinguish them as being one geographical and one statutory, like the two cities of Cicero, nor as being one national and one world-wide, like those of Philo, but as being one transitory and one eternal. 'Let us grasp the idea,' he says, 'that there are two commonwealths – the one, a vast and truly common state, which embraces alike gods and men; the other, the one to which we have been assigned by the accident of birth. This will be the commonwealth of the Athenians or of the Carthaginians, or of any other city that belongs, not to all, but to some particular race of men. Some yield service to both commonwealths at the same time – to the greater and to the lesser – some only to the greater. This greater commonwealth we are able to serve even in leisure – nay, I am inclined to think, even better in leisure, so that we may inquire what virtue is' (*On Leisure* IV, i). And in one of the *Moral Letters:* 'The human soul is a great and noble thing: it permits of no limits except those which can be shared by the gods. First of all, it does not consent to a lowly birthplace . . . The soul's homeland is the whole space that encircles the height and the breadth of the firmament, the whole rounded dome within which lies land and sea.'

The terms of these successive descriptions widen out like ripples in a pond. If we turn away from them toward a factual account of the long struggle recorded in the history of Rome, we find the positions of the contending parties summarised by the historians in rhetorical passages, imaginary debates and fictitious letters, in accordance with the literary tradition which made every character the spokesman for an idea.

The histories are full of speeches inserted into the narrative to sum up the views of the characters or those of their parties. At the same time, they give us an indication of the opinions of the historian himself, who may be using the past as a weapon in the political struggle of his own day.

Following this custom, Livy puts a speech advocating a vast, idealistic policy of social levelling into the mouth of the tribune Canuleius, who demanded the legislation of intermarriage between plebeians and patricians, in 442 B.C. The speech of the consul, on the other side, expresses the conservative point of

view. His words express the intolerant attitude of a class for
whom social levelling is a rebellion against the law of Heaven:
'What and how enormous schemes had C. Canuleius set on
foot! He was introducing the confounding of family rank, a
disturbance of the auspices, both public and private, that nothing
may remain pure, nothing uncontaminated; that all distinction
being abolished, no one might know either himself or his family'
(Livy, IV, ii, 5).

Besides the patriarchal attitudes to morals and family life,
Livy here shows an acute psychological understanding of aristocratic exclusivity, and makes a penetrating analysis of the slow
decline of patrician authority. To people habituated to a restricted circle made up of a small number of families, governed by
customs which seemed destined to last for ever, the mingling
of the classes seemed a blasphemy.

In his reply, the tribune pronounces what can only be called
a declaration of the rights of man. He put forward the theory
of the Empire as an instrument of the levelling process – a theory
expressed for him by the historian in the language of the Augustan period, four hundred years later, by which time a much
wider ruling class had supplanted the original closed caste of the
patricians. According to Livy, the tribune went back to the
remotest precedents in order to convince the senators. He
mentioned the various origins of the kings of Rome. Numa had
been a Sabine, Tarquin the son of a Corinthian, Servius a
bastard whose mother was a slave. He called on the senators to
remember the non-Roman origin of their own families: 'That
nobility of yours, most of you, the progeny of Albans or Sabines,
possess not in right of birth or blood, but by co-optation into the
patricians, having been elected for the honour either by the
kings, or after the expulsion of the kings, by the order of the
people' (Livy, IV, iv, 7).

The speaker also rises above the individual precedents, to
formulate the principle of assimilation in set terms – in words
found for him by Livy, writing in the very period of the Empire's
metamorphosis into the fatherland of the whole civilised world:

'So long as no stock was disdained, no race rejected, wherein appeared sparks of virtue, the Romans' Empire became mighty, and flourished' (Livy, IV, iii, 13).

The tribune, so remote in time from the historian, is none the less made the mouthpiece for his views, which are expressed in terms borrowed from the Hellenistic cultural heritage. But Livy is also fully sensitive to the burden that the patricians must have felt on their consciences when they remembered their own origin and that of their families, coming as they did from various areas – immigrants from the rustic hamlets of the hills of Latium, who had become settlers, bringing their own gods with them. 'No question here,' we can imagine the levellers saying, 'of a chosen race, or dynasties of divine stock.' Even the proudest Roman aristocrats may well have been conscious that the secret weakness of their class lay in its composite origins.

The accusation of rabble-rousing was always levelled by the ruling classes at those who favoured an extension of rights. Marius granted Roman citizenship to a thousand auxiliary soldiers from Camerinum, for valour in the field against the Cimbrians and the Teutons. This step was considered illegal, and condemned by some people (Plutarch, *Marius,* 28), but the general ignored these criticisms. It was, in fact, almost always the military leaders who were most generous with concessions, either to gain the votes of new electors, or to reward those who had fought well for them. When Marius wanted the supreme command in the war against Mithridates, he induced first the tribune Sulpicius, and then, a year later, the consul Cinna, to propose that all the Italians who had been admitted to Roman citizenship since the Social war should now be organised into tribes with voting rights.

Sallust was credited[6] with having advised Caesar to introduce large numbers of foreigners into the state – a suggestion we find in the famous *Letters* attributed to the historian. He anticipates the objections of the patricians to this vote-catching manoeuvre : 'The nobility will cry out that the Republic will

39

be converted from a free state into a monarchy!' (*Letter to Caesar*, VI, 1).

Caesar gave certain Gallic magnates the right to wear the *latus clavus* (a toga with a broad purple stripe, previously reserved for the Roman nobility). They may have been from Gallia Narbonensis, which had been Romanised for half a century, or have given him especially meritorious assistance in his military campaigns. He was then made the object of lampoons with an unconsciously prophetic ring : 'He who led the Gauls in triumph seats them in the Senate House . . .' (Quoted by Suetonius, *Life of Julius Caesar*, LXXX, 2).

The years that separate Sulla from Augustus are the critical period of ideological change. Men like Cato, fiercely hostile to the granting of Roman citizenship to the other inhabitants of Italy (Plutarch, *Cato*, 2), began to seem an anachronism. Those whose ambitions were aimed at autocratic power were all inclined toward vast projects of racial levelling – for there is an historic link between dictatorship and demagogic concessions.

Whether this development sprang from inner conviction or from opportunism, it can be followed stage by stage in the pages of contemporary authors, from Cicero onwards. In his younger years, the orator was very sensitive about his country origin. The nobles looked down on him not only because he was an upstart, a *homo novus,* of an undistinguished family, but also because he had been born outside the City which acknowledged as her legitimate sons only those with generations of residence within her walls. The scorn shown by Catiline toward Cicero is not the contempt of a patrician towards a member of the middle classes, but the disdain of a citizen with roots in the past of the City, who is as proud of them as of any noble title. How, he asks, can the Senate expect a man to give true service to Rome, when he is merely one of the City's lodgers. The word '*inquilini*', or 'lodgers' is explained by the historian Appian for the benefit of his Greek readers as meaning 'those who occupy houses belonging to others.'[7] When Cicero, a man from Arpinum, achieved the office of consul, 'most of the nobility were moved with jealousy, and thought the consulship was in some degree sullied, if a *homo novus,* however meritorious, attained it' (Sallust, *Catilinarian War,* XXIII, 6).

Marius,[8] who also came from Arpinum, maintained the military prestige of the provincial soldiers, as against the sprigs of nobility. Similarly, Cicero often praises the peasant frugality and tenacity of the inhabitants of the country districts, in which he sees a hope for the improvement of political morality and complacently remarks that *he* did not achieve high office through the merits of his ancestors.[9] He seems to enjoy dwelling on the devotion shown to him by the inhabitants of other parts of Italy. Was there perhaps a sort of tacit solidarity between non-Romans? He mentions, for example, in his *Letters to Atticus* (IV, i, 4; 57 B.C.) how a great crowd of them flocked to Brundisium to greet him on his return from exile.

To be known as *'Civis Romanus'* was not only a title much sought after, which gave its holder certain rights – it amounted to a family connection (Cicero, *Verrine Orations* II, v, 172). It gave general protection to the bearer everywhere, and could be relied on to do so even in the remotest countries. In the speeches against Verres, Cicero speaks of the privilege with the fervent enthusiasm of a man who knows what it is like to be without it. 'You,' he says, 'even as a stranger among strangers, among a people inhabiting the farthest and remotest regions of the earth, would have been well served by your claim to that citizenship whose glory is known throughout the world' *(op. cit.,* II, v, 166).

But Cicero takes his stand with the proud supporters of a policy of exclusion, when people are under discussion whom he cannot – as yet – consider his equals. In 69 B.C., when he defended Fonteius, a governor of Gaul who had been accused of embezzlement by the inhabitants, he bases his case on the argument that the word of members of an inferior race is not to be accepted. 'Do you think that nations like that,' he asks, 'are influenced, when they give evidence, by the sanctity of an oath or by the fear of the immortal gods?' ... 'Is any the most honourable native of Gaul to be set on the same level with even the meanest citizen in Rome?' (*Pro Fonteio*, XIII, 30 and XII, 28). But a few years later Cicero, finding it convenient to embrace the views of those then in power, dissociated himself from the dogma of Roman racial superiority, and put forward the argument in favour of a process of assimilation on a much wider base than the recent absorption of the other inhabitants of Italy. This idea was in process of becoming an accepted theory; not so much because Pompey and Caesar had adopted it as a clearly formulated policy, as because it was suited to the stage of development reached by Roman politics at that time, and in keeping with the internal logic of the Empire.

In 62 B.C., Cicero pleaded for the admission to Roman citizenship of the poet Archias, a Greek whose verses, written in his own tongue, hymned the glorious achievements of Marius against the Cimbri and the Teutons, and those of Pompey against the kingdoms of the East.

The few years that had passed between Cicero's speech in defence of Fonteius and his speech in favour of Archias show what a change had taken place in the Roman mentality as a result of the new political atmosphere. Archias was a foreigner, of course – but he was a Greek, and Cicero is torn between a proud awareness of the vast extent of Empire and a clear recognition of the inferiority of Roman culture to Greek: 'Greek literature is read in nearly every country under heaven, while the vogue of Latin is confined to its own boundaries, and they are, we must admit, narrow. Seeing, therefore, the activities of our race know no barrier save the limits of the round earth, we ought to be ambitious that whithersoever our arms have penetrated, there also our fame and glory should extend' (*Pro Archia*, X, 23).

In 56 B.C. – in the middle of the Triumvirate – Cicero pronounced his most famous oration in favour of racial levelling. He was defending the Spaniard Lucius Balbus, a personal friend of Caesar and also of Pompey.

Something of the coming dictatorship of Caesar was in the air, and Cicero, going with the tide, scented it. So he did not merely defend the individual cause of Balbus – the provincial whose right to Roman citizenship rested on his services to Caesar in Spain – but vigorously proclaimed the legitimate nature of a policy of unlimited assimilation, which he treated as the cardinal principle, ideologically speaking, of the Roman Empire. 'What has undoubtedly done most to establish our Empire,' he said, 'and to increase the renown of the Roman people, is that Romulus, that first founder of this City, taught us by the treaty which he made with the Sabines, that this State ought to be enlarged by the admission even of enemies as citizens. Through his authority and example, our forefathers never ceased to grant and bestow citizenship' (*Pro Balbo*, XIII, 31). The different views expressed by Cicero in different speeches may of course be attributed to the varied requirements of the individual cases, rather than to the evolution of his own opinions. But he would certainly always follow the general trend of the time at which he was speaking. The mainstream of public opinion is therefore reflected in his speeches, and its direction is towards an extension of the City's boundaries to coincide with those of the Empire.

To reassure those who feared that the rising tide of advancement for other peoples would finally submerge the original stock of Rome, and change its traditional characteristics, the most ancient possible precedents were invoked. The case of Romulus is quoted not only by Cicero, but by Livy (I, xii, 2), and by Plutarch (*Romulus*, 16). The steady growth of the power of republican Rome was due to the system initiated by the founder of the City. 'And indeed there was nothing that did more increase the greatness of Rome, than that she did always unite and incorporate those whom she conquered into herself' (*Romulus*, 16). 'Do you wish, according to the example of your ancestors, to augment the Roman state by admitting the vanquished among your citizens?' (Livy, VIII, xiii, 5).

'We too, though foreigners, have reigned' are the words Livy puts into the mouth of the widow of Ancus Marcius, as she tries

43

to overcome the hesitation of Servius Tullius. 'Consider who you are, not whence you are sprung' (Livy I, xli, 3). 'Nor is it at all new with the Senate and People of Rome,' writes Velleius Paterculus, in the reign of Tiberius, 'to consider the most meritorious as the most noble' (II, cxxviii, 1).

The new ideas were promulgated directly from the throne in the reign of Claudius, who himself proposed the admission to the *jus honorum* in A.D. 48 of the leading families of the Gallia Comata – Transalpine Gaul excluding Gallia Narbonensis. This not merely gave them equality of legal rights, but also made them eligible for the highest offices. Claudius was unpopular with the conservatives, perhaps because he was considered a champion of the policy of assimilation. His mania for putting men newly issued from barbarism into togas was ridiculed even by the plebeians, according to Dio Cassius.[10]

Behind these noble aspirants to the *latus clavus* stood the rest of the Gallic nation, sure of the favour of an emperor it regarded as its own. (Claudius had in fact been born at Lyons, while his father was making war against the Germans.)

The senators were against the proposal, which might have reduced the number of honourable appointments open to them, and Tacitus reports their objections. Some were based on national pride: was Italy sunk so low that she had call on men who were barbarians but yesterday to infuse new blood into the Senate? Other objects were inspired by patriotic feelings: they had not forgotten the long resistance of Vercingetorix, nor the recent uprisings of Julius Florus and of Julius Sacrovir, (A.D. 21). Others, finally, had well-founded apprehensions about their own interests: 'What distinctions will be left for the remnants of our noble houses, or for any impoverished senators from Latium? Every place will be taken by these millionaires!' (Tacitus, *Annals,* XI, xxiii).

The account by Tacitus of the speech in which Claudius replied to the objections has the appearance of a verbatim report. We happen also to have the text of the speech as actually delivered. A bronze tablet, on which his words were gratefully inscribed by the Gauls they benefited, came to light many centuries later at Lyons.[11]

A comparison of the speech as rewritten by Tacitus with the truly authentic text of the bronze tablet shows certain differences, which may well be largely due to considerations of style – perhaps also to subtle, tendentious motives on the part of the historian, which need not detain us here.[12] The interesting point is that both the emperor and the historian quite openly plagiarise Livy, borrowing from the speech of the tribune Canuleius in favour of the granting of rights of intermarriage to the plebeians (IV, iii, 4). A pleasing display of erudition, this plagiarism by an emperor who prided himself on his historical learning. It also reveals an historical awareness of the close analogy between two social developments. The advancement of the plebeians in the fifth century B.C. corresponded to the advancement of the provincials in the first century A.D. The scale of these concessions grew wider and wider, until the precincts of the City embraced the whole territory of Gaul.

Claudius seems very conscious of the fact that the argument which carried most weight with the senators is the appeal to precedent. 'I deeply regret,' he says, 'the opposition you show today's proposal, as if it were an innovation. I urge you, on the contrary, to consider how many changes have taken place in this City from its earliest days. . . . At one time the kings were the masters of this City – yet they were not able to transmit their powers to successors of the same family. . . . So strangers came in, some of them even from other countries: Romulus was followed by Numa, who was born a Sabine – a neighbouring nation, no doubt, but still a foreign one at that time. Ancus Marcius was followed by Tarquinius Priscus, son of the Corinthian Demaratus.'

Claudius goes on to enumerate the offices of state which had been successively introduced to cope with increasing social pressure and widening territorial and administrative responsibilities – the posts of consul, military dictator, and tribune of the people; finally the participation of the plebeians not only in positions of authority, but also in priestly offices. Then he quotes the names of Augustus and Tiberius, his venerated predecessors and members of his own family, as emperors who had voluntarily made similar concessions to deserving candidates. There is no other surviving evidence of these concessions except the bronze tablet which has emerged to the light of day after so many centuries of burial in the soil of France.

Then Claudius, just like Canuleius, goes on to make telling use of the non-Roman origin of many of the patricians themselves. The tribune of the people had quoted this precedent (according to Livy) in the fifth century B.C., when the movement of the noble families from the hamlets of Latium into the City was still a matter of living memory. When Claudius made his speech, however, the reference had a legendary character, of sentimental rather than legal significance. 'Clausus, the most ancient of my ancestors,' says the emperor, 'was a Sabine, who was admitted to Roman citizenship and to patrician rank on the same day.'[13]

Claudius finally answers the objections of the nationalists. The Gauls, it is true, opposed the advance of the deified Julius for ten years – but that was a century ago, and since then they have given proof of their unshakable loyalty. (The emperor does not mention the rebellions of Florus and Sacrovir in A.D. 21). 'Thanks to the Gauls,' says Claudius, 'my father Drusus, when he undertook the subjection of Germany, had a steady and secure situation behind him, which was guaranteed by the Gallic respect for peace.'[14]

The demand for a widening of the City's boundaries to include the provinces slowly passes from practical reality to ideological expression. Its formulation is carried out by provincial and Christian writers in the period ending with the fall of Rome.[15]

NOTES TO CHAPTER

1. *Dum nullum fastiditur genus, in quo eniteret virtus, crevit imperium Romanum.*
2. *De Legibus*, II, ii, 5. The significance of this passage, on a juristic rather than philosophical plane, is emphasised by E. De Ruggiero, *La patria nel diritto pubblico*, Rome 1921, p. 9 (note 4) and p. 12.
3. *De Legibus*, I, xxiii, 61; see also I, vii, 23 and I, xiii, 35.
4. Philo, *On Dreams*, I, 39; *On Joseph*, VI, 29; *Moses*, II, 51–3; *On the Creation*, 142–4. See also E. Bréhier, *Les idées religieuses de Philo J.*, Paris 1950 (3rd ed.); E. Goodenough, *The Politics of Philo J.*, New Haven, London 1938; S. Tracy, *Philo and the Roman Principate*, Williamsport 1933; A. J. Festugière, *La révélation d'Hermès Trismégiste*, Paris 1949, II, 521.
5. Ideas common to all the schools and widely published, as for instance, the περί κόσμου (*De Mundo*), an apocryphal work of Aristotle of uncertain date, in which the description of the universe is a devout contemplation of the work of God – 'that Great City which is the world.' *De Mundo*, VI, 400, B 25–30, in A. J. Festugière, *op. cit.* II, 475.
6. The authenticity of the *Letters to Caesar* has been often examined; it is denied by R. Syme, *Sallust*, Berkeley, California 1964, Appendix II, 'The False Sallust', pp. 318–27. See S. Mazzarino, *Il pensiero storico classico*, Bari 1966, Vol. III, *passim*.
7. Appian, *Civil War*, II, i, 2; see also Sallust, *Catilinarian War*, XXXI, 7.
8. Sallust, *Jugurthine War*, LXIII, 3.
9. Cicero, *Pro Murena*, VII, 16; *De Lege Agraria*, II, i, ii, iii; *Catilinarian Orations*, I, xi, 28. See also Velleius Paterculus, II, cxxviii, 1–3; J. Vogt, *Homo Novus*, Stuttgart 1926, reprinted in *Gesetz und Handlungsfreiheit in der Geschichte*, Stuttgart 1955, pp. 81 ff.; Plutarch, *Cato the Censor*, 1. The consul Mummius was the first *homo novus* to be allowed to adopt a title taken from the name of the enemy he had conquered, calling himself 'Achaicus' after the capture of Corinth in 146 B.C. (Velleius Paterculus, I, xiii).
10. LX, 17, 5. See also Seneca, *Apokolokyntosis*, III.
11. *C.I.L.*, XIII, 1668. See also P. Fabia, *La table claudienne de Lyon*, Lyons 1929; J. Carcopino, *Les étapes de l'impérialisme romain*, Paris 1961, Chap. V, p. 174; E. G. Hardy, *Roman Laws and Charters*, Oxford 1912, p. 133; A. N. Sherwin White, *The Roman Citizenship*, Oxford 1939.
12. The two texts are analyzed and compared in R. Syme, *Tacitus*, Oxford 1958, Vol. I, pp. 317–19.
13. Tacitus, *Annals*, XI, xxix. See also Livy, II, xvi, 4–6. The period here is 504 B.C.

47

14. Except where otherwise stated, the quotations are from the inscription (*C.I.L.*, XIII, 1668) and not from Tacitus, (*Annals*, XI, xxiii).
15. *Panegyric* X, xxxv to Constantine: *Senatus dignitas non nomine quam re esset illustrior cum ex totius orbis flore constaret* (313 A.D.). Also Rutilius Namatianus, *De Reditu*, I, 14: [*Senatus*] *nec putat externos quos decet esse suos* (417 A.D.).

III

Cultural Factors
and the Ecumenical Idea

I have not one single city, but the whole world
in which to live.

CRATES[1]

IN THE decades that followed the Punic wars, the Romans, aware that their zone of influence now extended far beyond the shores of Italy, began to understand what their mission was to be, and to shoulder its burden.

If we are to believe Livy writing much later, the men of that time already had a clear idea of the Roman mission. It was perfectly clear to Greek political observers, according to the historian, that the aims of Rome included not only free navigation in the narrow seas between Sicily and the African coast, not only trade outlets in the eastern markets, but also the destruction of Carthage and the take-over of her sphere of influence. 'All mankind are now in a state of anxious suspense,' says the ambassador of Locri to the senators of Rome, 'whether they are to see you or the Carthaginians lords of the world' (Livy, XXIX, xvii, 6; 205 B.C.).

After the conquest of Spain and North Africa, the Romans felt insecure because of the possibility of alliances being formed between the Carthaginians and the Hellenistic kings. The government of the Republic made a show of solidarity with the various peoples under monarchical rule, and found in this an excuse for intervention. The Romans, according to a letter from

49

D

Antiochus the Great to the King of Bithynia, were coming to abolish all kingly governments, so that there should be no empire in any part of the world, save that of Rome (Livy, XXXVII, xxv, 5–6; 190 B.C.).

Looking back from the pinnacle of power attained by Rome under Augustus, and writing in an atmosphere of world-wide imperialism, Livy indicates clearly the turning-point of history, the moment when the expansionist policy became a conscious driving force in the minds of the Romans themselves, and was fully appreciated in all its importance by the onlookers. Before attacking the King of Syria, in 191 B.C., Acilius Glabrio made a speech which, in the version given by Livy, is an undisguised manifesto of aggression. 'You will open a way for the Roman power into Asia and Syria, and all the most opulent realms to the extremity of the East. What, then, must be the consequence, but that, from Gades to the Red Sea, we shall have no limit but the Ocean, which encircles in its embrace the whole orb of the earth; and that all mankind shall regard the Roman name with a degree of veneration next to that which they pay to the divinities? Nerve yourselves to be worthy of such high rewards!' (Livy, XXXVI, xvii, 14–16).

Nerve yourselves to be worthy of the rewards! This was precisely the task to which Rome addressed herself in those critical years: finding a theoretical justification for the Empire; making the spirit of the people, as well as their institutions, ready to cope with it. The process took several centuries, because it involved the conversion of a restricted social system into a world-wide administration, the abandonment of a traditional policy in favour of one of much wider scope, and the acceptance of the responsibilities of conquest by those who enjoyed its profits.

In those same decades, Greek thinkers, orators and literary men arrived in Rome, as immigrants, as hostages, and as guests. Roman intellectual circles had been open to Greek influence for over a hundred years; now they were exposed to direct contact with Greek thought and its stimulating effects.

But the new ideas did not come through in a suitably gradual manner. These were the years of miraculous growth – a growth too vast and too rapid for its full scope to be understood at the time. The first two Punic wars lasted sixty years, and ended in 202 B.C. The Macedonian wars ended in 168 B.C., with the victorious battle of Pydna. The whole Mediterranean, from east to west, was now a Roman lake.

The achievement of power carried with it the duty of communicating a significant cultural message to the Empire's new subject peoples. These were the very years in which the Romans were absorbing the precious spiritual sustenance of Greek civilisation. They were overpowered by it before they had time to distinguish just how much of its content was right for them. Rome received the multifarious imprint of an ancient civilisation, which contained certain confused and mutually contradictory elements. Her thinking began to be very deeply coloured by ideas which had been worked out by another people, as the culminating result of a spiritual travail caused by very different historical circumstances.

One reaction to the theoretical and abstract nature of the new ideas was a hardening of the provincial and inflexible aspects of the Roman character. For in the early stages of their imperial career, the Romans absorbed a body of theory which had no relevance to their own current stage of development, because it came from a country already far advanced on the road to collapse. The Greeks had explored the problem of good and evil in every way of which the human mind is capable. Faced with the basic question how men ought to live together, they had worked out various solutions – some systematic and Utopian, others more extreme and disruptive. It was natural that the Romans found these speculations attractive, and eagerly absorbed the principles on which they were based. It was also understandable that they could not make immediate use of them in the legal and practical aspects of government – just as a young man, at the age of free decision and constructive effort, cannot base his actions on the advice of a teacher already grey with ex-

51

perience, even if he listens to the old man's views with the greatest respect.

In Athens, the principle of the equality of all citizens before the law had been established even before the Persian wars. The victories of the little republics blazoned the worth of their free institutions for all to see. Those years saw the birth of the idea that only the free citizen, the hater of tyrants, has the right to fight for his country, or the right, for example, to carry the blocks of marble for the buildings on the Acropolis. From this springs the conviction that other peoples are incapable of democratic self-government, and are fit only for slavery, since they do not possess institutions like those of the *Polis* – institutions of divine inspiration which the free man obeys willingly because they are his protection against both tyranny and anarchy. 'The people must fight to save its laws, as it fights to protect the walls of the city,' says one of the fragments of Heraclitus.[2] For the citizen, obedience to the laws of the City is a spontaneous act, because they coincide with the moral law. 'Stranger, tell the Spartans that we lie here, obeying their orders', says the epitaph for the fallen at Thermopylae. On the pediment of the temple of Zeus at Olympia, a race of calm, impassive beings strikes down the brutal Centaurs, the slaves of intemperance. This is the message of Greek art and of Greek thought – the triumph of Reason.

The Carthaginian threat in the third century B.C. aroused the Romans to a jealous love of their little country. At that time, Rome was still a walled city-state, for whose citizens the gods were the divine protectors of the nation, the Senate were its fathers, and strangers were an object of suspicion. The common peril drew them together, awakened their racial consciousness, and suggested the advisability of planting one or two strategic colonies at suitable points. The first annexations – those of Sicily, Sardinia and Spain – were inspired by motives of defence, not by overpopulation or the desire for foreign markets.

The political evolution of Rome had reached this point when she began to expand towards the Aegean, this time for fear of being encircled from the east by the Carthaginians. This, too, was a move on the Mediterranean chess-board which could not be put off any longer. But on this occasion, the consequences were of the highest importance, through the increase in the cultural influence of the Greek states.

Rome now encountered Greeks who had left her present stage of psychological development three centuries behind them – the stage, that is, of patriotic fervour and pride in free institutions. Their later experiences, and the defeats they had suffered, had given the Greeks ideas very different from those which had been appropriate in the years of their victories over Persia. Faith in the supreme excellence of the democratic city-state was a thing of the past, and so was devotion to its laws, which could no longer exact unquestioning obedience from men who now knew all about the diversity of human nature. The influx of prisoners and the mingling of different peoples in the seaports had taught the Greeks how varied the customs and the laws of different nations can be.

The idea of a natural law began to spread abroad, a law valid for all men, standing above all legal codes, and sometimes contradicting them. The Sophists reached the stage of a deliberate and emphatic affirmation that mankind was one and indivisible. For Antiphon, there is a universal law which stands above the laws of individual states, and abolishes all distinctions between races and between classes. 'We are all of the same substance,' he says, 'both barbarians and Greeks.' Laws, for the Sophists, are 'chains imposed upon nature', which no longer inspire inner consent. 'In my eyes,' says Hippias, 'ye are all members of one family, citizens of one city, not according to the law, but according to nature. . . . For the law, that tyrant of mankind, does violence to nature. . . .' 'I have not one single city,' says Crates of Thebes, 'but the whole world in which to live.' 'For the wise man,' says Democritus, 'the whole earth is a suitable home; and so the fatherland of virtuous spirits is the world.'[3] When Socrates was asked from where he came, he did not say that he was an Athenian or a Corinthian, but that he

53

belonged to the Universe (*Epictetus,* I, ix, 6). Diogenes Laertius, too, when asked the same question, replied 'I am a citizen of the world' (Diogenes Laertius, VI, 63).

These ideas emerged slowly from the stream of Greek thought, with its strong national tendency towards generalisation and abstraction. They drew added strength from the variety of experience that had enriched the Greek spirit. The Greeks had shown themselves capable of mourning the Trojan Hector with Homer, and of participating with Aeschylus in the agony of the Persians they had just defeated. As the centuries went by, the varied panorama of human life, of wartime destruction, the political convulsions and social upheavals of post-war years, all combined to divert men's thoughts from the affairs of their own little states to wider horizons. Looking back on that period, Plato writes of the extraordinary speed with which laws and customs broke down and collapsed.[4]

The minds of men escaped from the distressing sight of factious party politics, and from the dissatisfaction caused by their own frustrated ambitions, by losing themselves in longing for an ideal society. The City of Justice, ruled by lovers of the higher good, is the object of the noblest minds; and working for its realisation becomes something very like a religious vocation. But the City of Justice remains far out of reach of the little community huddled round the temple on the hill top. The life of the universe may have begun with the act of Creation, but the sequel has been entrusted to mankind, and it consists in the advance from the level of the brutes to the point where our will knowingly coincides with the law. It is the task of the best of mankind, schooled by the State in the art of government, to instill into the complex and changeable material of humanity a principle which undeniably also exists in Nature, however hard it may be to decipher – the principle of Law. Their eyes fixed on the Absolute, these leaders will guide the destiny of the City, and try to achieve in it the realisation of the laws of beauty, justice and virtue.[5]

The City of Justice, then, must mirror an eternal model, and

must be governed by men of thoughtful and severe tempera-
ment – perhaps even by one such man. With their usual lack
of prejudice, the Athenians, as represented by Xenophon, select
earthly models drawn from enemy countries – the Sparta of
Lycurgus, the Persia of Cyrus. A vision appears of a monarchy
so moderate and beneficial that even the most independent
spirits will be glad to be numbered among its subjects, since the
king rules only by virtue of being the best of men. Philosophy
will teach him how to achieve religious and political unity, to
realise in this world the intentions of the God who has given order
to the universe, and so to establish peace between the rival city-
states – which indeed might well be all combined into a federation.

Alexander was the first to expand the idea of the fatherland
to embrace the whole world. To the philosophers of the next
age, this suggested a plan for universal brotherhood. Greek
thinkers, who wanted to bring the changeable and inconsistent
world of reality into line with the perfection of the Absolute,
conceived the idea of a unified world of men, resembling the
cosmos with its single Divine ruler. 'The much-admired *Republic*
of Zeno, the founder of the Stoic sect, may be summed up in this
one main principle: that all the inhabitants of this world of ours
should not live differentiated by their respective rules of justice
into separate cities and communities, but that we should consider
all men to be of one community and polity, and that we should
have a common life and an order common to all' (Plutarch,
On the Fortune of Alexander, I, 6).

For Zeno, the first leader of the Stoics, and also for his
successor Chrysippus, the idea that the *Polis* is the centre of
religious, moral and political life is a thing of the past. All men
are citizens of the world, and should obey the precepts of a Law
which is both divine and human, because it rules over gods and
men alike, and coincides with both the voice of nature and the
promptings of reason. From the fragmentary writings which have
come down to us, it is not easy to extract a Stoic system of
political theory. But it is certain that the egalitarian and cosmo-

politan principles which were an integral part of the Stoic doctrine inspired the work of many political reformers.[6] Men like Sphaerus, the teacher of Cleomenes at Sparta, and Blossius, who taught the Gracchi at Rome and went on to teach Aristonicus at Pergamus, sought to establish a society based on the abolition of social distinctions and even the abolition of slavery.

These were the years in which the Roman Empire was born. For Cato and the other patriots who were loyal to the old conception of Rome as the dominant city whose gates must be kept closed to foreigners, the Empire should rightly be no more than an extension of the old Roman sphere of influence – a widening circle of outworks, designed to hold off the threat of invasion and to embrace certain territories which promised good supplies of recruits, raw materials, or tribute.

But territorial growth brought with it certain human contacts which had an insidious effect on those convictions. After the Macedonian wars, there was an influx of Greek scholars into Rome. It was Polybius, the guest of Paulus Aemilius and later the close friend of Scipio Aemilianus, to whom the Romans owed the conception of the Empire as an ecumenical organism. Sent to Rome as a hostage in 168 B.C., Polybius began to consider what reason there could be for the territorial gains so miraculously achieved by the Romans in the last fifty years. He concluded that the explanation lay in the perfection of their constitution, in their devotion to religion, and in their severe morality. Thus his account of their imperial system contained an admission of Roman superiority in the ethical and political fields as well as in military matters. The Rome he described was worthy to impose her rule on the world. His explanation of the genesis of her power was to provide a theoretical basis for its continuance.

Not being a Roman, Polybius was free from the prejudices and inhibitions which fettered Latin writers. He felt no need to dig up noble and disinterested motives for every declaration of war. In his very first chapter, he attributes a programme of universal dominion to the Romans after their victory over Carthage. He is generous with praise for the Roman political system, which has a useful adjunct, he says, in Roman religion. His high esteem for the religion is thus based on practical rather than theoretical grounds. He regards both the political and the religious elements in Roman life as ideally organised for purposes of world domination – which, in his view, is the objective toward which the Roman people is on the march.

The earlier empires of Persia, Sparta, and Macedon were limited, temporary affairs: 'but the Romans have subjected to their rule not portions, but nearly the whole of the world (*oikoumene*), and possess an empire which is not only immeasurably greater than any which preceded it, but need not fear rivalry in the future' (Polybius, I, 2, 7).

Sparta, of course, was the model always preferred by the moralists and idealised by the conservatives,[7] and might well appear worthy of special praise, with its austere way of life and its equal distribution of goods. But these virtues, says Polybius, tend only to preserve a city, and not to make it greater (VI, 50). Men often expected to find the image of their own past reflected in the contemporary republic – but Polybius had an instinctive understanding of the imperial vocation of Rome, which consisted in precisely the gift of assimilation which Sparta had always lacked.

Once installed in Rome, the ingenious Greeks did not limit themselves to the setting of high spiritual targets. Sometimes they raised subtle doubts about the legitimacy of conquest. Sometimes they sowed seeds of revolutionary thought even in the exclusive circles of the aristocracy,[8] with varied results. Scipio became convinced of the need for the removal of privilege on the horizontal plane, and saw instinctively that Roman civilisation must become a single harmonious entity, embracing all peoples without any racial barriers, and following a single leader. But Tiberius and Gaius Gracchus became the first champions of the abolition of privilege on the vertical plane, for they realised that if the Empire were to endure it must win the willing support of the lower classes, who were then subject to harsh disabilities.

Though later Latin historians sometimes criticise Scipio for giving himself the airs of a superman, they generally have very high praise for this statesman. But they have only condemnation for the Gracchi. For the sake of expansion, it seems, Romans were willing to accept despotism, but not the elevation of the lower classes.

As the consolidation of the Empire went forward, there was a constant shift in the forces on which it was based. It would not be long before members of the equestrian order, freedmen, veterans, auxiliaries, provincials and petty officials of varied origin would claim equality of rights and of opportunity to achieve high office, either for themselves or for their sons. These pressures favoured the work of the levellers, and led to doctrines which bestowed an ideal meaning on daily practice. But during the years when intellectual life at Rome was dominated by Greek thinkers, very few Romans felt inclined to espouse these doctrines. The ideas they embodied had many years of underground development to come, before they could bear the fruit of practical innovations.

In many cases, the Stoic ideal of moral perfection led men to a complacent contemplation of their own virtuous conduct, as of some rare and beautiful sight, rather than to active participation in public life. Gravity, decorum and impassiveness were gentlemanly virtues, which could be regarded as identical with the virtues of one's ancestors; but it was not very easy to convert them into tasks achieved for the benefit of society. And the other philosophy absorbed by the Romans, that of Epicurus, urged men to flee from responsibilities, material interests, and the cares of the world, to keep away from the *profanum vulgus* and take refuge in the world of books and the arts.

The main tendency was therefore toward a sterile spiritual isolation, which made the pride of the upper classes still more overbearing, and helped to introduce narcissism into the life of the mind, and anachronism into its ideals. The imperative demands of private life prevailed over those of the common weal, and the moral demands made on the individual considered as a human being began to be different from those made on him as a citizen.

The Empire came into being in the middle of this inner conflict between the spiritual aspirations of the individual and the official beliefs of the good citizen. To the Greeks of that age, these steps toward the end of racial boundaries and of religious and social distinctions formed but one normal stage of the onward march of human thought toward truth – the particular section which had been allotted to their own generation. Considered in conjunction with the actual course of events, Greek aspirations toward the unity of all peoples might be excessively Utopian, but they did coincide in time with the break-up of the old separatist political units in the Hellenistic world, and to that extent were in harmony with the course of history. In Rome, on the other hand, the same ideas could only be artificially superimposed on a system of thought which demanded the supremacy of one race over the others by virtue of its political superiority and its military strength.

The policy of expansion was bound to reach the stage of cosmopolitan egalitarianism; but at the time of its first impetus, its own inner nature demanded a period of autocratic rule, based on the assumption of the physical and moral pre-eminence of the conquering race.

All these elements mingled in Latin literature. The conflict between the morality appropriate to the growing power of the City and the ideas of the universalists reveals itself in the inconsistencies of both writers and politicians. Cato accused the philosophers of corrupting the youth of Rome, and in fact proposed and carried a motion in the Senate that they should be expelled from the City;[9] yet he too was a follower of Greek thinkers. Plautus echoes the disrespectful comments of the public on these foreign pedants, who preached abstinence and lived the lives of parasites in the households of the nobility. 'They stalk along with their sage observations, fellows you can always see guzzling in a tavern when they've stolen something' (Plautus, *Curculio*,

288 ff). Yet the plots of his comedies come from the Greek theatre.

There was a general widening of the horizons of the spirit, thanks to the influence of Greek thought. The walls of the City ceased to be a barrier, for the dead as well as for the living. Memorial inscriptions of the republican era reflect the closed atmosphere of a restricted society, and portray characters who are niggardly even in their virtues. But in the first century the tone changes to one of generous humanity.[10]

Military and civic merit counts for less than it did; a larger moral standard, suited to a world-wide community, has come into existence.

NOTES TO CHAPTER

1. Crates of Thebes. See H. Diels, *Poetarum Philos. Fragmenta*, p. 127.
2. Heraclitus, *Fragments*, 44. See. H. Diels, *Herakleitos von Ephesus*, Berlin 1909. For Antiphon, see Timpanaro Tardini, *I Sofisti*, Bari 1923, p. 120. For Hippias, see Plato, *Protagoras*, 337 C-D. For Democritus, see P. Natorp, *Die Ethika des Demokritos*, Marburg 1893, Fragment 168.
3. H. C. Baldry, *The Unity of Mankind in Greek Thought*, Cambridge 1965. The references to Antiphon are on pp. 43–5, and to Crates on p. 109.
4. Letters, VII, 325 D. The doubts about the authenticity of Plato's epistles which were prevalent at the beginning of the last century have been dispelled by modern scholarship. See C. Turolla, *Platone, i Dialoghi, l'Apologia e le Epistole*, Milan 1953, Vol. III, p. 753; N. Abbagnano, *Storia della filosofia*, Turin 1966, p. 74; D. Ross, *Plato's Theory of Ideas*, Oxford 1951, p. 3, which fixes the date of the epistle quoted here as 353–2 B.C.; Glenn P. Morrow, *Studies in Plato's Epistles*, University of Illinois, 1935, p. 47; A. Maddalena, *Platone, le lettere*, Bari 1948, p. vi.
5. Plato, *Republic*, VI, 484D, 500C; VII, 520C. See A. J. Festugière, *Contemplation et vie contemplative selon Platon*, Paris 1936, p. 454: 'Si l'état est juste c'est parcequ'il obéit au sage, qui, de son côté, obéit à l'idée.'
6. See T. A. Sinclair, *A History of Greek Political Thought*, London 1951, Chaps. XII and XIII; M. A. Fisch, *Alexander and the Stoics*, in *Am. J. Philol.*, LVIII, 1937, pp. 59–82, 129–51; W. W. Tarn, *Alexander the Great and the Unity of Mankind*, London 1933; M. E. Reesor, *The Political Theory of the Old and Middle Stoa*, New York 1951.

7. F. Ollier, *Le mirage spartiate*, Paris 1933 and 1943.
8. P. Grimal, *Le siècle des Scipions*, Paris 1953; F. W. Walbank, *Political Morality and the Friends of Scipio*, in *J.R.S.*, LV, 1965, pp. 1 ff.; W. Capelle, *Griechische Ethik und Römischer Imperialismus*, in *Klio*, XXV, 1932, pp. 86 ff.
9. Plutarch, *Marcus Cato*, 22. The expulsions took place in 173 and 161 B.C.
10. *Nullo odio sine offensa*, is the epitaph of one professional soldier: F. Buecheler, *Carmina Epigraphica Latina*, Leipzig 1886, 372–3.

IV

Gradual Penetration
of New Ideas

Through conquering we have been conquered.
We are the subjects of foreigners.

PLINY, *Natural History*, XXIV, i, 1[1]

THE TEACHING that all peoples are one slowly spread abroad and
found its way into the hearts of men, gaining in consistency
until it provided the true basis of Roman thought. It is conspicuous in the writings of Cicero, who echoes, quotes, or perhaps
plagiarises, the Greek thinkers who had been active in Rome
during the period he regards as the golden age of its culture
–the century of the Scipios. Being an eclectic, he throws together
opinions gleaned from the most contradictory sources – but his
whole work is permeated by faith in a single God, present in the
hearts of men, without Whom there could be no universal
conception of humanity. Cicero absorbed from the Stoics the
concept that the only valid law is the law of nature, which towers
above all human provisions. 'True law is right reason in agreement with nature,' he says; 'it is of universal application, unchanging and everlasting; there will not be different laws at
Rome and at Athens or different laws now and in the future,
but one eternal and unchangeable law will be valid for all nations
and all times' (*De Republica,* III, xxi, 33). And again : 'If the
principles of Justice were founded on the decrees of peoples,
the edicts of princes, the decisions of judges, then Justice would
sanction robbery and adultery' (*De Legibus,* I, xvi, 13).

The City gates which the Romans have guarded so long and so jealously are now flung wide open. Cicero's Philus speaks to Laelius about 'that home which is not shut in by the walls we build, but is the whole universe, a home and a fatherland which the gods have given us the privilege of sharing with them' (*De Republica*, I, xiii, 19).

In the same work, Scipio looks down from the starry heavens on the little City where he had played the leading part during his life-time. Though he knows that it has since become the capital of a world-wide Empire, he finds it totally unimpressive, when seen from a cosmic view-point. 'The earth itself seemed so small to me,' he says, 'that I was scornful of our Empire, which covers only a single point, as it were, upon its surface' (*ibid.*, VI, xvi, 16).

From these phrases we can see that certain political influences have made their way into the universal religion that has taken possession of the hearts of men. The Hellenistic doctrine that the City of mankind is the whole earth, and that all its inhabitants are equal, has been transposed into a political conception of world-wide scope. The literate classes of the last few decades of the Republic knew very well that a new theory of the State had to be formulated, which must be valid for the whole world.

The Empire had, indeed, reached its world-wide stage. The conquests of the Scipios, to which Polybius and the masters of the Middle Stoa had borne witness, were followed by those of Lucullus, Sulla, Pompey and Caesar. The theatre of operations had spread out to cover regions so vast and remote that a cosmic view of geography, at least, was needed to follow it.

It was no longer a matter of theorising, in learned conversations, essays or lectures about a Utopian plan for a single world government and a legal system based on the law of nature — the time had come to put it into practice. To regard the Empire as a world-wide political organism was no longer a flight of fancy — it was a statement of fact. Words and concepts of universal significance begin to appear. *Orbis terrarum,* for example, is an expression often used by Cicero and the other authors of his time, to indicate the vast extent of the Roman Empire.[2]

The military prowess of the Romans has now mastered the whole world,[3] and the Empire comes to be generally regarded as a beneficent, indeed providential organisation. Cicero refers to the Romans bringing 'safety to the world' in the *Pro Lege Manilia*; in the *Catilinarian Orations* he calls Rome 'the light of the world and the refuge of all nations' and describes the Senate as 'the most august, the most important [assembly] in the world'; 'our government,' he claims in the *De Officiis*, 'could be called more accurately a protectorate of the world than a dominion.' Sulla is referred to as one who 'guided the Republic and swayed the world', in the *Pro Roscio Amerino* – and in fact the dictator did put a globe on his coins. Political observers, he says in *Pro Milone,* begin to be aware of the fact that the Roman can swagger and domineer anywhere in the world, and can distribute crowns to his favourites.[4]

When we come to Pompey, Cicero frequently reminds us that his victories have put the whole world at the feet of Rome.[5] Lucan repeats the same message equally often, a hundred years later. It is fully realised by the contemporaries of Caesar and Pompey that the outcome of the war between the two generals will determine the destiny of the whole human race.[6]

Pompey's triumph was of a kind to convince even the most obtuse spectator that the whole world was laying its treasures at the feet of Rome. The theatre that Pompey built in 55 B.C. – the first stone-built theatre in Rome – was decorated with statues representing the conquered peoples, each with its national characteristics (Plutarch, *Pompey,* 42–52). This fancy is repeated on the coinage of Hadrian, and before his temple; and also around the altar at Lyons, where Drusus put up statues representing the sixty tribes of Gaul. The nations of the world now offered themselves in effigy to the gaze of the Roman people.

When hostilities broke out between Caesar and Pompey, the boundless extent of the battle-fronts, and the vast number of different nations and races taking part, caused much bewilderment. Pompey, it was thought, might march through Germany to the attack of Gaul (Cicero, *Letters to Atticus*, X, ix). Alternatively, he might pass through Africa and invade Spain. And the roll-call of nations fighting under his flag was most impressive. 'All his fleet,' says Cicero, 'from Alexandria, from Colchis, from Tyre, from Sidon, from Aradus, from Cyprus, from Panphilia, from Lycia, from Rhodes, from Chios, from Byzantium, from Lesbos, from Smyrna, from Miletus, from Cos, is being got ready to cut off the supplies of Italy and to blockade the grain-producing provinces.'[7]

A century later Lucan repeats the same theme when he devotes 120 lines of his epic[8] to the list of the nations who thronged to swell the ranks of Pompey's army : Greece, Colchis, Thrace, the Troad, Syria, Cilicia, India, Cappadocia, Armenia, Arabia, Mesopotamia, Ethiopia and Scythia – he does not arrange them in any particular order. Other peoples are recorded only by the names of the seas that wash their shores – the nations of the Caspian and Black Seas – or by the names of their rivers – the tribes of the Nile and the Don. The poet sums up the stupefaction of contemporary observers of this duel between two rivals, both belonging to the restricted ranks of the Roman elite, and fighting it out on a battlefield as wide as the world itself. 'In order that the fortunate Caesar might receive everything together, Pharsalia offered him the whole world to conquer at once.'[9]

Caesar, for his part, had been recruiting auxiliary troops among the Germans from an earlier period – that of the most difficult stage of the Gallic revolt. But Cicero, a contemporary witness, speaks only of Gallic soldiers, said to have volunteered for the war against Pompey. At a time of world-wide mobilisation, he says, they 'offered to serve at their own expense, for ten years' (*Letters to Atticus*, IX, xiii).

Gauls and Germans undoubtedly followed Caesar in his subsequent campaigning across the world. He himself speaks of seeing them dead on the soil of Africa (*African War*, XL). As Marius had broken the law and the customs of Rome by enrolling the poorest classes in the legions, so Caesar swelled the ranks of his army with foreigners, who had been hostile savages a few years earlier.

Romans who lived through this period of racial, social and spiritual transformation, of collapsing institutions, of foreign infiltration into the Roman organism, experienced the same dismay that the patricians had felt when the plebeians had started claiming the right to marry their daughters, to hold the high offices of state, and to penetrate into the closed circle of the priests. In 54 B.C., Cicero wrote: 'The State, my dear Pomponius, has lost not only its sap and its blood, but even all its colour and outward semblance' (*Letters to Atticus,* IV, xviii, 2). In the *De Republica,* written in the same year, he says: 'It is through our own faults, not by any accident, that we retain only the form of the commonwealth, but have long since lost its substance' (V, i, 2).

The old, narrow fatherland began to be lost in the vastness of this new world. 'The individual who had proudly called himself a citizen of his own city and had felt the full value of the civic bond, now found no sense of liberation in the acknowledged universality of his new, world-wide fatherland, but rather a feeling of emptiness and isolation. . . . In a world which had become too vast for him, he began to feel that there was no other road to self-affirmation except that of renunciation. . . . Faced with this new fatherland, with which he had so little intimate connection, he no longer felt bound to devote his own activities to its welfare. . . . But he could still keep his own ideals locked up in his own heart, as if in a sacred shrine.'[10]

NOTES TO CHAPTER

1. *Vincendo victi sumus: paremus externis.*
2. J. Vogt, *Orbis Romanus,* Tübingen 1929; F. Christ, *Die Römische Welt-herrschaft in der Antiken Dichtung,* Stuttgart 1938; F. Kaerst, *Die Antike Idee der Oikumene,* Leipzig 1903.

3. Cicero, *Pro Murena*, X, 22: *Haec[virtus] orbem terrarum parere huic imperio coëgit.*
4. *Pro Lege Manilia*, XXII, 64; *Catilinarian Orations*, IV, vi, 11 and I, iv, 9; *De Officiis*, II, viii, 27; *Pro Roscio Amerino*, XLV, 131; *Pro Milone*, XXVII, 73.
5. *Pro Sestio*, XXXI, 67; *Pro Lege Manilia*, XV, xvi; *Pro Balbo*, VI, 16.
6. *Pharsalia* II, 583–95, 632–49; III, 169–297; VII, 70, 132, 205–6.
7. Cicero, *Letters to Atticus*, IX, ix, 2. See also Caesar, *Civil War*, III, 3; Velleius Paterculus, II, li, 1; Appian, *Civil War*, II, viii, 49; Plutarch, *Pompey*, 64; Dio Cassius, XLI, 55; Lucan, *Pharsalia*, III, 169–297.
8. See Note 6 above.
9. Lucan, *Pharsalia*, III, 296–7. *Acciperet felix ne non semel omnia Caesar Vincendum pariter Pharsalia praestitit orbem.*
10. G. De Ruggiero, *Storia della filosofia*, Bari 1921, II, pp. 98–101.

V

Foreign Religions

My unique divinity is adored through all the
world, in divers images, in various rites, and
by many names.

APULEIUS, *Golden Ass,* XI, v[1]

FOREIGN RELIGIONS brought another universalist element into the
heart of Rome. The Romans had always admitted the gods of
immigrants, or summoned the gods of the enemy into the City,
in order to win the favour of powers they might have offended.
Annexation of the denizens of Heaven was one of the most
characteristic features of the Roman policy of absorption. But
the eastern cults brought with them, in their tumultuous
invasion, the emotional sustenance for the hearts of men that
both the state religion, based on politics, and the philosophers'
religion, based on reason, had failed to provide.

In mixed communities such as those of the larger Hellenistic
cities and the sea-ports, foreign settlements sprang up. Friendly
societies and funeral clubs were founded, and held periodical
meetings at which the members worshipped their native gods,
and sometimes displayed them in public, during the celebration
of splendid and deeply mystical rites.

The gods of Rome, on the other hand, were satisfied with
rustic sanctuaries and country offerings. In this cult, with its
unchanging liturgy and its archaic language, the Romans saw
the simple and modest faith of their ancestors. 'For my part,'
said Cato, addressing the Senate, 'I prefer these gods to be
propitious, and I hope they will continue to be, if we allow

them to remain in their own mansions' (Livy, XXXIV, iv, 4).

The beneficial powers of each god, in fact, were thought to be inseparably linked to the site of his cult, and his effective authority was commensurate with the degree of regularity in the performance of his rites. The gods were a group of beings who kept watch over the City's destiny and guarded the City's administrators. In the words he attributes to Cato, Livy is trying to recall the feelings of the past – feelings which Augustus wanted to revive in Roman hearts: they amount to a faith that every god charges the site of his worship with a magic power which can be neglected only at peril of incurring the divine wrath.

'I have held the conviction that Romulus by his auspices, and Numa by his establishment of our ritual, laid the foundation of our State, which assuredly could never have been as great as it is had not the fullest measure of divine favour been obtained for it' (Cicero, *De Natura Deorum,* III, ii, 5).

The rites were performed within a consecrated enclosure, by a priest whose head was veiled. The liturgical actions had to be carried out with the strictest precision. Endless care surrounded the execution of gestures which were repeated from century to century in an unchanging form, which helped to preserve them unimpaired when the foreign religions invaded Rome. There were often caves or underground hiding-places nearby, where sacred objects could be stored when they were not in use, to keep them from the contact of unconsecrated hands.

In its magical elements, the cult aimed to utilise the forces of good, to avert the powers of evil, and to attain specific objectives such as good harvests, victory in war, the ending of epidemics and the ensuring of human and animal fecundity.

The main thing was to obtain the 'peace of the gods' – a good understanding with powers capable of unforeseen acts of wrath. The gods to whom sacrifice and prayer were addressed were therefore feared by man, because they were touchy, vindictive and unsleeping. They were not worshipped in love, or in the hope of receiving from them solace in misfortune.

The vocabulary of the cult betrayed this need to propitiate hostile powers, by the use of such words as *piare, placare, expiatio, piaculum*. Sacrifices, offerings and other rites were not acts of adoration, but attempts to obtain the protection of powers which were omnipresent even if invisible, and may have been unintentionally offended. 'Do thou, goddess, appease for us the springs and their divinities; appease the gods dispersed through every grove.'[2]

A mystic sense of the divine presence, hidden but always watching, was infused into every wood and every spring. By a series of penalties, each harsher than the one before, the Codex of Theodosius shows clearly that the paganism of the country-side was the last to disappear, because of its links with the tasks of rural life. This religion had no articles of faith, but merely ritual laws, the inobservance of which by an individual might lead to the punishment of a whole community. Thus the defeat of Lake Trasimene in 217 B.C. was attributed to the failure of the consul to perform certain sacrifices correctly (Ovid, *Fasti*, VI, 765–70). The defeat of Carrhae was blamed on the indifference of Crassus to unfavourable auspices (Plutarch, *Crassus*, 18).

And yet this formalistic, dry, contractual religion had its merits, for its laws coincided with those of the land. Greek observers, from countries that had reached a more advanced stage of mental and spiritual evolution and absorbed a deeply sceptical spirit of critical enquiry, found this divinely sanctioned discipline a most healthy institution (Polybius, VI, 53–4; Dionysius of Halicarnassus, II, 19). Polybius especially approved of the cult of the dead, the watchful and unending presence of ancestral figures alongside the living members of each family. He admired the solemn inspiration which the Romans drew from the virtues of the departed, recorded for ever in the wax masks which were kept in the hall of every house. In funeral processions, they were worn by the mourners who followed the bier, as a symbol of the everlasting nature of the bonds of blood and custom between the ancestors and their remotest descendants.

The Roman religion arose from a mixture of different rites

which had been brought in during the archaic period by immigrant family groups. The acceptance of their gods was often a gradual affair, though sometimes divinities were specifically invited to transfer themselves to Rome, as protectors or as healers, in times of danger or of pestilence. Apollo was brought in during the year 431 B.C.,[3] and Aesculapius, the god of medicine, in 293. A sharp contrast to these private cults, frugal and rustic in their nature, and to the severe liturgy of the public ceremonies, came with the importation of the religions of the Aegean, whose celebrations were open, collective and joyful. *Ludi* were introduced – competitions of a religious character, in honour of a god, of a victorious general, or of someone who had died. Later, these celebrations came to be held annually. The gods took human form, and banquets were given for them, at which an empty couch symbolised the invisible divine presence.

A conception of the gods began to emerge which allowed a direct dialogue between divinity and worshipper, without the intermediary of the priesthood. There began to be a feeling of brotherly solidarity between men of the same sect, irrespective of differences of nationality and social class. Initiation, which had been an aristocratic privilege, became accessible to everyone. The relationship between the believer and his god became more intimate. Non-observance of ritual ceased to be a civil crime, and became a personal sin. Spiritual loyalty began to be not so much a duty of the citizen towards the divine patrons of his city, as a passionate devotion to the unseen. Sacrifices were replaced by fasts.

In this way, the national religion was gradually supplanted by an individual conception of the Godhead. Certain rites were symbolical representations of events supposed to have been historically experienced by the gods during their stay on earth; these appeared as a secret presage of the possibility that similar experiences might fall to the lot of the believer. The rites which recalled the cycle of the seasons – the burial of the seed when the plant dies, the rebirth of the seed at germination, the resurrection of Spring – acquired a universal and eternal significance, centred on the theme of survival after death.

To be sure of winning this supreme prize, the novice had to submit himself to occult initiation ceremonies and rites of purification. These were sometimes brutal and obscene, but always designed to ensure redemption. Poor citizens and even slaves were no longer excluded from the holy places, as they had been when Cato wrote the *De Re Rustica*. In a dry, peremptory style which recalls that of the Twelve Tables, he instructs those in a dependent position to restrict their religious observances to a minimum, and to leave the celebration of prayers, sacrifices and offerings entirely to their masters (V, 3–4) – whereas in the earliest Christian places of burial we find slaves buried next to their masters.

The new rites were very stimulating to the emotions. In the religion of Dionysus, the faithful searched for the body of the slain god at night, by torchlight, and gradually lost all sense of their own personality, becoming mystically identified with the god himself. In their ecstasy, they experienced a feeling of spiritual communion which transcended their existence as individuals, and therefore necessarily submerged all memory of differences of race or class in collective harmony.

These mystical experiences were destined to free the worshipper from the fears which chained him to the laws of his country. Even in Greece, as Pettazzoni remarks, the religion of Dionysus, with its mystical, rustic and collective elements, was opposed to the Olympian gods of the City-State. Its spread, he says, coincided with 'the successive steps of the lower classes towards the winning of political power.'[4] This aspect of the cult did not escape the notice of the Roman Senate, which tried to hold it off with a series of prohibitions.[5]

In spite of these precautions, the gods installed themselves in Rome. From a boat on the Tiber, Evander's mother prophesied the acceptance by Vesta of the Trojan gods;[6] and Saturn, fleeing from Jupiter, sought shelter and a hiding-place in Latium, which is said to derive its name from this fact.[7]

Gods arrived from various lands, some finding their way into the City by the strangest routes, others expressly invited to make the move. There was an archaic ritual by which the besiegers of a city would respectfully ask its patron deity to desert its walls, to abandon his worshippers – now doomed to become the slaves of the conquerors, and to make his home with the victorious nation. Rich offerings and flattering promises might have a favourable effect on the mind of the god. Perhaps this ancient and poetic custom shows an intuitive understanding of the fact that the submission of the conquered can only be maintained if the victor both respects and absorbs their beliefs.

Camillus invited the Juno of Veii to come to Rome, with the alluring promise of a temple on the Aventine (Livy, V, xxii, 6–7; Plutarch, *Camillus*, 6). Scipio invited the goddess of Carthage. The formula which he pronounced with all due solemnity on this occasion has come down to us almost verbatim, thanks to the antiquarian zeal of Macrobius, a pagan author of the fourth century A.D.[8]

For the invitation to be successful, the besieger had to follow certain rules with the utmost rigour; and, above all, he had to know the real name of the god – a name kept secret with the very object of preventing its invocation from outside the city walls. It would only be known to a very small number of initiates, and was never to be spoken aloud even by them.

Further rites were introduced, from more and more remote lands. The religion of Cybele, or Magna Mater, was the first Asiatic cult to be officially accepted. It was a serious time for the nation; the Carthaginian threat was close at hand. The Senate decided to bring the Divine Mother to Rome. Besides being the Mother of all the gods, she stood in an especially maternal relationship to Rome, for she was a Phrygian deity, and Aeneas ought to have brought her with him from Troy in the first place, but the time was not then ripe. So now she was invoked to protect the land which had offered refuge to the fugitives from Troy. A mission was sent to the King of Pergamus, to ask for the black meteorite stone worshipped at Pessinus, which was

73

regarded as an image of the goddess, in 204 B.C.[9] Two years after this idol had been installed on the Palatine, the battle of Zama showed how well Cybele liked her new home.

The legend of Claudia was a favourite subject with artists.[10] She was a virtuous matron, unjustly accused of immorality. When the ship bringing the goddess was stranded near the port of Ostia, she refloated the vessel with ease. This story gives a typically Roman flavour to the fateful meeting of Rome and the East: thus chastity, the virtue most highly esteemed among the Romans, escorted the goddess of procreation into the City. Cybele represented the primaeval force of animal reproduction, and brought with her a highly emotional cult. At her side came Atys, the god of vegetative fertility, who, according to the legend, was once a young shepherd beloved by Cybele. As a result of breaking faith with her, he castrated himself, lacerated himself with sharp rocks, and finally threw himself over a precipice. The goddess mourned him after his death, and her worshippers mourned with her, for a whole day of lamentation and fasting. His resurrection, on the 27th day of March, was celebrated by scenes of exultation no less exaggerated than the preceding rites of sorrow. The worshippers repeated in their own persons the tortures and the mutilation which the god had inflicted on himself, in order to attain, by renunciation, the resurrection of the spirit which he had achieved. This was a chastity preserved by mystical ecstasy, or by ferocious mutilation, very different from the virtue which Roman matrons attained by simple self-control.

Other cults of a similar kind, such as those of Isis and of Atargatis, also acted out the tragic adventures of goddesses cruelly bereaved of their loved ones, but later fortunate enough to find them again, miraculously risen from the dead. The various sects had similar liturgies, and their rites amounted to a sacred drama. The faithful felt themselves at one with the god-head, both in the inevitability of death and – perhaps – in the possibility of resurrection.

An element of doubt began to creep into the spiritual life of

74

individual worshippers, who saw an underlying similarity between all these divinities which aroused profound questioning. Could they be only various aspects of a single God? The measures outlawing conversions to foreign religions were praised by Cicero, and also, at a short interval of time, by Dionysius of Halicarnassus[11] – but those measures undoubtedly had very little effect. Equally inadequate had been the precautions taken by Romulus, who was said to have built Rome inland, so that its institutions and customs might avoid the degeneration so common in sea-ports.[12] Countless mystical influences broke down the barriers of tradition, and made their way even into the Capitoline citadel. The Iranian sun-god Mithras whose birthday, on December 25, falls a day or two after the solstice, had places of worship right in the very middle of Rome, many of which have been excavated.[13]

The divinities of the Mediterranean area resembled each other so deeply as to encourage the belief that they were all personifications of the same godhead, varied to correspond with needs of individual cities. Apuleius, indeed, affirms that this is the case, at the beginning of his description of the festivities dedicated to Isis. The goddess appears to him rising from the waves, and says:

'I am she that is the mother of all things that exist in Nature, mistress and governess of all the elements, the initial progeny of worlds, chief of the powers divine, queen of all that are in hell, the principal of them that dwell in heaven, manifested alone and under one form of all the gods and goddesses. At my will the planets of the sky, the wholesome winds of the seas, and the lamentable silences of hell be disposed; my name, my unique divinity is adored through all the world, in divers images, in various rites, and by many names. For the Phrygians, who are the first of all men, call me the Mother of gods at Pessinus; the Athenians which are sprung of their soil, Cecropian Minerva; the Cyprians, which are girt about by the sea, Paphian Venus; the Cretans which bear arrows, Dictynnian Diana; the Sicilians, which speak three tongues, infernal Proserpine; the

75

Eleusians, their ancient goddess Ceres; some Juno, others Bellona, others Hecate, others Rhamnusia; and principally the Ethiopians which dwell in the Orient and are enlightened by the morning rays of the sun, and the Egyptians which are excellent in all kinds of ancient doctrine, and by their proper ceremonies accustom to worship me, do call me by true name, Queen Isis.'[14]

A relative uniformity of ideas therefore emerged from all these religions. Intelligent and well-read people were well aware of this, and found a common ground of certainty on the irrational plane which philosophy could hardly achieve. So even the well-born and well-educated saw nothing discreditable in joining many different cults at once, as is shown by a large number of inscriptions of the fourth century A.D.[15]

But for a long time those who were wedded to the institutions and the feelings of the past continued to oppose this powerful infiltration of universalist influences.[16] They did so both through racial and social conservatism, and because they were intuitively aware that Rome could not maintain her institutions and traditions if she swallowed so large a draught of other nations' ideas and customs.

'Barbarian superstition' is Cicero's description of the religion of Israel, two years after Pompey annexed Judaea (61 B.C.) Unlike every other subject people, the Jews seemed to the orator to be impossible to assimilate. 'Each city, o Laelius, has its own peculiar religion – we have ours. While Jerusalem was flourishing, and while the Jews were in a peaceful state, still the religious ceremonies and observances of that people were very much at variance with the splendour of this Empire, and the dignity of our name' (*Pro Flacco*, XXVIII, 69).

But the plebeians were open to this cult. 'I have no religious scruples!' exclaimed Horace impatiently to a tiresome fellow who urged him not to violate the repose of the Sabbath day. 'But I have!' was the reply, 'I am less certain about these things – *like so many others*.'[17]

And there really were many such others – ready to believe, longing to believe that one day wickedness would be abolished, the arrogant would be punished, and a higher justice would be established. Absurd as it might seem to the rationalist, this hope rang out in prophetic tones, in the poetical ravings of the Sibyls, and announced the coming revenge of the humble and meek against their oppressors. What is more, it coincided with the political propaganda directed against Rome by the Asiatics.

Ever since the upheaval of the Exile had freed the religion of the Jews from its original narrow nationalism, it had been oriented towards universalist conceptions.[18] Judaism had been widely preached even in the world of Rome itself. Unlike the religion of the City, it refused to be sullied by other sects, no matter how similar to itself, and it dispensed with outward formalities. 'I will not take calves out of thy house : nor he-goats out of the flocks. . . . Offer to God the sacrifice of praise, and pay thy vows to the Most High.'[19] The holy books of Israel contained a reply to the doubts and sorrows of the oppressed, even before the Gospels isolated and stressed this element, which became their main theme. 'They that sow in tears shall reap in joy.'[20] 'The Lord . . . healeth the broken of heart, and bindeth up their bruises. He telleth the number of the stars, and calleth them all by their names. The Lord lifteth up the meek, and bringeth the wicked down even to the ground.'[21]

The western world believed the Jews to be in possession of hidden truths; but it regarded their monotheism as a sign of contempt for the other gods (Pliny, *Natural History,* XIII, ix, 46). The firm solidarity which Jews showed towards each other was seen as neglect of civic duties, and aroused suspicions – especially among those who knew about the links that still connected the Jews of the Roman world with those living beyond the Euphrates.

The underlying theme of the Jewish message is clearly to be seen in the works of Philo[22] – though he also summarises and adopts as his own many Greek ideas. His conception of history is a theological one, totally foreign to the Roman mental system. If a Roman official has permitted the Jews of Alexandria to be persecuted,[23] the Divine retribution is minutely, precisely designed to match the pains suffered by the Jews through his fault: the law of retaliation is strictly enforced. Philo also hints, not very definitely, at the fate of an earlier persecutor – which reveals the nature of the Jewish writer's ambitious aim. His object is to warn the whole world that this is what happens to the enemies of Israel. The rigidly legalistic idea of the relationship between man and man, and also between gods and men, which was in force at Rome, received a rude shock. So God can intervene in cases of oppression by those in authority? So rights and duties have the same significance for those who hold sway as for their subordinates? This amounts to a sudden transfer of politics and administration from the practical to the metaphysical sphere. Offences committed against the humble and meek acquire a disproportionate prominence. In the person of the Jews of Alexandria every man is afflicted. In the person of Flaccus, all persecutors of the innocent are punished – including Cain and Judas, according to a norm of historical writing which we find repeated in Lactantius, Tertullian, Orosius, and St Augustine.

Other works of Philo assert the identity between the laws of the small city and the eternal laws of the universe. 'Whosoever will carefully examine the nature of the particular enactments, will find that they seek to attain to the harmony of the universe, and are in agreement with the principles of eternal nature' (Philo, *Moses*, II, x, 52). 'Particular polities are rather an addition to the single polity of nature on which supreme authority is conferred. . . . The cities which we see are unlimited in number, and subject to diverse polities and laws by no means identical. . . . The cause of this is the reluctance to combine all fellowship with each other' (Philo, *Joseph*, VI, 28). The true citizen of a city is not the man who is born there, lives there and carries out the functions of government there, if he is a wicked man. The true citizen is rather to be found among 'those who have never been placed upon the burgess rolls, or have been condemned to disfranchisement or banishment'.[24] And who are these men who have the rights of citizenship in the spiritual

City. They are the good, the honest, those who live wisely, like brothers.

The servants of Isaac found four wells – and that is all the story means to those who have limited powers of vision. 'But those who are on the roll of a greater country, even this whole world, will be quite sure that four things propounded as a subject of enquiry, are not four wells, but the four parts of the universe – land, water, air, heavens' (Philo, *On Dreams,* VII, 39).

Man is therefore a citizen of the world. Philo, who was not of course a Roman, represents the meeting-point of Greek thought and Jewish religion. But he lived and worked in the world of Rome, which may be why his vision of a universal city, governed by an ideal ruler, has a theoretical relationship to the Roman Empire.

It was because Caligula expected his subjects to worship him as a god that Philo disapproved of him. Philo's dream was indeed of a single monarch to rule over all mankind. He wanted him to be as wise as a philosopher, as mild as a shepherd, as alert as a helmsman. He wanted him to be endowed with a natural majesty of soul, which is the gift of Heaven and cannot be learnt. This majesty must therefore come of divine right, and be universal in scope because of its divine origin. It must be a spontaneous mental attitude, showing itself outwardly in temperance and in dedication to the tasks of government. These doctrines can be found in the works of Plato and the writings of the Neo-Pythagoreans. Caligula made a clumsy attempt to proclaim himself a god and affirm theocracy in the very years when Philo was perfecting their theoretical expression on the abstract plane.

Such ideas, rites, and feelings made their way through the mixed populations of the cities, moved with the troops to far-off frontiers, flocked in with auxiliary troops from their distant homes. Little by little there sprang from them a common feeling, a unifying vision of mankind: the equality of all mortal men in the sight of the Godhead made them all citizens of the same spiritual community. The levelling process took place first on the

79

ideological plane, and was ratified by the law only at a later stage. And monotheistic ideas were widespread before the idea of monarchy as a unifying force was officially adopted as the informing principle of the Roman system.

NOTES TO CHAPTER

1. *Cuius nomen unicum multiformi specie, ritu vario nomine multiiugo totus veneratur orbis.*
2. *Tu, dea, pro nobis fontes fontanaque placa   Numina, tu sparsos per nemus omne deos.* Ovid, *Fasti,* IV, 759–60.
3. J. Gagé, *Apollon Romain,* Paris 1955. *Bibl. des Ecoles Franc. d'Athènes et de Rome,* Vol. 182.
4. R. Pettazzoni, *La religione della Grecia antica,* Turin 1954, p. 99. See also H. Jeanmaire, *Dionysus,* Paris 1951, Chap. IX, p. 422. E. Rohde, in *Psyche,* London 1950, Chap. VIII, p. 253, sees Dionysus as a barbarian god who slowly penetrated into the Greek world. L. Gernet and A. Boulanger, in *Le génie grec dans la religion,* Paris 1932, pp. 120 ff., think of him rather as the expression of a mystical tendency, inherent in the spirit of man, which breaks out in times of social and economic instability.
5. In 426 B.C. (Livy, IV, xxx, 11) and 186 B.C. (Livy, XXXIX, viii-xviii).
6. *Iliacos accipe, Vesta, deos!* Ovid, *Fasti,* I, 528.
7. Ovid, *Fasti,* I, 238; from *latere,* meaning: to hide.
8. Macrobius, *Saturnalia,* III, ix. See V. Basanoff, *Evocatio,* Paris 1944, p. 49.
9. Livy, XXIX, x, 6, 8. See Ovid, *Fasti,* IV, 182 ff.
10. Ovid, *Fasti,* IV, 305–47. Livy, XXIX, xiv, 12–13. See C. Pietrangeli, *I monumenti dei culti orientali,* Rome 1951, plates II and IV.
11. Cicero, *De Legibus,* II, viii, 19. Dionysius of Halicarnassus, II, 19.
12. Cicero, *De Republica,* II, iv, 7.
13. M. J. Vermaseren, *Corpus Inscriptionum et Monumentorum Religionis Mithriacae,* Hagae Nijhoff 1956. Prudentius describes the initiation ceremony in *Peristephanon,* X, 1011–50, (A.D. 405).
14. Apuleius, *Golden Ass,* XI, v. And in another work, *De Mundo,* Apuleius emphasises this idea: 'For all that he is one, [God] is invoked under many names owing to the great number of his aspects.' (XXXVII, 370).
15. See G. Reville, *La religion à Rome sous les Sévères,* Paris 1886; F. Cumont, *Les religions orientales dans le paganisme romain,* Paris 1929; J. F. Toutain, *Les cultes païens dans l'empire romain,* Paris 1911; A. Loisy, *Les mystères païens et le mystère chrétien,* Paris 1930; G. La Piana, *Foreign Groups in Rome During the First Century of the Roman Empire,* in *Harv. Th. Rev.,* XX, 1927, pp. 183 ff.

16. The cult of Dionysus receives hostile mention from Horace, *Odes*, I, xviii, 11 ff.
17. Horace, *Satires*, I, ix, 70–2. '*Nulla mihi, inquam, Religio est. At mi: sum paullo infirmior; unus Multorum.*' See also *Satires*, I, iv, 142.
18. M. Radin, *The Jews among the Greeks and Romans*, Philadelphia 1915; J. Juster, *Les Juifs dans l'empire romain*, Paris 1914; M. Ginsburg, *Rome et la Judée*, Paris 1928.
19. *Psalms*, XLIX, 9, 14 – *RV*, L, 9, 14. The author's biblical quotations are based on the approved Catholic Bible, which often differs from the English Authorised and Revised Versions both in interpretation and in the numbering of chapters and verses. The translator has reproduced these quotations as far as possible by the corresponding passages in the official English Catholic Bible – the Douai-Rheims version. Where chapter and verse references differ, he has given both – Catholic first, Revised Version second.
20. *Psalms*, CXXV, 4 – *RV*, CXXVI, 5.
21. *Psalms*, CXLVI, 3, 4, 6 – *RV*, CXLVII, 3, 4, 6.
22. E. Bréhier, *Les idées religieuses et philosophiques de Philon*, Paris 1950, (3rd ed.); E. R. Goodenough, *The Politics of Philo Judaeus*, New Haven, London 1938; *The Political Philosophy of Hellenistic Kingship*, in *Yale Cl. St.*, I, 1928, p. 53; S. Tracy, *Philo Judaeus and the Roman Principate*, Williamsport 1933; J. Daniélou, *Philon d'Alexandrie*, Paris 1958.
23. See Philo's, *On the Embassy to Gaius* and also his *Flaccus*.
24. Philo, *Every Good Man is Free*, I, 7. See Cicero, *Acad. Prior*, ii, 136: *Sapientem . . . civem, insipientes omnes peregrinos.*

F

VI

The Precedent of Alexander

He bade them all consider as their fatherland
the whole inhabited earth.

PLUTARCH, *On the Fortune of Alexander*, I, 6

A THIRD INFLUENCE, working alongside the new philosophical
and religious doctrines, helped to open up new horizons to the
Romans and their power-based policy. This was the precedent
of Alexander.

At the beginning of his brief career, the Greek cities looked
to Alexander as the great captain under whose leadership they
would march to the final destruction of Persia. But after his early
death, they began to give further consideration to the nature of
his achievement – perhaps to twist it to their own ends – and
certain aspects came to acquire special prominence. The first
of these was the idea of monarchy as a mystical and levelling
force. His biographers, especially Plutarch, credit him with a
clear-cut programme of universal brotherhood. In fact, this idea
probably grew up in his mind by slow degrees, inspired by the
requirements of his expanding empire or by the influence of
Persian and Egyptian cultural factors.

He had a definite object when he caused himself to be proclaimed the 'Son of God' by the Egyptian priests (who used a
slightly ambiguous form of words). He was well aware of the
glaring differences that separated from one another, the peoples
he had conquered and he wanted to unite them in the fold of a
single religion.

According to the later version of the story, his policy has an iron consistency, which it cannot really have possessed at all. 'That we should consider all men to be of one community, and that we should have an order common to all – this Zeno wrote, giving shape to a dream, or, as it were, a shadowy picture of a well-ordered and philosophic commonwealth; but it was Alexander who gave effect to the idea' (Plutarch, *On the Fortune of Alexander*, I, 6).

As his astonishing expedition carried him further and further away from Greece, he seemed to lay aside his original task of establishing Pan-Hellenism as a world system. This object had been suggested to his father before him, and was recommended not only by the nationalists of the city-states, but also, it was said, by his master, Aristotle. The philosopher instructed him to impose the leadership of the Greek cities on the whole world, and to be very careful not to extend the rights of their citizens to people of other races. Courage, talent, and membership of a chosen race were the privilege of the few – an aristocratic theory later repeated by Statius. So Aristotle, according to Plutarch's *On the Fortune of Alexander*, taught his pupil to 'treat the Greeks as if he were their leader, and other peoples as if he were their master; to have regard for the Greeks as for friends and kinsmen, but to conduct himself towards other peoples as if they were animals or plants. But as Alexander believed that he came as a heaven-sent Governor to all, he brought together into one body all men everywhere, and bade them all consider as their fatherland the whole inhabited earth.'

These ideas were attributed to Alexander later on – after they had been broadcast by the Stoics in the years immediately following his death, or after the Roman Empire had given reality to them by uniting the world under a single government. The authors who credit Alexander with this high philosophical objective all lived in the time of the Roman emperors, except for Eratosthenes, a disciple of Zeno, and were all of provincial origin. Arrian a disciple of Epictetus, was invested with high office by Hadrian, who influenced him in his Stoic doctrine and in his broad pacific vision; Plutarch's spirit was open to religious impulses; their portrait of the young king favours the interests of their provincial compatriots, and is coloured by the universalist views generally accepted in their own day.[1] One episode among the many which have come down to us seems particularly significant. The Macedonians became jealous of the favour shown by Alexander to the Persians, and threatened to leave him and return to their homes. But the king invited Greeks, Persians, and Macedonians to a feast and reconciled them, 'praying for all sorts of blessings, and especially for harmony and fellowship in the empire between the Macedonians and Persians' (Arrian, *Expedition of Alexander*, VII, xi, 4–9).

It can hardly be maintained that the young king really followed an ideological plan which he had worked out in advance. It is much more probable that he picked up his divine honours by stages, in accordance with the needs of his eastward progress, and was intuitively aware that he would have to adopt the beliefs and the customs of the conquered if he wanted to gain their hearts. Accidental events, which he may not even have foreseen, perhaps determined him to convert half-formed ideological leanings into positive action. The vastness of his new empire, and the necessity of controlling a most diverse group of nations, may well have led him to a friendly understanding of their habits and their mentality. The same factors certainly contributed to his decision to cause himself to be proclaimed as the Son of God; for nothing but common devotion to a God-King could hold together a state so recently formed from such varied elements.

But, on the other hand, it must also be admitted that Alexander, with his Greek cultural background, may have been able to extract certain elements from the teaching of the Sophists or the Cynics – the few universal ideas, transcending nationality, which suited his own political activities – and combine them into a plan, to which he could then lend the prestige of his own authority.

There is also room for a third hypothesis. The cosmopolitan element in his policy may have been emphasised after his death, and may reflect the times and the spirit of the world-wide Roman Empire of many years later. Provincial writers of biographical or rhetorical works may have laid stress on the levelling elements in the incomplete life-work of Alexander, and invested them with a mystical glamour, intending to bring them allusively to the attention of the emperor to whom their writings were addressed.

If we turn to the Latin authors, we find a contrasting interpretation of the life of Alexander, which demonstrates the ideological differences that divided Roman thinkers. Some writers condemn the Macedonian as a great captain who degenerated into a tyrant, and present his leanings towards theocracy as a sign of moral decadence. For traditional republicans, Alexander is a fine example of the corruption which overtakes the mighty when they yield to a craving to be first in all things. Cicero asserts that the young king could never have extended his conquest so far into Asia if he had not grabbed a great deal of other people's property (*De Republica,* III, ix, 15). He also says that Alexander, though a great man, was often contemptible (*'turpissimus'*) (*De Officiis,* I, xxvi, 90). Livy says that when he conquered the peoples of the East, he did not subject them to Greek law, but adopted their customs. The historian speaks of him a little later on as 'commanding an army who had forgotten Macedonia, and were degenerating into the manners of the Persians' (IX, xviii, 4). Pompeius Trogus deplores Alexander's attempts to lord it over his equals and his friends (IX, viii, 17) and still more his use of the royal robes and diadem of the Persian kings, which had previously been 'unknown to the kings of Macedonia' (XII, iii, 15).

Curtius Rufus, who probably lived in the reign of Claudius, represents the traditional Roman view. He condemns the young king's progressive abandonment of his national customs, especially his demand that his companions in arms should prostrate themselves in his presence in the Persian style. An old Scythian – the typical unspoilt savage of classical literature – is chosen by the historian to be the spokesman for the doctrines of the Stoics.

'With you, each victory is the parent of a new war,' says the wise barbarian to the monarch, reminding us of the non-involvement preached by the philosophers (Curtius Rufus, VII, 8). According to Philo, who lived about the same time as Curtius, an Indian thinker also gave Alexander the benefit of his advice, sending him a letter full of praise for the inviolable freedom of the human spirit. A man who is worth anything must refuse to flatter the mighty, and must not fear their threats. 'If they threaten him with exile, he can reply: "All lands are my fatherland".' (*Every Good Man is Free,* XX, 145). A few years later, Seneca contrasts Alexander with his supposed ancestor, the god Hercules, instead of dwelling on their resemblances. The generous divinity always acted on behalf of the oppressed, and never for his own benefit, whereas the Macedonian had behaved like a bandit right from his earliest youth. 'A plunderer of nations, a scourge alike to his friends and his foes,' Seneca calls him. And Lucan, for his part, describes him as a 'fortunate brigand'.[2]

In spite of the ideological opposition he aroused, Alexander was the first to diffuse a new idea into the minds of men in the West – the idea that certain leaders are made of superhuman stuff, and that a god is incarnated in them, which gives them the right to rule over the whole human race and to subject it to a uniform system of laws.

This seemed a perverse idea to the holders of republican views, in a city where even religion was controlled by democratic rules, so that even heroes could only hope for immortality on a basis of proven military and civic achievements. The Roman distaste for theocracy can be seen in Curtius Rufus's account (VIII, v) of a dispute said to have occurred at Alexander's table. One party proposed to give the king divine honours immediately; the other was also in favour of his ascent into heaven, but only after his death.

In Rome, the first signs of this sort of personal aggrandisement marked the decay of the two basic principles of the City's constitution, which laid down that the high offices of state must be shared between two or more individuals, and that they could only be held for one year. The institution of provincial governorships was the first step towards a military regime. In wartime, the distances that separated the battle-fronts from the capital reduced the subservience of the consuls toward the Senate. As it stretched out to cover ever vaster areas, the web of Roman administrative institutions grew thin and frail. Something more than civic spirit was needed to bind the hearts of new and varied subject populations to the ruling City. The best chance of a really effective bond lay in following the precedent of the gorgeous monarchies of Asia and Egypt. This meant the deification of the head of state, and there were some precedents for this in the traditions of the Republic. The figure of a Roman general on the day of his triumph, standing erect in a chariot drawn by white horses, his head crowned with oak-leaves and his face painted with red lead, bore a resemblance to the figure of Capitoline Jove.

It gradually became possible for military leaders to obtain the supreme command without being constitutionally invested with it by the Senate. Marius obtained it in the Jugurthine war by a plebiscite proposed by the tribune of the people (108 B.C.). Sulla followed his example in 88 B.C., and so in their turn did Pompey, Caesar and Crassus.[3]

It was natural for an *imperator,* hailed as saviour by the citizens, drawing power from the people, worshipped by the troops, to nurse the ambition of emulating Alexander. For Pompey, the comparison with the Macedonian was a flattering one;[4] but the same comparison was used as a weapon against Caesar by opponents who wanted to emphasise his monarchical designs.[5] His biographers commented unsympathetically on his passion for imitating Alexander. In his *Letters to Atticus,* Cicero speaks of the moderating influence that Aristotle exercised on Alexander, at least in his earlier years, and regrets not having succeeded in playing the same role with Caesar. He also deplores Caesar's inevitable verging from military leader into despotic ruler.[6]

For the whole of the first century of the emperors, the name of Alexander provides the text for sermons on the frailty of human fortune, and especially on the impossibility of the virtues of justice and temperance for a man in supreme power. This shows the continuing vital force of the ideas held by republican thinkers – though the historical reality they represented had ceased to exist.

In the days of Antoninus Pius and Marcus Aurelius, the Empire took on the appearance of an ideal system of government, the best that human imperfection could achieve. Then historians began to present a totally different picture of Alexander, whereby he was transformed into a deliberate promoter of universal brotherhood. Plutarch speaks of him, after his conquest of Persia, as 'wisely considering that whilst he was engaged on an expedition which would carry him far from thence, it would be wiser to depend upon the good-will which might arise from intermixture and association as a means of maintaining tranquillity, than upon force and compulsion. . . . As for his marriage with Roxana, it was indeed a love affair, yet it seemed, at the same time, to be conducive to the object he had in mind' (*Life of Alexander*, 47).

The Roman emperor who followed the example of Alexander in a later period carried the power of his country so far afield from his starting point that the essential character of the capital city itself was blurred. The same thing had happened to the Greek city-states. When they submitted to the control of Philip and Alexander, it was with a view to making use of them for the time being and discarding them later when they had achieved the object of all the Greek cities – Greek hegemony in Asia. They were even prepared to hail the Macedonian king as a god, if he could 'make all the barbarians slaves of Greece', to quote a letter of uncertain authenticity, traditionally supposed to have been addressed by Isocrates to Philip (*Letters*, II, 5).

The opposing party – the followers of Demosthenes – foresaw that a military leader invested with absolute power would inevitably interfere with the internal politics of the cities in the end, but even they wanted to establish Greek supremacy over the rest of the world. However, neither Demosthenes nor the Roman senators of a later period could be expected to foresee that this policy was inconsistent with the maintenance of the fundamental institutions and spirit of his own city.

The reproaches levelled by Roman authors against Alexander may seem to be based on pure morality. This, however, masks an intuitive feeling that any imitation of his policy, with its inevitable tendency towards the abolition of racial discrimination, would lead to the disappearance of the oligarchic system. Any community planned by a deified king would hardly conform with the aristocratic, socially stratified isolationist nature of the original City of Rome.

If the republicans held Alexander in doctrinaire horror, those who aspired to theocratic power took him as a model. His physical likeness must have been familiar to the Romans after Metellus defeated the Macedonians and brought a collection of Greek statues to Rome, in 148 B.C.,[7] and from then on he had no lack of imitators.

After his death, Alexander was compared with Hercules;[8] he may indeed have claimed descent from him during his lifetime. Hercules was not then regarded primarily as a symbol of strength, but rather as the benefactor of the humble, noted for moral rather than physical prowess.[9] It was this view of him which led a number of emperors to proclaim him as their tutelary deity, and even to try to achieve personal identification with him.[10]

Another deity who had smiled on Alexander was Dionysus. These religious affiliations are indicative of the promise of social progress which was implicit in the idea of monarchy. High hopes were based on the advent to power of a ruler who claimed these mythical figures as his predecessors.

Alexander's triumphal advance to the Caspian,[11] and the story of his symbolical closure of the Caspian Gates against any further advance by Westerners, or any future intrusion by invaders from the East, contributed to a legend that had an aura of mystical glory about it. The unifying principle on which his cosmopolitan authority was based necessarily involved international unity in religion and politics. This in turn could only mean monotheism and monarchy.

The legendary figure of Alexander and the precedent set by his career gave a name and a form to a mass of confused ambitions.[12] His unfinished life-work was always in the thoughts of those who believed theocracy to be the only way to achieve the eternal desire of enlightened spirits – the bringing of the world of men into harmony with the single all-embracing order of the universe.

In Rome, the first sign of these tendencies appeared immediately after the first direct contacts with the Hellenistic world. A mysterious light was said to shine from the forehead of Scipio, according to Silius Italicus (XVII, 398); his hair was long, which for a Roman was most unusual and a sign of supernatural power; he was believed to have secret conversations with the gods. Some of these details come from later records, but may be presumed to derive from the legend that sprang up around Scipio in his life-time. It was said that he was a favourite of the gods – perhaps the son of one of them.[13] He certainly had most remarkable personal qualities, which could wring praise even from the most unexpected of all admirers – Hannibal himself (Livy, XXXV, xiv, 7). His personal authority was such that he could dare to take the most dangerous of all steps for a Roman, and set himself above the law. 'He alone was the head and pillar of the Roman Empire; a state which was mistress of the world lay sheltered under the shade of Scipio; his nods were equivalent to decrees of the Senate, and orders of the people.' Such were the murmurings of the Conservatives (Livy, XXXVIII, li, 4).

One of the two vital aspects of Roman political thought is typified by Scipio, and, later, by Caesar and by Antony. The other side is represented, in strong contrast, by Cato the Censor and Cato of Utica, the spiritual heirs of Fabricius and Cincinnatus.

For the first three statesmen, the leadership of a single man is seen as expressing the rational principle which governs individuals no less than it governs the universe. By subjecting all men to a unified government, monarchy performs on mankind the operation originally performed by the Creator on primeval chaos. Thus the leader appears as the intermediary of the Divine Will, the interpreter and the representative of the deity, perhaps even its incarnation. The ruler must clearly be a man of extraordinary personal gifts. It will not be the votes of his fellow-citizens that raise him to power, nor the sort of moral virtues and services to the State that might have won him election to the magistracies – it will be his superhuman qualities that turn the scale.

'There has been in truth,' admits Cicero with some reluctance in the *Pro Lege Manilia* (XVI, 48), 'in the case of some most illustrious men, good fortune added as some contribution of the gods to their glory.' This is the first sign of predestination. Appian's *Civil War* (II, xxi, 149–50) describes Caesar as 'a man most fortunate in all things, superhuman,' and as 'worthy to be be compared with Alexander . . . since, just as the Macedonian calmed the waves at the crossing of the Gulf of Pamphylia . . . so did the Roman impose his will on the Adriatic, crossing it in the heart of winter.'

The eyes of the conservatives, however, were not turned toward distant, world-wide horizons, but piously focussed on hearth and altar, on the virtue of submission to the ancient laws of the great Roman family to which they belonged. Their effort to find a peaceful solution of social problems followed a more practical course than those of the other party. Their devotion was not to a deified tyrant, but to a principle. Their guiding light was duty – the duty of defending a society which, with all its limitations, had shown itself capable of providing the world with a code of rules for human coexistence which had no rival at that time. They held the proud conviction that their domination over other countries was made lawful by the special favour of the gods, which the Romans had earned by their unfailing moral excellence.

These two threads of political thought, contrasting in colour though parallel in course, run together through the web of Roman history. Sometimes both surface together in the pages of a single author, or in the character of a single historical figure. Sulla ensured his personal popularity with the plebs by certain supernatural pretensions. He took the title of FELIX and of FAUSTUS[14] and his arrival was heralded by the mysterious call of an invisible trumpet. This last prodigy was paralleled by one that fell to the lot of Caesar on the eve of the Battle of Pharsalus, when the augurs told him 'the gods indicate a great change and revolution.'[15] These stories show the historical insight which underlies the popular imagination. They also show that there was a wide-spread feeling, during the years that separate Sulla from Augustus, that the days of the old order were numbered – a feeling that had in it something like the expectation of a Messiah.

Caesar certainly welcomed comparison with Alexander, and the analogy did not escape the notice of his contemporaries. It was a basic element in the judgement of later historians on Caesar. But their views of men and events were formed at a time when universalist, equalitarian ideas were no longer confined to a handful of idealists, and their upholders were no longer regarded as dangerous cranks by the ruling classes. Cosmopolitan ideas were now preached in literary gatherings, discussed in philosophical debates, and given wider circulation in the sermons delivered to the populace by street-corner speakers. Rhetoricians even preached them to the emperors themselves. Then these principles began to appear in the legal code, and to enlighten the practice of everyday politics. It became common form that the parallel between Alexander and Caesar did not consist merely in their fatal passion to excel in all things, as the moralists had maintained, but in the miraculous good fortune (*felicitas*) which the gods had granted to both men in consideration of the higher aims whose fulfilment was their unique task. On the political plane, Alexander and Caesar were alike in rising above the idea of racial superiority and domination, in favour of a broad humanitarian outlook.

The career of Alexander, says R. Pettazzoni, meant 'the end of the *Polis* and the triumph of the monarchical idea ... the absorption of the *Polis* in a multi-national imperial state, ruled by one man. The religion of the city-state, based on the old gods, gave way to the religion of the imperial state, based on the double status of ruler as god and man.'[16]

Dying young, at the height of his fortunes, Alexander remained a special case, and soon came to be regarded in an almost mythical light. But Caesar, whether intentionally or not, became the founder of a system, the first of a long series of successive rulers, who took his name as a title. He himself was removed from the scene by enemies with clear cultural and political aims, and his historical image was therefore distorted by hostile commentary. The picture of Caesar drawn by later writers derived many of its features from the shadow cast by Augustus, who very wisely drew attention to the conservative and legalistic aspects of his own policy. His image, in the eyes of his contemporaries, was meant to be as different as possible from that of Julius Caesar. He wanted to appear as the spiritual heir of Romulus and Numa rather than of Alexander. In the exaggerated paeans of praise which Augustus drew from the poets of his time, comparison with Alexander, except of a very indirect kind, was totally absent.

Writers of the senatorial school lay special emphasis on one feature of Julius Caesar's career – that it is extraneous to the mainstream of Roman history. Julius Caesar, for the historians of the opposition, is the heir of Alexander and the precursor of Caracalla – the originator of the idea of a world in which the spirit of Rome is to act as the mortar in the edifice of a universal civilisation, but Rome herself will no longer be the supreme City, and Italy will be reduced to the level of the other provinces.[17]

Considered in the light of later interpretations, the well-known story of Caesar's tears at the sight of a statue of Alexander[18] stands out like an additional detail in a portrait which is already sufficiently complete. The ghost of the Macedonian must have caused the Roman magistrate a shock of self-revelation, which disclosed his vocation to him – a vocation of unlimited expansionism, a mission to unify the world. At the time of the episode, Caesar was at the most westerly outpost of the known world, at the furthest limit set by the facts of geography to expansionist ambitions – the point where Hercules had reached but not passed. Perhaps Caesar compared it in his mind with the corresponding limit in the East – India, which Alexander in his turn had reached but not passed. At the same time, Caesar received a hint of his future greatness from religious authorities and, it should be noted, not Roman ones. The sequel to this story, in fact, bears an obvious resemblance to the type of anecdote which was told about Alexander. Caesar said that he had dreamed of possessing his mother, and the priests explained that he was destined to possess the Earth, which is the mother of all men.

There is an obvious analogy between this prophecy and one which Alexander had received – again from priests of a foreign religion – in the temple of Ammon (Arrian, *Expedition of Alexander*, III, iv).

In private life, too, Caesar showed himself a follower of Alexander. He was said to have had a law permitting polygamy ready for submission to the Senate (Suetonius, *Life of Julius Caesar*, LII, 3). The power he derived from Rome was that of a military commander, which, according to the constitution, was a temporary appointment that could be taken away from him; he could add a permanent and hereditary element to it by becoming the prince-consort of the Queen of Egypt, who claimed to be the descendant and the legitimate heiress of Alexander.[19] Another story is that Caesar considered transferring the capital of the Empire either to Alexandria or to Troy, the fatherland of his ancestors (Suetonius, *op. cit.* LXXIX, 3). It has been ingeniously suggested[20] that these tales were spread abroad in a later period by Mark Antony, with the specific object of creating a precedent for his own marriage with Cleopatra and his own permanent transfer to Egypt.

Autocratic tendencies, in the rulers of Rome, are invariably accompanied by imitation of Alexander. Caligula, for example, had the hero's tomb opened up, so that he could wear his breastplate. He also pretended to have secret colloquies with the gods, like the Macedonian, and insisted on being worshipped as a god himself.[21]

After the death of Caesar, we can trace a continuous ideological connection between the political figures who reflect this tendency to a greater or lesser extent. The historians – traditionally a conservative breed – always represent these autocrats, with their strain of mysticism, as greedy, vicious, cruel tyrants. A family resemblance between Alexander and these later public figures is also traceable in certain common features that appear in their statues and on their coins – the young king's image was that of a curly-haired youth, with tilted head, eyes looking moistly up to heaven, absorbed in rapt attention to the words of some divine voice.[22] Roman sculpture[23] – an attractively realistic art – traditionally depicted a magistrate entrusted by his fellow-citizens with temporary responsibility for well-defined tasks. Only by degrees did the Roman portrait undergo a transformation into an ever more stylised representation of a being sent from heaven. Resemblance to the sitter ceased to be important; the public for whom the work was intended had not known him since he was a child, had not chosen him and raised him to supreme power, and were in no position to depose him. All that mattered was that the stylised face should exude a suggestion of majesty, of supernatural prestige.

Of the Romans who attained power in the years following the death of Caesar, those who, like Antony, Caligula and Nero, inherited this tendency, all had yearnings toward an oriental empire. When they died, there was much talk of their resurrection. Their return was expected – or feared – for many years.

As the figure of Alexander began to loom more and more

impressively on the Roman horizon, the analogy between the Roman emperors and their illustrious model became steadily clearer. A corresponding analogy emerged between the attitude of the supporters of the Greek city-states and that of the supporters of the Roman Republic. The destinies of the two groups were also similar. The Roman republicans had the same longing for hegemony as the Greek statesmen, and also the same hatred of intrusive influences from abroad, and of the idea of monarchy; they shared the same basic political assumptions. Exactly like the Athenian leaders, they swallowed their objections to military dictatorship in the hope that it would help them to maintain their social supremacy at home and their racial supremacy abroad. But they knew in their hearts that the old constitution, on which their privileges were based, was not suited to the tasks of empire. If the *imperator* were to fulfil the new functions required by the new role of Rome, both in the field of defence and in that of administration, he would inevitably end up by assuming just those powers of government which they did not want to give him. Finally, they granted him those powers, on what they hoped was a temporary basis, hoping also to be able to guide him towards the achievement of their own ends.

But the Roman leader who rose to power in his capacity as defender of the frontiers, or as living proof of the superiority of one people over another, went on to free himself from all constitutional control. The demands of subject peoples, of the army, and of social classes seeking to improve their lot, led him to deviate from the route he was meant to follow, so that he did not become the instrument of a policy of enslavement, but the legitimate sovereign of a multi-national society. This made him a leveller. To the consternation of the senators, he threw off their yoke; he tolerated and even propagated cults that had nothing to do with the religion of the Capitol; he seated representatives of recently hostile states in the Senate House; he gave important appointments to freedmen and ex-barbarians; he took advantage of anti-Roman ideological tendencies to demand, or at least to accept, divine honours, without which it would have been difficult for him to achieve the blending of mixed populations into a harmonious whole. The most conspicuous characteristic of the sovereign, as portrayed on coins, in panegyrics, and in epitaphs is not the *invicta virtus* of earlier years with its connotation of robust strength, but rather *pietas*. The most favoured adjective is *sanctissimus*.[24] So devout a spirit could hardly fail to put forward a universalist political ideal. The place of the City-State is taken by the City of Justice, belonging to all humanity.

NOTES TO CHAPTER

1. For evidence of the priority of Alexander, see W. W. Tarn, *Alexander the Great and the Unity of Mankind*, London 1933; *Alexander the Great*, Cambridge 1948. On the other side, see M. H. Fisch, *Alexander and the Stoics*, in *Am. J. Philol.*, LVIII, 1937, pp. 59–92, 129–51; H. C. Baldry, *The Unity of Mankind in Greek Thought*, Cambridge 1965, pp. 113 ff.; W. Bruhl, *Le souvenir d'Alexandre et les Romains*, in *Mél. Arch. Hist.*, XLVII, 1930, p. 202; P. Treves, *Il mito d'Alessandro e la Roma d'Augusto*, Milan 1953; J. Gagé, *Hercules-Melquart, Alexandre et les Romains*, in *Rev. Et. Anc.*, XLII, 1940, pp. 425 ff.
2. Seneca, *De Beneficiis*, I, xiii, 3. Lucan, *Pharsalia*, X, 20: *Illic Pellaei proles vaesana Philippi   Felix praedo iacet.*
3. Lex Gabinia, 67 B.C.; Lex Manilia, 66 B.C.; Lex Vatinia, 59 B.C.; Lex Trebonia, 55 B.C.
4. Pliny, *Natural History*, VII, xxvi, 95.
5. Suetonius, *Life of Julius Caesar*, VII, 1. See also Plutarch, *Caesar*, 11. 'Both of them,' said Appian (*Civil War*, II, xxi, 151) 'aimed only at conquest.'
6. Cicero, *Letters to Atticus*, XII, xl, 2; XIII, xxviii, 3 – letters written in 45 B.C.
7. Velleius Paterculus, I, xi, 3–5; Pliny, *Natural History*, XXXIV, xix, 64; Statius, *Silvae*, I, i, 86 ff.
8. J. Gagé, *op. cit., loc. cit.*
9. Cicero, *De Officiis*, III, v, 25; Seneca, *De Beneficiis*, I, xiii, 1–3; Plato, *Symposium*, 177B; Isocrates, *Phil.*, 109.
10. Cornelius Nepos, *Hannibal*, III; Appian, *Civil War*, II, xxi, 149; III, ii, 16; Plutarch, *Antony*, 4, 36, 60; Vergil, *Aeneid*, VIII, 102, 287–303; Horace, *Odes*, III, xiv, 1 ff.; Philo, *On the Embassy to Gaius*, 78, 79; Dio Cassius, LXII, 20. See also J. Bayet, *Les origines de l'Hercule romain*, Paris 1926.

11. R. A. Anderson, *Alexander and the Caspian Gates*, in *Trans. Proc. Am. Philol. Ass.*, LIX, 1928, pp. 130 ff. Philostratus, in his *Life of Apollonius*, II, xx, xxiv and xlii (written in A.D. 216) writes that Apollonius, a Neo-Pythagorean philosopher of the first century, found bas-reliefs in India which represented the heroic deeds of Alexander, and a triumphal arch with his statue mounted on an eight-horse chariot.

12. See Plutarch, *Life of Pyrrhus*, 8. The Macedonians agreed that Pyrrhus resembled Alexander in character and in looks, while the other kings endeavoured to imitate the Macedonian 'in the purple attire, the number of their suite, the inclination of the head.'

13. Livy, XXXVIII, li, 8–12 and lviii, 8; Aulus Gellius, VI, i; Aurelius Victor, *De Viris Illustribus*, XLIX, 1–4; Appian, *Spanish Wars*, 23. See also Lily Ross Taylor, *The Divinity of the Roman Emperor*, Middletown, Connecticut 1931, pp. 3 ff.; E. Strong, *Apotheosis and After-Life*, London 1915, p. 62.

14. Velleius Paterculus, II, xxvii, 5; Appian, *Civil War*, I, xi, 97. For the relevant coinage, see E. A. Sydenham, *The Coinage of the Roman Republic*, London 1952, p. 124, no. 762; p. 145, no. 879; p. 146, no. 880.

15. Plutarch, *Sulla*, 7; *Caesar*, 43.

16. R. Pettazzoni, *La religione della Grecia antica*, Turin 1954, p. 267.

17. R. Syme, *Caesar, the Senate and Italy*, in *Papers of the British School at Rome*, XIV, 1938, pp. 3 ff.

18. Suetonius, *Life of Julius Caesar*, VII.

19. Propertius's allusion to the queen as being of 'the blood of Philip' (III, xi, 40) goes to show that such a claim seemed obvious to the Romans. Moreover she bore the same name as Alexander's sister (Diodorus Siculus, XVIII, 23). The founder of the Lagid dynasty was Ptolemy, son of Lagos and Arsinoe (of the royal house of Macedon), who was the king's brother according to Curtius Rufus (IX, viii, 22). It was he who supplied Arrian with details of the military campaigns of Macedon. See A. Bouché-Leclercq, *Histoire des Lagides*, Paris 1903, Vol. I, Chap. I.

20. Lily Ross Taylor, *op. cit.*

21. Suetonius, *Caligula*, XXII, 2, 3; Dio Cassius, LIX, 17, 3.

22. Plutarch, *On the Fortune of Alexander*, II, 2, 335; *Life of Alexander*, 4. See also the coins depicted in H. P. L'Orange, *Apotheosis in Ancient Portraiture*, Oslo 1947, pp. 20–1.

23. R. Bianchi-Bandinelli, *Archeologia e cultura*, Milan and Naples 1960, pp. 172 ff.

24. See the Arch of Gallienus at Salonica: *C.I.L.*, VI, 1106; Alexander Severus, *C.I.L.*, II, 3413; Maximian, *Panegyric*, III, xi; Maximian and Constantine, *Panegyric*, VI, v, vi, vii, xiii. See also M. P. Charlesworth, *Pietas and Victoria*, in *J.R.S.*, XXXII, 1943, pp. 1 ff.

VII

From Sulla to Augustus

> If you would trace it back to its beginning,
> Rome was but little; nevertheless, in that little
> town was hope of this great city. The walls
> were already standing, bounds too cramped
> for future peoples.
>
> OVID, *Fasti*, III, 179–81[1]

THE CONFLICT between the universalist conception of the Empire and the political heritage of the Republic stands out in ever sharper relief during the period that runs from the time of Sulla to the time of Augustus. Cicero compares Sulla with Jupiter. The god, for all his merciful nature, lets slip an occasional tempest: the dictator must therefore be forgiven if for all his vigilance, he lets slip an occasional oversight. 'He alone was governing the Republic and administering the affairs of the whole world' (*Pro Roscio Amerino,* XLV, 131).

Supreme power over the whole world, divine gifts of wisdom and intuition : such are the marks of the man of destiny. Though Sulla's intention had been to restore power to its traditional holders – the Senatorial aristocracy and the owners of great estates – he yielded to the flattering prospect of despotism; perhaps also to its historical necessity. To fortify his new position, he claimed to possess not only *virtus,* the manly attribute typical of the warrior, but also *felicitas,* that potent, superhuman power, that heaven-sent luck which is transmitted magically from the leader to his whole people. A suitable number of strange events underlined the miraculous aspect of his good fortune, so that his coming had a vague air of the millennium about it

99

(Appian, *Civil War*, I, i, 83). Advance notice of the opening of a new era was given by the sound of a mysterious trumpet (Plutarch, *Sulla*, 7, 11, 17). Within the cycle of the Great Year, made up of many centuries, the shock that accompanies the moment of change from one period to another is physically apparent to the senses. We find similar messianic stirrings during the career of Julius Caesar, and on the eve of the career of Augustus.[2]

After the proscriptions, the massacres which stained his victory with blood, a statue of Sulla appeared in the Forum with the prophetic inscription : SEMPER FELIX.

He skilfully spread the story of a revelation that he was destined to become a god.[3] These intimations of future glory were accompanied by the subjugation of the magistrates and the setting up of an inexorable despotism, based on the force of arms and arrayed in the prestige of the supernatural. Generous concessions, both social and economic, were the next stage, together with the creation of agricultural settlements. Sulla was the first to attempt to give the Empire an organisation appropriate to its vast size and to the variety of races which made it up. But, though his stated programme had been that of restoring power to the patrician aristocracy, whose support he sought by marrying into the family of the Metelli, the conservatives were not slow to notice that this supposed restoration presented features which boded no good to the republican institutions.

His contemporaries were well aware of this aspect. In later years, whenever there was a real threat of a new despot arising, Sulla was always mentioned as the precedent. '*Sullaturit*',[4] says Cicero of Pompey's activities, coining a sinister new verb from Sulla's name. Seeing that political advantage could be drawn from Cicero's analogy, Caesar cultivated the role of the avenger of one particular group of men – the men whom Pompey had put to death as a subordinate commander of Sulla.[5] This must have been a very frequent accusation among the popular party, for we find it echoed a hundred years later by Lucan.[6] The

Pompeians, on their side, made similar charges against Caesar.[7]

As a result of social war and the military new order, the unpropertied classes, and the peoples of Latium and the rest of Italy, had acquired a new importance. They carried more weight politically speaking, and played a conspicuous part in the economic life of the country. But a scornful attitude towards provincials, men of obscure origin and those born outside the precincts of the City, lingered on in the aristocratic citadel which dominated the heart of Rome.

Cicero was from Arpinum, and his pride was hurt by this arrogant attitude;[8] he remained a conservative in spirit and in his moral ideals, but turned away from the *optimates* to formulate the theory of a more broadly-based state. Not content with a social concord, *concordia ordinum,* which he thought he had achieved in the year of his consulate (63 B.C.), he hoped to see the *consensus omnium bonorum,*[9] or consensus of all right-thinking men.

This went further than a mere community of interest between the various ruling groups – the great agricultural land-owners on the one hand and the industrialists and tax-farmers in the provinces on the other. It meant a spirit of unity extending far beyond the Senate House and the Forum, to embrace Latins and Italians of every social class. The conception is still an abstract one, but it answers to the moral ideals of the orator, who remembers the simple virtues practised in towns such as Arpinum. These uncorrupted surroundings are the only possible starting-place for a healthy renewal of the country's political life. Alike in Cicero's speeches and his letters, we can trace the first appearances on the national scene of people emerging from previously obscure rungs of the social ladder – men who have been totally ignored by earlier theoretical writers, such as farmers, artisans and Italian provincials. In the *Verrine Orations* (II, v, 169), Cicero calls 'all Italy' the home of the Law; in the *Catilinarian Orations* (I, xi, 27), he calls Italy 'our true father-land, dearer than life itself'. Her sons are not a mere handful of arrogant patricians, but also the *ignobiles,* the *municipales,* the *rusticani,* the common throng, men of village and country-side; the orator likes to linger for a few words with them, to discuss the news, while Pompey is in flight from Rome (*Letters to Atticus,* VIII, xiii, 13). The same Italy is always in his thoughts, both when he reluctantly prepares to follow Pompey (*ibid.,* IX, i, 6), bewailing the situation that compels the exiles to make war on her, and when he tries to rally the whole country in support of Octavian against Antony.[10] His hope is that a spirit of unity will emerge on a vaster scale, both socially and racially speaking, than would be possible if only Romans were included.

But to rally the hearts of all men, bringing them into a single ideal harmony, the need for a single leader begins to emerge – a man capable of reconciling the conflicting interests, of blending together the voices of the upper, middle and lower classes, like a choir-master (*De Republica,* II, xlii, 69).

The spirit of Rome is imperceptibly taking on a new shape, which does not exclude the idea of rule by a single man as definitely as before. This tendency is strengthened by various disorders, by the deterioration of electoral institutions, and by the increasing personal power obtained by certain individuals.

Ideas stemming from Hellenistic lands, moreover, though not yet taking on a concrete form, showed an increasing tendency towards the expectation of a saviour – see Cicero's *De Republica,* I, vi, 11 and 12. The ideological development which paved the way for this new concept reflects an awareness that a new era is about to open, and jars with the old traditions of the City.

Those who wanted to justify the setting up of a single magistracy, tenable for life, had recourse to the ideas of Greek thinkers: in the same way that nature and the human soul are guided by a single rational principle, the social order requires a single ruler. He will be the earthly incarnation of the divine Mind. When he has proved himself the possessor of the warrior-like virtues and of all the moral attributes required by the Stoic doctrine, he will become the conciliator of the parties, the media-

102

tor between the classes and between the nations, the representative among men of the Godhead.

The pages of Cicero contain a profile of the *princeps* – the role which Augustus later tried to make his own, though his conception of it was more distinctively legalistic than the orator's.

Personal rule was inevitable in an empire of such vast size. In his *De Republica*, Cicero undoubtedly succeeded in providing the ideological content for the new system of government which was about to emerge. He raised it to the level of a doctrine, thus offering his own contribution to the cultural revaluation of Rome desired by patriotic spirits who were impatient of Greek superiority in this field.

Scholars have wondered about Cicero's motives in producing his picture of the ideal *princeps*. Was he expressing nostalgia for the Rome of Scipio, indirectly claiming the position of spiritual guide to the State for himself, or hinting that the long-awaited leader might turn out to be Pompey – or Caesar?[11]

As far as his own position was concerned, the ambitious provincial lawyer had now convinced himself that the nobles did not welcome his advancement; and he made up his mind, not without hesitation and moral repugnance, to take his stand alongside the holder of real power, whether it were Pompey or Caesar – though he saw the faults they had, and feared the faults they might acquire.

Social, economic and ideological factors all had their urgent importance. The conflict between the classes was matched by the deeper and more intimate conflict in the hearts of the Romans themselves – on the one hand, the knowledge of their own strength and the will to maintain undisputed supremacy over all nations; and on the other a leaning toward the ecumenical idea which had reached them from Greek and Asiatic countries.

There was a real incongruity between the privileged position of the Roman citizen in the eastern provinces and the awe with which even the most typical exponents of the Roman way of life regarded the local intellectuals. Cato of Utica was delighted to have been able to persuade the philosopher Athenodorus of Pergamus to follow him to Rome. Pompey lowered his *fasces* in salute when he passed the house of Poseidonius, and granted freedom to the inhabitants of Mitylene as a sign of gratitude toward Theophanes, his personal historian, who lived there.[12] The man who took upon himself the job of reorganising the State would also have to face the more difficult task of imparting a new value and a new self-confidence to the Roman spirit, together with a new consciousness of the Roman mission, so that the Empire could be presented to the peoples of the world as the vehicle of a universal idea.

It was no longer merely a question of composing disputes between classes within the walls of a single city, but of taking into consideration the social and spiritual unrest of a world in ferment, and finding a formula to express the ideological motives of empire.

Caesar reached the age of manhood during the Mithridatic wars. He had been initiated into the refinements of the East – and also, people said, into its corruptions – in Bithynia, during his stay with King Nicomedes, and in Cilicia and in Lesbos. During these visits, he saw the revolt of Asia at close quarters, and understood its motives.

Mithridates, who boasted of descent from Darius, had appealed for support to all the peoples of the East, and had made himself the centre of a vast rebellion. He had deposed the vassal-kings appointed by the Romans, and had successfully claimed the role of the liberator of Asia from the tyranny of the Roman tax-gatherer. He had emphasised the promise of innovation contained in his political message, and also its social and mystical elements, by adding the name of Dionysus, the god of the country labourer, to the name of Mithridates. No other divinity could have made so insistent an appeal to the spirit of universalism, or taken such easy strides across the boundaries of the Roman world. No other religion could have had the same disintegrating effect on the network of familial and social relationships that linked the other gods to the racial and communal

104

life of the City-State. No other faith could have deprived the ancient religion of the City of the prestige which it had derived from acceptance by the cultivated classes.

The beardless, wavy-haired image we see on the coinage of Mithridates shows that he drew his inspiration from Alexander.[13] The successes of the Romans did not seem to have the power to scathe him.[14] Sallust gives us a condensed version of the central theme of Mithridates' propaganda in a letter supposedly addressed by him to the king of the Parthians. 'They detest us as their rivals in power, and as likely to be the avengers of the cause of mankind' (*Letter of Mithridates*, 18, *Histories*, IV). The historian's intuition has summarised the deep-rooted causes of the Romans' confusion in this sentence – the fear of an Asiatic bloc, that might have effectively counterbalanced the still fluid and indefinite authority of Rome, and perhaps discredited it.[15]

The Hellenistic school of history, whose main themes can be seen in the work of Pompeius Trogus, brings out another delicate point regarding which the conquerors were very sensitive. In the *Epitome* of Trogus, Mithridates claims with lofty disdain that his kingdom is based on a right to rule which the Romans conspicuously lack – the right of an hereditary monarchy. 'It was not,' he says, 'the offences of kings, but their power and majesty, for which the Romans attacked them' (*Epitome*, XXXVIII, vi, 1). Such arguments show that divine favour and a pedigree to match had become absolute necessities for an aspiring statesman.

The consternation of the Romans at the idea that Mithridates might dare to drive towards the West is echoed in the pages of later historians. 'He sought to hasten through Thrace, Macedonia and Greece, and so to make a sudden inroad into Italy,' writes Florus (I, xl, 26), who adds the horrified comment: 'Even this did he conceive!'

Roman relief at the news of the death of Mithridates, in 62 B.C., can be judged from a letter written by Cicero to Pompey (*Letters to Friends*, V, vii, 1). He speaks of 'incredible joy,' anticipating the '*nunc est bibendum*' ('this calls for a drink') with which Horace greeted the death of Cleopatra.

These were the opening measures of an impressive motif : the revolt of the East against Rome – a revolt fed by the hatred which Pompey's annexation of Palestine inspired in the Jews, and by Parthian resentment at the aggression of Crassus. Both the mystical and the political elements of the propaganda emanating from Egypt under Antony and Cleopatra were to merge in it.

With the rich imagination and dynamic energy of his youth, Caesar could hardly fail to realise the advantages of getting out of the narrow field of Roman factional politics and into that boundless ideological debate, so that he could make use of those seething forces and enlist them in the service of Roman imperialism. Nor did he underestimate the personal glory to be gained from the submission of lands rich alike in history, in the arts, and in gold. Even before Pompey returned from the East and showed those who had stayed at home, by the splendour of his triumph, that their wildest dreams were founded on fact, Caesar had had his first glimpse of the opportunity he longed for. The testament of King Ptolemy XI, whether genuine or forged, had bequeathed Egypt to the Roman people. When his successor, Ptolemy XII, was driven into exile in 65 B.C., the Romans had both an excuse and a legal justification for annexing the country. If Caesar could have managed to add Egypt to the Empire, it would have been a far richer and more wonderful prize even than the three new provinces of Crete, Syria and Bithynia which Pompey was about to win for Rome.

To rule in Egypt was not merely to take up a magistracy like any other – it meant command over a distant and splendid monarchy, over sovereigns whose divinity was unquestioned; it meant the absorption of the most un-Roman ideas in the name of Empire; it meant that toga and sword would have a diadem added to them – perhaps even a halo. The proposed annexation, however, did not meet with general favour. Caesar's request for an extraordinary military command in Egypt was

106

rejected, and he had to shelve his eastern plans for the moment.[16]

He now had recourse to psychological devices of a typically Roman kind. The alternating threads of traditional Roman thought and the thought of the East are symbolised in Caesar's person and by his activities during these years.

The widow of Marius was Caesar's aunt; and when she died, he seized the opportunity of bringing out the images of the hero. This had been strictly forbidden since the days of Sulla. Not content with using Marius as a sort of moral predecessor, he asserted the right to the people's trust in another way, by a claim which had nothing to do with services to the State. On the same day, he announced, in the course of the funeral oration, that he was descended from Ancus Marcius on the father's side, and on the mother's side from Venus, through Ascanius, also known as Iulus, who was the goddess's grandson (Suetonius, *Life of Julius Caesar,* VI, 1).

This claim was repeated on the coins, struck many years later,[17] which show the famous scene of Aeneas carrying Anchises on his back. Others show Venus herself.[18]

For the first time, an attempt had been made to unite in a single person the two constituent factors of political power – military command, the shield of Rome against the barbarians, as personified by the rough-hewn features of Marius on the one hand, and on the other, the authority of divine right. The second nullified the fundamental republican characteristics of traditional military command, which had always been subject to appointment by the constitutional authorities of the state, and had lasted only for a limited period of time.

Now that Rome needed a form of government capable of overawing the whole world, the valour of her soldiers and the severe wisdom of her magistrates were no longer enough. Supernatural sanctions were also needed; and so Caesar developed a flair for archaeology and myth,[19] claiming ancestors of royal or heavenly stock for himself, and descent from the Trojans for the whole Roman people. (Recent archaeological discoveries suggest some historical foundation for the Trojan theory, though it remains largely a matter of legend.) Sulla had touched the same chord during his time in Greece, when he assumed the title of *'Epaphroditos'* – not merely one protected by Venus, but her very darling.[20] Venus was the patron goddess of the Romans, and the mother of Aeneas. Lucretius addresses her as 'Aeneadum genetrix'.

The distant memories of a migration to Italy from Asia Minor, of which there are some confused records at the beginning of the history of the Mediterranean peoples, were given increased substance and literary form after the battle of Cynoscephalae, in 197 B.C. Like all *nouveaux riches,* the Romans were ashamed of their lack of pedigree, and there was no dearth of willing hands to help in the search for ancestors. The question had hardly been mentioned previously in the writings of the Romans, and Greek references to the matter were vague and contradictory. Caesar took advantage of this cue. Trojan origin and the past glories of Marius became the two mainstays of his political propaganda.

The Roman principate of future years was to have two faces, which now appeared together for the first time. The two tendencies were permanently opposed to each other, and though each prevailed in turn, the loser never vanished altogether. On the one hand was the splendour of the divine right of Empire; on the other, the tradition represented by the rustic birthright of the obscure scion of the gentry from Arpinum in Latium – Marius, who boasted that he had no ancestors, unlike the haughty patricians of the Senate;[21] who had been called the new founder of Rome, and compared to Romulus and Camillus; who had made the army the instrument of political power. Marius had won the Numidian war, and had paraded King Jugurtha in chains before the eyes of the Romans in his triumph. But his political propaganda was very different from that of Sulla, with its anticipations of later claims to divine descent. Marius's message was a simple and homely one. His coins are decorated only with the head of Ceres, the goddess of farming, and with a team of bullocks ploughing a virgin terrain under the guiding hand of a colonist.[22] This to commemorate the colony of Eporedia, founded by Marius in Cisalpine Gaul (Velleius Paterculus, I, xv). Here is the old theme of the Gracchi – land must be given to the poor, and to soldiers returning from foreign service. Colonial expansion should be planned to give work and bread to the plebeians rather than to install garrisons at strategic points. But the greatest glory of Marius – though he declined a triumph after it – was his defence of the soil of Italy from its worst threat since the days of Brennus and of Hannibal. The Teutons had thrust their way as far south as Provence, and the Cimbrians had made their way through the Brenner Pass and invaded the plain of the Po right down to Vercelli.

The popular party shared in the glory of Marius's victories His whole figure breathed a rustic, homely spirit, with no suggestion of the legendary aura so easily acquired by conquerors returning from the East. Apart from a few unimportant miracles, a Syrian prophetess of doubtful reputation and a pair of tame vultures (Plutarch, *Marius*, 17–36), there is no sign of heavenly ancestors or supernatural guidance about Marius. His contemporaries did not give any credence even to these half-hearted impostures – as any miracle must obviously be if it is credited to a plebeian.

On his return from Spain in 65 B.C., Caesar again emphasised the theme of patriotic resistance to the barbarians. Having gained the favour of the people by offering them exceptional festivities at his own expense, he had statues of Marius erected on the Capitol under cover of darkness, together with statues of victory bearing trophies, and inscriptions celebrating his conquest of the Cimbri.[23]

The trophies and the threatening visages of the barbarians remained on the Capitol. Cimbri and Teutons were names of fear, indissolubly linked with the name of the hero. Those of Caesar's biographers who accentuate his ambitious leanings towards a theocratic principate do not give this episode its proper value. It showed that Caesar could already see the outlines of a

Roman policy in the West, a territory still partly unexplored, and inhabited by savages whose threatening hordes might again descend on Italy to rob and destroy. The man who carries the Roman standards into those lands will not find the ghost of Achilles or Alexander lurking behind ancient walls or splendid monuments to bar his passage, nor will he find marble palaces, thrones surrounded by eunuchs, nor yet sardonic historians or conceited men of letters. To introduce the Roman way of life into the West, to build temples, law-courts, baths and aqueducts, to drive roads through the forests, to direct these vast human resources to productive labour, to spread the knowledge of the law, and exploit the natural wealth of the area – here was a task which justified the brutality of war, for anyone who was not blindly attached to legalistic tradition. These territories might later provide a valuable counterweight to the excessive influence of the East on Italy.

Caesar's policy deliberately introduces the stimulating idea that the lands of the West have something more to offer than strategic positions carefully chosen to intercept the probable routes of future invaders; that their threat may be met by conquest rather than resistance, and that conquest can be regarded as a missionary activity.

Repulsing the invader is a traditionally sacred task, and the only legitimate basis for *imperium.* To perform this task, all that is traditionally needed is appointment by due democratic process. But it was now essential to provide a second element, and Caesar was instinctively aware of the need for it – a power drawing its authority directly from heaven.[24] Not content with the glory due to a descendant of Venus, he added to it the prestige due to the *pontifex maximus,* the high priesthood, a post which he obtained with great expenditure of money and intrigue, in 63 B.C. The dismay with which the Senate greeted the news shows the importance attached to the position (Plutarch, *Caesar,* 7).

The thread of supernatural authority is paralleled, in Caesar's writings, by the thread of republican activity. He clearly respects

110

the feelings of the political world in Rome, for whom he was writing. In the *Gallic War,* everything that Caesar does is done in the name of the Roman people. Whether he opposes the migration of the Helvetians, treats with Ariovistus, parleys with the Gauls, or builds a bridge across the Rhine in two weeks, he is always acting as the people's elected representative, and in their name. The national will has more weight, in the Roman scheme of things, than the grace of heaven. Similarly, when he tells the story of the civil war, Caesar tries to convince his reader of his firm determination never to break the rules of democracy – he was compelled, he says, to take up arms in self-defence, but he was always ready for any compromise and any sacrifice for the sake of the Republic.[25] He never forgets the political ideas on which he was brought up. He tries to give the impression of a man who has been given a temporary command because of his recognised ability to exercise it. He wants to keep the image of the general whose power is limited to the camp – the image of Marius, or even, going back through history to the border of legend, the image of Camillus. And yet another element can already be seen in his face and felt in his thought, an element derived more from the historical figure of Alexander and the mythical figure of Hercules than from those illustrious republican forerunners. The message of the Macedonian and the god had an element of idealism, which promised a single, beneficent government for all mankind, and therefore implicitly denied the validity of the special position enjoyed by the upper classes among the citizens of Rome, and by Rome among the cities of the world.

Turning from political theory to visual evidence – the most convincing testimony of all – we find that Caesar was the first man allowed by the Senate to put his own features on the coinage minted at Rome in his life-time. This showed that a single man had been chosen to symbolise the State, and to represent it in all the countries which were linked to the Roman economy – that he had been exalted above his peers. When writing the history of Rome, Cato the Censor had omitted the names of leading figures, in order to avoid the glorification of individuals.[26] But history now came to be seen as the work of a single, heaven-sent individual, rather than the result of the devotion of his numerous, modest, anonymous fellow-citizens.

The new coinage identified the dictator with the State, and promised the citizens liberty and dominion : the word 'Freedom' was on one side of the coins, and on the other, Rome with her foot resting on the globe.[27]

A profound ideological contradiction can be detected in the new coinage. Its message is two-fold, for the visual images just mentioned as tending to convert an individual into a symbol of the common will are accompanied by other images designed to appeal to the conservative classes. The traditional religious insignia are there – the fillets of the *flamen dialis* (a priesthood which Caesar had entered at the age of seventeen) are shown, and also the crooked staff of the *pontifex maximus*.[28] This last title had been especially sought after by the young Caesar, who foresaw the extraordinary prestige that could be obtained by adding religious authority to political power. This does not mean that there is any truth in the view, expressed by many authors, that Caesar had definite monarchical ambitions; nor that this view was held by his contemporaries.

Caesar simply tried to unite the two theories in his own person, the theme of the City and that of the Universe – to combine the features of Tiberius Gracchus with those of Scipio. To establish himself as the faithful servant of his country, he made masterly use of the threat of barbarian invasion. He saw how effective an argument this was on the minds of the masses. He knew that a man who had deserved well of his country in defence was exempt from the rigorous application of the laws of the City. The Senate had not been able to proceed with the trial of Marcus Manlius in the Forum, in sight of the Capitoline Rock where he had gloriously repulsed the Gallic invaders (Plutarch, *Camillus*, 36). And the indignant protests of the supporters of the letter of the law had no effect, when Scipio Africanus was thought to have exceeded its provisions.[29]

112

In view of these precedents, it is easy to imagine how deeply the conservatives must have distrusted a man who had deliberately gone and routed the barbarians out of their lairs. They must have foreseen the political use that Caesar would make of his military feats. The concision of his *Commentaries* can easily be misinterpreted. It is not the straightforward brevity of an army communiqué. A completely consistent logical thread runs through the long catalogue of military operations. Right from the beginning of the book, we can see him justifying himself against various accusations. We have no verbal record of them, but they are easy to guess. Caesar, they said, had provoked the war to add to his own importance; he had exaggerated the danger of the threat from the Helvetians; he had deliberately extended and prolonged operations in order to obtain booty and slaves, and to acquire a well-trained and devoted army for his own personal ends. The counter-propaganda contained in the *Gallic War,* eloquent though not explicit, aims at establishing the legitimacy of the means he employed and of the long duration of his command. The narrative of his actions overlies another strand – the justification of his motives. The 'barbarian peril' can seldom have been so thoroughly exploited.

Caesar gives a very full report of the Gallic chieftains' appeal for help against the Germans, who had been migrating across the Rhine in their thousands for years past, and settling in the lands of the Gauls. How could he betray the Gauls' trust? Other arguments, too, he introduces, of proven effectiveness. 'Becoming accustomed to crossing the Rhine and invading the territories of Gaul,' he says, 'the Germans would represent a threat to the people of Rome. Barbarians of such ferocity would not stop at invading Gaul, but would encroach on the neighbouring province, and thrust their way through to Italy itself, like the Cimbrians and the Teutons before them' (*Gallic War,* I, xxxiii).

Such fears were far from unfounded. The mention of the Cimbrians and Teutons echoes the demagogic theme of earlier days. Italy had not forgotten the past terrors of those names,

113

and Caesar had appropriated the name of Marius for his own banner.

He gave new heart to the legionaries when they were terrified by the stories of the ferocity of the Germans, and also alarmed at the thought of the disciplinary penalties involved in a war set in motion by the proconsul himself on his own initiative – a war which was unjust in itself and had never been the subject of a regular vote, in the words of Dio Cassius (XXXVIII, 35, 2). (The legal point is not mentioned by Caesar, but is emphasised by later historians.) So Caesar, according to his own account, was ready to parley with Ariovistus, and most willing to offer him fair terms; but the German chieftain, aloof and mistrustful, surrounded by armed guards, would not even deign to dismount from his horse. He justified his encroachments on Gallic territory as having the same grounds in law as the Roman encroachments in Gallia Narbonensis. Finally he proudly called on Caesar to withdraw. 'If he could get rid of Caesar altogether,' he said, 'he would be doing something welcome to many patricians and important figures at Rome. He knew this from them directly, for they had sent him special envoys bearing this message. . . . But if Caesar would withdraw, and leave him in uncontested possession of all Gaul, he would reward the Roman with vast sums of money. Then Caesar would be able to undertake any war he had in mind without difficulty or danger' (Caesar, *Gallic War*, I, xliv).

At this point Caesar makes a parade of his contempt for the military support offered to him to attack his own country, and for the barbarian's gold. He also exposes the patricians to the execration of all Roman patriots, accusing them of negotiating with the enemy for the destruction of those who were defending the soil of their country.

It will be seen that Caesar was very much alive to his compatriots' susceptibilities. Yet those who opposed him, because they shared the traditional objections to all territorial expansion that was not an obvious strategic necessity, or because they had distrusted the idea of too much power in one man's hands, were loud in condemnation of 'Caesar's war'.[30] Many others applauded his campaigns as a guarantee of future safety for the State.

After two years of war in Gaul, the Senate declared its intention of taking away one of Caesar's provinces, or even both of them, and entrusting them to the consuls for the following year. Then Cicero set out to explain his reasons for backing Caesar, basing himself both on constitutional[31] and patriotic grounds. Many others must have backed him for the same reasons.

Cicero admits that he had to overcome certain scruples before ranging himself on the side of the dictator;[32] he neatly points out, however, that the Senate itself had taken up an attitude that could only encourage him to do so. 'I admit that I formerly differed from Caesar, and agreed with you – and now I am still with you, no less than before. For it was you yourselves who decreed public prayer in honour of Caesar for a greater number of days than has ever been done before for a single general and a single war.'[33]

This oratorical subtlety betrays the embarrassment of Cicero. Many senators let him feel the weight of their disapproval for this *volte-face*. But at the same time, his words clearly betray the inward conflict, the inner contradiction inherent in Roman patriotic thinking. Despite economic difficulties,[34] the Senate had not hesitated to satisfy all the demands that reached it from Gaul, whether they requested the celebration of religious ceremonies or the despatch of financial help. At the same time, the senators had expressed unfavourable judgments on the military leader, who had followed a policy opposed to that observed by his predecessors and that expected by the strategists of the Senate House.

'For our generals at all times,' says Cicero, 'thought it better to limit themselves to repulsing those nations, than to provoke their hostility by any attack of our own. Even that great man Caius Marius . . . was content to check the enormous multitude of Gauls . . . without endeavouring to penetrate into their cities and dwelling-places. . . . But I see that the counsels of Caesar are

115

widely different. For he thought it his duty, not only to war against those men whom he saw already in arms against the Roman people, but to reduce the whole of Gaul under our dominion. . . . Nations which were either hostile to this empire, or treacherous, or unknown to us, or at all events, savage, barbarian, and warlike – nations which no one ever existed who did not wish to break their power and subdue them. Nor has anyone, from the very first rise of this empire, ever carefully deliberated about our republic, who has not thought Gaul the chief object of apprehension to this empire. But still, on account of the power and vast population of those nations, we never before have had a war with all of them; we have always been content to resist them when attacked. Now, at last, it has been brought about that there should be one and the same boundary to our empire and to those nations.'[35]

Nature, Cicero goes on, had previously protected Italy with the Alps, 'not without some special kindness of the gods in providing us with such a bulwark. . . . Now, indeed, the Alps are at liberty to sink down if they please; for there is nothing beyond those lofty heights as far as the ocean itself which can be any object of fear to Italy.'[36]

A year later, in 55 B.C. Cicero confirmed his support of the dictator in even more explicit terms, expressing, perhaps, the feelings of many republicans at that crucial moment : the overcoming of moral repugnance or prejudice, the renunciation of civil liberties in view of the tasks of expansion and the civilising mission which history had assigned to the Romans. For those tasks could only be fulfilled by new methods and new ideas. Cicero never tires of repeating how Caesar had paid homage to his virtues and made various flattering propositions to him. 'But even if he had always shown himself implacable and irreconcilable towards me, still I could not feel otherwise than friendly towards a man who had performed and was daily performing such mighty actions. Now that he is in command, I no longer oppose and array the rampart of the Alps against the ascent and crossing of the Gauls, nor the channel of the

Rhine, foaming with its vast whirlpools, against those most savage nations of the Germans. Caesar has brought things to such a pass, that even if the mountains were to sink down, and the rivers to be dried up, we should still have Italy fortified, not, indeed, by the forces of Nature, but by his victory and great exploits.'[37]

These arguments may well have been suggested to the docile propagandist by Caesar himself, so that the prolonged struggle for territorial expansion could be justified by the strategic value of the new territories. For Caesar, defence was still the Leitmotif. It was left for Augustus to bring ideological justification into play. Caesar's only concern was to obtain acceptance for his war. For this end he made use of all possible means – he distributed thrones in the provinces to the young men who were recommended to him, and he watched over the interests of the Romans' clients, even in the heat of battle.

No Roman, whatever his position, could be unaware of the economic advantages of conquest. The Romans had been exempt from taxation since the time when the eastern provinces began to pour their tribute into the exchequer. The *publicani* made immense profits out of farming the taxes. Everywhere in Gaul were merchants, middlemen and industrialists who had a vested interest in the growth of business and in the opening of new markets in those technically undeveloped lands, from which raw materials could also be imported. Some Romans bought land in Gaul, and made enormous profits out of it. Later on, when colonisation of Gaul was completed and, after a census, full value began to be obtained from the system of tribute, it could be claimed that 'the provinces of Gaul tamely pay almost the same tribute as all the rest of the world' (Velleius Paterculus, II, xxxix, 2).

Among those who favoured Pompey, however, there were murmurs that Gaul, Germany and Britain were rustic, backward, inhospitable territories, of small economic interest, and that this was why the great captains of the past had never bothered with them. With the foundation of the Narbonese colony in 118 B.C., a pawn had indeed been thrust forward into enemy territory, a control post set up on the lines of communication between Spain, the lands of Gaul, and the Mediterranean. The German invasion that swept across the Rhine and Danube a few years later had confirmed the Romans' belief that the coastal strip they had won from Gaul was a most valuable strategic acquisition, guarding the Ligurian approaches to Italy which were the peninsula's most vulnerable point. But no one had ever thought of setting up a system of protectorates based on the local dynasties of Gaul, of creating a network of vassal states, as had been done in Greece and in Asia.

Up to that moment, Roman territorial acquisitions had been piecemeal in character and wholly defensive in object. Expansion had followed a haphazard course. There had been no guiding policy of conscious imperialism before Caesar. Caesar himself may have followed that policy, but he certainly did not draw up the theory. Rome had always tried to maintain a balance of power in the Mediterranean, by exercising authority over its satellite states. The provinces were regarded as military districts, to be entrusted of officials whose *imperium* could be prolonged as necessary. Because of the distrust of the ruling classes, and the difficulty of controlling and maintaining distant garrisons, the Empire had always had the character of a protectorate, which might be harsh and grasping but exercised its power indirectly. The Macedonian and Jugurthine wars, for example, had not been followed by annexation. The Romans preferred to regard the conquered nations as a sort of game reserve. They exploited them by taxation and by the operations of commerce, but did not want to administer them directly from Rome.

But the serious danger into which the Mithridatic wars plunged the Roman sphere of influence around the Aegean, and the length of the struggle against the pirates compelled the Roman generals to assume direct control over the territories in question, especially those bordering on the sea. Pompey understood the importance of maritime countries, and subjugated

118

Syria, Cilicia, Judaea, Crete and Cyprus. But he left the inland monarchies intact. He allowed Tigranes, the most formidable ally of Mithridates, to retain the kingdom of Armenia, for example (66 B.C. – see Plutarch, *Pompey,* 33).

Caesar claims to have tried to win over the Gauls with a similar policy. He summoned a council of Gallic leaders, and flattered them with promises of personal honours and a share of booty in all future campaigns in which they took part. But the long resistance of the Gallic nation, and the vastness of the territory, convinced him that direct rule was indispensable. Thus Rome found herself unexpectedly committed to the reorganisation and the garrisoning of an immense area, which was vulnerable to German attack.

Those years saw an extraordinary enlargement in the Romans' ideas about the proper geographical extent of their empire, and also their feelings about its duration and ideological meaning. A globe, signifying world-wide power, appeared on the coinage of Sulla in 82 B.C.[38] The feet of Caesar's statue also rested on a globe, according to Dio Cassius (XLIII, 14, 6). Caesar was said to have extended the Empire of Rome to the limits of the inhabited world by his conquests (Cicero, *Pro L. Balbo* XXVIII, 64). In the same period, the phrase *orbis terrarum* came into common use, as a term to describe the area occupied by Roman arms. It was treated as equivalent to *orbis Romanus* – the difference between the two concepts seemed to have vanished. *Humanum genus* came to indicate the subject peoples of Rome considered as a whole. The pun on the words *urbis* and *orbis* (City and world) made its appearance,[39] the first being mystically represented by Vesta, the guardian of the traditional Roman values, and the second by Cybele, the Asiatic divinity who was mother of all the gods. The ecumenical concept, first introduced into Roman political thought by Polybius, took on a more concrete form. Vast, resounding terms began to be used to describe areas of command, the spread of the provinces, and the Roman sphere of influence. *Aeternitas* became the common term for the duration of the Empire – always subject to the

119

fundamental condition that the original Roman virtues will not be lost. Let Rome control her greed, and return to her ancient austerity, and 'the State will be immortal, and its empire will be eternal,' according to Cicero.[40]

The Romans realised that an unpunished outrage may form a precedent, whose consequences may extend to the whole world. An attack on the majesty of the Senate is an insult to Rome, and hence to the whole world.[41] It amounts to 'laying siege to the government of the whole earth' (Cicero, *Philippics,* IV, vi, 14). The Romans know how important it is to train newly conquered peoples to appreciate the rights granted to them by a constitutional government (Cicero, *Letters to Friends,* X, viii, 3).

A new cult was instituted for the great City – 'the light of the world, the guardian of all nations,' according to Cicero (*Philippics,* IV, vi, 14), the City which, thanks to the valour of her sons, has 'imposed obedience on the whole world' (Cicero, *Pro Murena,* X, 22). Sallust calls Rome the 'controller of the nations' (*Oratio Lepidi, Histories,* I, 11) and describes the Romans as 'born to command' (*Jugurthine War,* XXXI, 11). So the laws of Rome now possess a universal scope, a world-wide validity. How vast a responsibility rests on the man who is called upon to decree those laws!

The above quotations belong to a period earlier than that of Augustan literature. They prove, however, that the prophetic inspiration and the universal spirit which permeate that literature are not derived solely from the demands of Octavian's propaganda department. From the time of the Romans' victories over Carthage and over the Macedonian succession states, there had been a growing conviction that a huge and splendid historical development like the Roman Empire could not have come about unless it had been deliberately willed by the gods. So vast a power could only fulfil itself on a universal and eternal plane. Thus ideas which had been latent since the second century B.C. found expression in more and more precise and explicit words during the periods dominated by Sulla, Pompey and

Caesar. The almost supernatural valour of the three men, and the fabulous renown of their deeds, appeared as the worthy fruition of those half-formed aspirations. Under Augustus, the same aspirations acquired lustre and prestige, and became the guiding lights of the imperial ideology.

The Roman State took on the shape of a single organism – a blow at any part of it, however remote, was felt by the whole body. And though the State was coming to be identifiable with the universe, 'it all depended on the spirit of one man,' according to Cicero (*Pro Marcello,* VII, 22 in 46 B.C.). Terror was felt at the thought that he may be subject to the ordinary weaknesses of the human condition, and prayers were offered for his health. He was the soul of the universal State, its centre, its intellect, its creative force, its spiritual guide. If he should perish, no one could be saved. These thoughts can be traced in the pages of Cicero, long before they became common property with the Augustan poets.

Among Julius Caesar's legislative measures, Suetonius mentions the reform of the calendar – a step appropriate to his office of *pontifex maximus.* To reorganise the months, so that they corresponded with the solar year instead of the phases of the moon, was a necessary innovation on practical grounds. But a theocratic and universalist element can also be traced in his action. When Romulus founded Rome, his first action had been to institute the old ten-month year (Ovid, *Fasti,* I, 27–8). One of the prerogatives of mythical kings and founders of states is to initiate a new era, to impart a fresh rhythm to the movement of time. Almost as if they wanted to re-establish the ancient course of events, the conspirators chose March 15 – the feast of Anna Perenna, which had been New Year's Day in the old calendar – to murder the man who had subverted the very sequence of the days.

Caesar's astronomer, Sosigenes, was an Egyptian, and therefore inclined to trace a connection between the rhythm of the seasons and the movement of the heavenly bodies on the one hand, and the fates of men on the other.[42] Poseidonius, another of Caesar's masters, regarded all created things, including the heavenly bodies as parts of a unitary cosmos. How far, we may ask, had these two thinkers influenced Caesar's ideas, and how much attention may he have paid to the aspirations that were in the air, calling for a mystical, universal revolution, the advent of an era of world-wide peace? There is a certain messianic flavour about the final passages of Cicero's *De Republica,* written as early as 54 B.C., while four years after the Ides of March the *Fourth Eclogue* of Vergil salutes the rebirth of the world, and expresses 'the aspiration towards renewal which had been wide-spread among the peoples of the Empire for several decades at least.'[43]

The poets of the Augustan age were not slow to celebrate the beneficial effect of Caesar's star on the crops.[44] Ovid, in fact, treated the reform of the calendar as a presage of Caesar's inevitable deification. According to the poet, Caesar formed a definite intention of inspecting the vault of heaven, so that he might acquaint himself with his promised home in the firmament even before he gained admission to it in his capacity as a new god (*Fasti,* III, 159). The order of the earthly City perfectly matches that of the heavenly one, says Manilius : In the sky there is a crowd of stars constituting different classes just as here we have senators, equestrians and plebeians.[45]

NOTES TO CHAPTER

1. *Parva fuit, si prima velis elementa referre, Roma: sed in parva spes tamen huius erat. Moenia iam stabant, populis angusta futuris.*
2. J. Carcopino, *Virgile et le mystère de la IV éclogue,* Paris 1930.
3. Appian, *Civil War,* I, xi, 97; Velleius Paterculus, II, xxiv, 3.
4. Cicero, *Letters to Atticus,* IX, x, 6; xi, 3; xiv, 2.
5. Cicero, *Letters to Atticus,* IX, xiv, 2.
6. *Pharsalia,* VII, 307: *cum duce Sullano gerimus civilia bella.*
7. Cicero, *Letters to Atticus,* XI, xxi, 3.

8. For the reaction to Cicero's attainment to the consulate, see Sallust, *Catilinarian War*, XXIII, 6, quoted on pp. 40-1 above.

9. See P. Grenade, *Remarques sur la théorie cicéronienne du Principat*, in *Mél. Arch. et Hist.*, LVII, 1940, pp. 32–63; *Essai sur les origines du Principat*, Paris 1961; A. Oltramare, *La réaction cicéronienne et les débuts du Principat*, in *Rev. Et. Lat.*, X, 1932, pp. 58 ff.; E. Lèpore, *Il princeps ciceroniano*, Naples 1954, pp. 33–4, 105–18.

10. *Philippics*, III, xiii, 32: *Italia tota ad libertatem recuperandam.*

11. See P. Grenade, *Remarques*, p. 63; E. Lèpore, *op. cit.*, pp. 18, 68 note 8; M. A. Levi, *Il tempo di Augusto*, Florence 1951, p. 14; J. Béranger, *Recherches sur l'aspect idéologique du Principat*, Basle 1953; E. Ciaceri, *Il trattato di Cicerone 'De Republica'*, in *Rend. R. Acc. L.*, XXVII, 1918, pp. 312 ff.; A. Oltramare, *op. cit.* P. Boyancé, in *Etudes sur le Songe de Scipion*, Bordeaux 1936, maintains that the figure of the man who has deserved well of his country and for whom a place is reserved in Heaven is meant to be Cicero himself; and that the 'princeps' mentioned is Authority as an abstract conception, the word 'orator' being used similarly, (p. 139, note 4). See also E. Meyer, *Caesars Monarchie und das Principat des Pompeius*, Stuttgart 1922; J. Gagé, *De César à Auguste: où en est le problème des origines du Principat?*, in *Revue Hist.*, CLXXVII, 1936, pp. 279 ff.; W. Allen, *Caesar's Regnum*, in *Trans. Proc. Am. Philol. Ass.*, LXXXIV, 1953, pp. 227 ff.; E. Ciccotti, *La civiltà del mondo antico*, Udine 1935, p. 126.

12. Plutarch, *Cato*, 10, 15; *Pompey*, 42.

13. W. H. Waddington, T. Reinach, *Monnaies grecques d'Asie Mineure*, Paris 1890, I, p. 12.

14. Cicero, *Pro Murena*, XV, 33; *Pro Lege Manilia*, III, 8.

15. E. Bikerman, *La lettre de Mithridate dans les Histoires de Sallust*, in *Rev. Et. Lat.*, XXIV, 1946, pp. 131 ff.

16. In 59 B.C., when Caesar was consul, he induced the Senate to grant Ptolemy XIII recognition and the title of 'socius et amicus', which, practically speaking, put the king at the mercy of Rome.

17. E. A. Sydenham, *The Coinage of the Roman Republic*, London 1952, p. 168, no. 1013; p. 182, no. 1104.

18. E. A. Sydenham, *op. cit.*, p. 169, nos. 1016–21; p. 170, no. 1022; p. 177, nos. 1059, 1060, 1062, 1064.

19. J. Perret, *Les origines de la légende troyenne de Rome*, Paris 1942, p. 529.

20. Appian, *Civil War*, I, xi, 97; Plutarch, *Sulla*, 34.

21. Plutarch, *Marius*, 9; Sallust, *Jugurthine War*, LXXXV, 38.

22. E. A. Sydenham, *op. cit.*, p. 119, no. 744 a, b.

23. Plutarch, *Caesar*, 6; Suetonius, *Life of Julius Caesar*, XI.

24. M. A. Levi, *La lotta politica nel mondo antico*, Verona 1963, p. 205: 'A man deemed to possess the faculty of *imperium* as a personal gift could dispense with the normal investiture.'

25. M. Rambaud, *L'art de la déformation historique dans les Commentaires*, Paris 1953.

26. Cornelius Nepos, *Life of Cato*, III. For the coinage, see E. A. Sydenham, *op. cit.*, p. 213, nos. 1362–4, for 45–44 B.C.; p. 177, nos. 1060–3, for 44 B.C.; p. 178, nos. 1067–74, for 44 B.C.; p. 179, nos. 1075–6, for 44 B.C.

27. E. A. Sydenham, *op. cit.*, p. 159, no. 949 – coin of 48 B.C. showing Rome with her foot resting on a globe; p. 179, no. 1076 – coin of 44 B.C. showing a globe on the pediment of a temple inscribed 'Clementiae Caesaris'; p. 176, no. 1055 – coin of 44 B.C. showing Venus on a globe. The series is continued in later years.

28. E. A. Sydenham, *op. cit.*, p. 177, nos. 1056–60; p. 167, no. 1006; p. 179, nos. 1075–6.

29. Livy, XXXVIII, li, 4–6; Aulus Gellius, IV, xviii, 3.

30. Suetonius, *Life of Julius Caesar*, XXIV, 3; Plutarch, *Cato*, 33.

31. The Lex Vatinia gave Caesar full powers up to March 54 B.C. See E. G. Hardy, *Some Problems in Roman History*, Oxford 1924, Ser. II, Chap. VI, p. 150.

32. Cicero, *Letters to Atticus*, IV, vi, 5.

33. Cicero, *De Provinciis Consularibus*, X, 25.

34. Cicero, *Pro Balbo*, XXVII, 61.

35. Cicero, *De Provinciis Consularibus*, XIII, 32.

36. *Ibid.*, XIV, 34.

37. *In Pisonem*, XXXIII, 81–2.

38. J. Vogt, *Orbis Romanus*, Tübingen 1929; F. Christ, *Die Römische Weltherrschaft in der Antiken Dichtung*, Stuttgart 1938.

39. See Cicero, *Paradoxa Stoicorum*, II, 18: *Mors terribilis . . . exilium autem iis quibus quasi circumscriptus habitandi est locus, non iis qui omnem orbem terrarum unam urbem esse ducunt.*

40. *Pro Rabirio Perduellionis*, XII, 33. See also *Pro Marcello*, VII, xxii, and *Philippics*, II, xxi, 51.

41. Cicero, *Catilinarian Orations*, I, iv, 9: *hoc orbis terrae sanctissimo, gravissimo consilio.*

42. Macrobius, in *Saturnalia*, I, xvi, 39, gives it as certain that Caesar's ideas on astronomy came from Egypt, and says that he composed a treatise on the subject. See G. Pasquali, *Cesare, Posidonio e Platone*, in *Studi Italiani in Filologia Classica*, 1931, pp. 297 ff.

43. A. La Penna, *Orazio e l'ideologia del Principato*, Turin 1963, p. 32.

44. See Vergil, *Eclogues*, V, 78–80 and IX, 47–8.

45. Manilius, *Astronomica*, V, 734–9.

VIII

Augustus

Why should I tell over the barbarous nations
and the peoples dwelling by either Ocean?
Whatever is habitable in the world shall belong
to him.

OVID, *Metamorphoses*, XV, 829–31[1]

AFTER THE murder of the dictator, strife was clearly inevitable
between Caesar's official heir, Octavian, and his spiritual heir,
the consul Antony.

Victory was reserved for the candidate who might prove
more sensitive to the feelings of the citizens, and also more open
to the needs of the Empire. At this point the politician, however
immersed he might be in the main struggle and in its contingent
difficulties, had to show the thoughtful vision of a philosopher
and a historian's grasp of perspective. Awe-inspiring tasks
awaited him – the finding of answers to the practical problems
of defence and pacification, and of the administration of a
disturbed and fragmented empire. Above all, he had to give it a
soul.

Octavian's gradual achievement of all this was a remarkable
performance. He was especially sensitive to the yearning for self-
affirmation which was active in the Roman soul. If the will of
heaven and the valour of her sons have given Rome power over
the world, the City has no intention of being absorbed by her
own dominions – she claims the right to impose her own spirit
and her own principles on the lands over which she holds sway.

Beneath the surface of a culture based on feeble imitation

125

of Hellenistic models, a new current was flowing – one of nationalist reaction. If the task had merely been one of encouraging this tendency, of refusing to accept cultural and spiritual forces of foreign origin, there would have been little difficulty. The Eastern Mediterranean lands, however, which had been converted into protectorates or annexed, from the time of the Macedonian wars until the recent conquests of Pompey, were not merely areas for exploitation, like Africa, Spain and Gaul. They were also the source of a wave of discontent which assumed subtly threatening forms, and of theories which enjoyed great prestige among the Romans themselves.

One possibility was to adopt these theories as one's own. The policy of Augustus was in fact one of partial absorption of the foreign ideas he outwardly rejected, and of revaluation of the traditional thinking of his countrymen.

Within the City, the constitutional organs of government had long ago lost many of their functions and much of their prestige. Most ancient historians regard the first triumvirate – that short-lived truce preceding the struggle of Caesar against Pompey – as the beginning of the end for republican institutions. But even before the triumvirate, the tyranny of Sulla and the immense prestige of the young Pompey had provided a foretaste of the absolute rule which everyone expected to come[2] – including the senators themselves, who hoped for a ruler with a firm hand and a due respect for their own political and economic prerogatives.

Octavian was cautious and farseeing despite his extreme youth, when he found himself in the treacherous atmosphere left behind by the recent murder of Julius Caesar. It must certainly have seemed preferable to him to win the good-will of the Senate, rather than to lean solely on the memory of Caesar. The forces responsible for Caesar's death had, after all, drawn their strength from republican thinking. Octavian was aware, however, that the dictator had bequeathed him a moral and political heritage that it would be madness to waste – the affection of the soldiers and of the lower classes.

The first political moves made by Octavian were designed to re-evoke the prestige of his dead uncle. Within two months of his death, the young man was trying to exhibit in public the golden chair that the Senate had offered Caesar, the crown that he had refused. Forbidden to proceed with this plan, he was not discouraged. In July, a celebration of the dictator's past victories was dedicated not merely to the memory of Caesar himself, but also to the divine ancestor of his family, *Venus Genetrix*. The chance that a comet appeared at about that time gave him the opportunity to claim that the dictator's soul had been converted into a beneficent guardian star.

His second step was to acquire an army. He did this by promising the legions five times the pay offered by Antony, the consul in office. The senators were struck by the strange blindness which is an infallible sign of approaching eclipse for a political class. They showed no alarm, but hoped that republican institutions would be defended, and legality assured, by none other than the heir of the late dictator – 'A young man, almost a boy, gifted with incredible, divine genius and courage,' to quote Cicero (*Philippics,* III, ii, 3). The orator was confident that he would be able to guide the actions of this respectful lad as long it suited him to do so. He did not detect the untamable strength concealed in that immature, sickly frame, and thought it an excellent idea to persuade the senators to entrust themselves to Octavian, who had come forward of his own accord, at his own expense, to save the liberties of all men. To this disinterested patriot all authority should be granted, not to mention all the official honours which Octavian, according to the constitution, was too young to enjoy.[3]

A private citizen who provided himself with military forces at his own expense, enticing them away from the constitutional authorities, thereby made himself an outlaw. Antony made what he could of this, exposing Octavian to the scorn of the legally minded. But the young man had already realised that he could operate on two fronts, presenting himself to the populace and

127

the soldiers as the sole interpreter of the thoughts of Caesar, and to the Senate as the protector of republican institutions.

During this gestation of his future policy, he may have been inspired by the one Roman authority in the field of political doctrine – Cicero. In his voluminous works, composed on the lines laid down by Greek thinkers, it was not difficult to find arguments to justify even the illegal aspects of Octavian's actions. 'If it is a question of defending the rights of the citizens, no one should consider himself as a private individual': Cicero had written these words ten years earlier in the *De Republica* (II, xxv, 46) – the work which was supposed to fill a serious gap in the culture of Rome, and provide it with the master-piece of political theory it lacked. Had not the noblest deeds in Roman history been carried out by the initiative of private individuals? Brutus had expelled Tarquin, Scipio Nasica had slain Tiberius Gracchus;[4] the younger Brutus, ignoring the links of personal affection, had conspired against Caesar. In extra-ordinary circumstances, actions that would normally be crimes are no longer criminal.

Under the influence of these admonitions and precedents, the young man took on the task of defending the republican institutions against the forces of monarchy, which seemed to be represented by Antony. At the end of his career, looking back on those early days, Augustus uses the very same words in the Ancyran inscription that Cicero had used in the *Philippics* to defend his actions.[5]

In moments of crisis, we need a leader, a guide, a helmsman, Cicero had written in 53 B.C. So he had held this conviction for a considerable time. Perhaps he had hoped at one time to be the man of destiny himself; then he had cast Pompey for the role, and finally Caesar. He had hoped for a *rector, moderator, tutor, auctor* – words which define the spiritual qualifications for a ruler, rather than his constitutional position.

The continuing ideological conflict which underlay Roman political thought reflected the two coexistent aspects of Roman imperialism: lofty supremacy over barbarian nations on the one

128

hand, and the cosmopolitan principle on the other. These two threads could be seen woven together in the person of Caesar, and were both implicit in the political heritage he left behind him. In the struggle between Octavian and Antony, the two elements seemed to split apart once more.

Octavian won because he knew how to claim the role of defender of the republican institutions. Cicero was convinced by this performance, thinking to recognise a kindred spirit in Octavian. To persuade the orator to present him to the Senate as the champion of the constitution, Octavian wrote to him twice a day, in the autumn of 44 B.C. He besought him to leave the country home to which he had prudently retired and come back to Rome, so that he could interpret Octavian's thoughts to the Senate. To get Cicero on his side, the young man skilfully used the infallible weapon of flattery. He reminded him of the happy consequences of his famous consulate, and implored him to 'save the Republic for a *second* time'. Cicero did not remain deaf to these appeals. 'I would not care to be absent,' he wrote, 'when honour demands that I should be there.' But he had moments of clearsightedness when he could not trust a champion of republican liberties who held out his arm towards the statue of Caesar whenever he spoke in public.

Even the appeal to all Italy, which was subsequently the key-note of Octavian's propaganda at the time of Actium, may have been suggested to him by Cicero. In the *Third Philippic,* the orator exhorts the Senate to form a holy alliance against Antony, affirming that 'all Italy has risen to recover her liberty.' These words were borrowed by Augustus for the Ancyran inscription.[7]

The youth somehow succeeded in persuading the elders of the Republic that his intervention was heaven-inspired, and that bribing the legions away from the consul in office was a legal action. With Cicero's help, he persuaded the senators that a return to legality could best be achieved through illegality. 'In him we place our hopes of liberty; from him we have already received salvation' says the orator (*Philippics,* V, xviii, 49).

129

I

There is no proof that Octavian drew his inspiration directly from the works of Cicero; there was a vast Greek literature on the subject of political theory. But the end which he finally achieved – the possession of an *auctoritas* which was not a usurpation of power, but the product of moral prestige – fitted as closely as possible with the ideal portrayed in the *De Republica*.

His struggle against Antony lasted more than ten years; but the slow rise of Octavian's fortunes never lost the sanctified aura of legality. The absolute power he attained was the summation of the high offices of state which he held one after the other – always refusing them when first offered. To get so far, tenacity and cunning were not enough : treachery and cruelty were also required. But once he was transformed into Augustus, the Princeps contrived that Octavian – the heir of a dictator assassinated for much milder presumption – should be forgotten.

The achievement of which he boasted most loudly was the pacification of the world. But the controlling figure who closes the doors of the temple of Janus against barbaric threats and fratricidal wars is really of secondary importance. There is another side to the character of Augustus, which explains the completeness of the consensus in his favour, and makes his reign a turning point of history, his person the link between past and future. He had interpreted the idea of absolute rule into terms suited to the Roman mentality, and accessible to the Roman psychology, and he had reduced the Empire, that historically burdensome, geographically crushing fact of life, to the scale of the City.

A call to unbridled expansionism, a claim of divine right to rule, can undoubtedly be heard in the literature of the Augustan age. But the mythical features which the writers introduced into their portrait of Rome cannot possibly discredit the traditional picture, contained in the Ancyran inscription. Expressing the real views of Augustus, this text manages to reassure those who are bewildered by the sheer size of the Empire, or confused by the many strange emotional disturbances that originate from it. The ruler of the Empire, according to the short paragraphs of the

Index, is an ordinary magistrate like those of an earlier age. If he has been granted exceptional powers, he has won them by his merits, in accordance with the ethics of Stoicism and the customs of the City. At the end of his day, he feels a moral obligation to render an account of what he has done, like a conscientious book-keeper. Nothing portentous or supernatural emerges from the list of his actions. He has never taken a single step which went beyond the bounds of the rigid procedural formality of Rome. It is the Senate (mentioned twenty times in the thirty-five paragraphs of the *Index*) and the People of Rome who have laden him with special honours and the highest offices, and none of this has been done in a way contrary to ancient custom (*Res Gestae,* VI). When he first appeared on the political scene, Octavian had Cicero to introduce him as the guarantor of legality, the supreme good of the citizen. In his old age, he takes extraordinary care to insist that he has never assumed extra-constitutional office, and never abused the powers which the People and Senate repeatedly and insistently offered him, and which he always accepted in the end.

The Empire is administered not like the Universe, in keeping with the Divine Mind, but rather like a small farm, where the steward accounts for every penny spent. The obsessive fantasies of world dominion, revolution and disaster take flight at those peaceful, down-to-earth words. Rome is a City-State, just as she used to be. She will never degenerate into the mere principal town of a region, like the capitals of the other countries which form part of the huge international community. The Empire will never absorb the City, will never place her, like the other cities of the earth, under the control of a hieratic, levelling leader. The City, on the contrary, will model the Empire in accordance with her own traditional criteria, spreading her own systems, her own laws, that have stood the test of centuries, across the face of the earth.

For the City to assume the role of head of the world, *caput mundi,* it would be necessary to give full value to its spirit and its ethnic characteristics, and impart a mythical quality to its past. That would help to provide it with the ideal platform it lacked. To assure its future, the Empire must be furnished with a moral justification and a supporting prophecy. In the time of Augustus, the conviction did in fact grow that the Empire was a well-deserved reward for the valour of the ancient Romans on the one hand, and a working-out of the long-term plans of the gods on the other.

These ideas helped to restrain the ideological offensive from overseas,[8] which had increased immoderately during the years that separated Augustus from Sulla. The opposition that resisted Caesar was much the same as that which had resisted the Gracchi and the Scipios; the position of Cato of Utica was not very different from that of Cato the Censor. For Augustus, however, senatorial opposition could quickly be liquidated if it formed a serious obstacle; but it was not so easy to resist the flood of cultural, religious and political ideas which poured in from Greece, from the provinces of the East, and from the examples of Persia and Egypt.

The Princeps studied the scope of these ideas, and saw that he could neutralise the disruptive forces only by making full use of the moral and religious values of the past, which were still alive, still fertile, though partly obscured from view. By following this plan, he gave meaning to the deep, confused yearning of Roman civilisation to find its own identity, instead of being a mere marginal presence in the scheme of Hellenistic culture.

Cultural circles in Rome were aware of their own inadequacy, which was further aggravated by the falling birth-rate. Amid the numerical decline and the economic impoverishment of the patrician families – greatly reduced by the civil wars and by a sort of death-wish – Augustus encouraged the growth of a *petite bourgeoisie,* a middle class that he saw as destined to take on the spiritual heritage of the upper class, which had failed at the very time when it should have shown itself fit to safeguard the moral and religious traditions of the City. Cancellation of taxes, distribution of land to veteran soldiers, public works, support for agriculture, the formation of new colonies, and the construction

132

of a new senatorial and aristocratic class, often coming from the Italian municipalities[9] – these were the steps necessary to produce a new people, heir to the ancient moral inheritance, but open to larger ideas than their predecessors.

A new patriotism, Italian rather than Roman in character, grew up around the Princeps. The Italian communes' struggle for equal rights was still a recent memory – the Latin colonies of Central Italy had gained the status of *municipia* in 89 B.C., and those of the Po valley in 49 B.C. But now the recognised fatherland is Italy.[10] This was the rich farm-land that had been assigned to the fugitives from Troy, who had greeted it with an excited cry of 'Italia!' an exultant shout, as soon as they saw its low skyline on the horizon.[11]

The whole of Italy, not just the City of Rome, is now celebrated as better than richly-wooded Media or the lands of the Ganges.[12] After civil war and famine, she rises again, thanks to her provident, far-sighted leader, who renews her ancient arts and protects her like a patron god.[13]

The gratitude of those who benefited can be heard in the words of Tityrus.[14] The Government's political interest in the new land-owners can be traced in the *Georgics,* that long poem dedicated to the small-holders of the Italian municipalities by a provincial author from the Po valley, an area not long Romanised.

Frugal ways, attachment to the soil and to the small-holding, the annual rituals of the agricultural life – everything that survived of the habits and feelings of a closely-bounded society such as the republican City of the immediately preceding period had been – had to be emphasised and broadened to bring it up to the level demanded by the Empire. Augustus resurrected the spiritual forces and the moral values of the past, so that the constitution of the little city became the creed of the City of the world.

The 'universal consensus', of which Augustus speaks in his *Res Gestae* (paragraph XXXIV) had been laid down by Cicero as something his ideal ruler should have, and it was also a requirement of the old democratic electoral practice. For the leaders of other peoples, this total consensus came from hereditary or divine right; for Augustus, in accordance with the principles of Stoicism, it must be based on his own worth as a man and a citizen.[15]

Though based on the restoration of things past, this policy looked towards the future, to distant times, and far-off places. It was destined to recall to the path of Roman patriotism those who had strayed after various mirages, and at the same time to satisfy the needs of the eastern half of the Empire. Augustus realised how important it was to provide the Roman image with clear and unmistakable features, in order to set it in firm and permanent contrast with the East, whose influence permeated into the Western world through a thousand chinks. Its advance on the political plane might seem to be checked by the murder of Julius Caesar; but it reappeared on the frontiers of the Roman world in the person of Labienus, the renegade Roman General of a Parthian army, and of Antony, the Roman propagandist of a theocratic system. On the cultural plane, these ideas were widely diffused in Roman opposition circles, and on the religious plane they were insinuated into the hearts of men by the proselytising of the Jews and other immigrant groups.

Augustus proceeded to lay special emphasis on his devotion to the ancestral religion and on the orthodox nature of his policy – thereby implicitly setting it in contrast with the policies of Antony and of Julius Caesar. He summoned up a ghostly bodyguard of the unassuming fathers of the Republic, and claimed them as his spiritual predecessors, from Fabricius to Cato. In the eighth book of the *Aeneid,* Vergil lists the names of the heroes who are to spring from the Trojan stock, and describes the pride Aeneas felt at learning of their future deeds – among them is Cato (VIII, 670). Horace, in his turn, puts Cato among the spiritual fathers of Octavian's new order (*Odes,* I, xii, 36).

In foreign policy, Augustus adhered to the views of the Senate, both in the avoidance of aggressive wars and the formal respect he paid to areas of local autonomy. But his legalistic attitude, so perfectly in keeping with the old-fashioned hegemony of the Republic, had a new quality about it, an aura of divinity. Augustus played the part of an ordinary magistrate, but at the same time he took on the character of an Olympian being, lord of all nations. His role is that of the great conciliator, preferring the use of clemency to that of force.[16] He aims at moral supremacy, rather than the ends of colonialism. That pleased the nationalists and helped to cover up the impossibility of taking on the burden of new territories, which might well be both treacherous and turbulent. In terms of Roman prestige, the highest possible prize was the formal submission of the previously victorious Parthians; when he achieved it, Augustus proudly claimed to have followed the ancient traditions of the City, and entrusted the throne of the conquered populations to local dynasties.[17]

It was the psychological side of territorial expansion that he mainly emphasised – the loyalty of men's hearts, the respectful trust of the nations. They asked for the friendship of Rome, and sent their young princes to the imperial court. The City widened her motherly boundaries; the barbarians sought a Roman education for their sons, and promised recruits for the legions.[18]

There is a certain contrast between the paternalistic attitude of the Princeps, faithful to the traditional prudence of the Senate on the one hand, and the Augustan literature of Rome on the other. The literature is animated by a spirit of boundless imperialism. The poets implore Augustus to extend the sway of Rome to the lands of legend, to the ends of the earth; but as he grew older, the Princeps, perhaps owing to an inner bent as well as to gain popular favour, moved away from any hint of imitation of Alexander, the traditional model for conquerors. In the early days of the principate, he had used first a seal showing the head of a sphinx, and then one depicting the head of Alexander; but later on his seal bore his own face, with its

135

regular features and air of inexorable concentration. On arrival at Alexandria, Octavian had visited the tomb of the Macedonian, and exhumed his body; but this youthful whim was followed, in later years, by a considered rejection of all such ideas. Though Augustus in fact realised Alexander's dream, and became the divinely appointed head of a unified world, he would have nothing to do with the trait said to have been most typical of Alexander – the acceptance of foreign manners.[19]

The flattering anecdotes recorded by the worshippers of Alexander must have been a severe temptation to Augustus, who could easily have adapted them to his own life-story. In fact, his biographers did precisely that. But Augustus himself made every effort to present himself as the antithesis of Alexander. He wore the modest dress of a Roman citizen, a simple toga rather than a purple robe. He carefully re-established the old Roman ways, the ferocious military discipline, the religious traditions. He resurrected old priesthoods and ceremonies that had fallen into disuse, and ancient rituals,[20] following the example of Camillus, who had been called the second founder of Rome (Livy, V, iv, 2). He restored no fewer than eighty-two ruinous temples, and he prohibited Asiatic religions and the cults of Egypt, as unbecoming to the dignity of Rome.[21] To those who tried to obtain exemption from service as Vestal Virgins for their daughters, he replied indignantly that if he had had a daughter to offer to the Vestal order, he would have been proud to do so (Suetonius, *Augustus*, XXXI, 4). To preserve the national character, he insisted on Romans wearing the toga.[22] Livy quotes the views of Augustus as an expert authority on the details of the enemy general's armour brought back as a trophy by Cornelius Cossus, and kept in one of the temples later restored by the Princeps. The historian also interrupts his narrative to quote, in pious detail, the words of the sacrificial formula pronounced by Decius when he devoted his life to the infernal gods. 'I thought it not out of place,' says Livy revealingly, 'to report all this in the exact words ceremonially used at the time and handed down by tradition – though

136

nowadays anything new and outlandish is generally preferred to the ancient customs of the fatherland.'[23]

Augustus had the genius to close the gap between the habits of a civic administration and the demands of world government. His originality lay in the fact that he was able to make himself the instrument of a process not uncommon in history – the mutual absorption of two opposing tendencies.

We do less than justice to the figure of Augustus, if, following the example of certain nationalistic historians, we exalt his genius and gloss over the doctrinal ideas which inspired it and helped to give it its shape.[24] In his actions, we see not only the firm resolution to revivify the national institutions, but also an aspiration the source of which is doctrinal, and the object of which is to emphasise the ethical element in the principate, and stress that moral superiority is a precondition of supreme power. These are the principles of Plato and of the Stoics. The *auctoritas* which he exercised was equivalent to the prestige won by his merits; the golden shield presented to him by the Senate stood for the ultimate recognition of his extraordinary qualities. As regards the wide-spread messianic content in the literature of the Augustan period, there are no indications that this was planned by the Princeps himself. The writers of the period, on the contrary, far from obeying directives emanating from the court, appear to have had a special sensitivity to certain spiritual needs which were very widely felt at the time, and indeed to have shared those feelings, so that it was natural for them to apply the monarchical and universalist concepts that were in the air to the person of the Princeps.

When Julius Caesar died, Octavian was in Illyricum, waiting for the opening of the campaign against the Parthians. He at once returned to Italy. The westward direction of this journey can be regarded as a premonition of the course of his life – the return to Rome, the return to a concept of power based on a constitutional foundation, the realisation that a man who wanted to lead the world must first win the highest place in the City.

His journey symbolised, above all, the renunciation of eastern adventure.

The renunciation was necessary, at that time, though the prospect was extremely tempting – the weakness of the armies of Asia was common talk and everyone knew that all the most exquisite and precious things in the world came from the East, and that the defeated had much to teach the victors.

Contingent factors had their effect on Octavian's attitude – Italy and the West were allocated to him in the division of territory which took place at Brindisi in the autumn of 40 B.C., for example. It might have been thought that this was bad luck for him. The economic situation in Italy was bad, the veterans were demanding reward, essential food imports were being interrupted at sea by Sextus Pompeius, and the Gallic territories were in a state of threatening unrest.

But Octavian realised that Rome contained the springs of political power. . . . Pompey had left Italy when Caesar invaded it, withdrawing to the eastern lands that had been the scene of his earlier triumphant campaigns. But he had not in fact done so in the spirit of proud confidence attributed to him, long after his death, by his admirer Lucan. Contemporary witnesses speak of surprise and sorrow at Pompey's departure. Antony made the same choice, and thereby alienated the hearts of his countrymen.

Rome inevitably favoured those who showed that they preferred her themselves, both as a home and a way of life; even though she had become the ruler of the world, she was still the City-State she had always been, for those who exercised power in her name were still all members of the narrow ranks of her ruling class, still all linked to each other by ancient ties of relationship; a tight group of families.

The Empire was still viewed as a vast extension of the capital. Rome was still the essential fatherland, coming before Italy and before the Empire. 'You will say that the fatherland does not consist of walls,' wrote Cicero. 'No, indeed – but it does consist of altars, of hearths.' During the civil war between Caesar and

138

Pompey, it was above all the City that caused anxiety to Cicero, who trembled at the thought that Rome might be abandoned to pillage or to the flames. Never, never, he said, should Pompey have left the City, for that was to leave the fatherland, for which and in which it is so good to die.[25]

With the passage of the years, this feeling grew ever stronger in the heart of Augustus, as if a regressive influence were working on him, bringing his political ideas closer and closer to the old system of the ancestral city-state – all of which was in complete contrast with the universalist tendency of the events and the aspirations which surrounded him and with the universalist aura of Augustan visual art and literature. This return to the ancient ways may have been motivated by the knowledge that the ideas of Antony had survived his defeat and death, so that for Augustus to complete the overthrow of his late rival on the ideological plane, he would have to stress the anti-Hellenic, anti-barbarian character of Actium, and spread the gospel that the rule of Rome now had universal extent, both in space and in time.

When he had obtained satisfaction from the Parthians who had defeated Crassus, and eliminated, or at least silenced the direct challenge to Rome posed by the rivalry of Egypt and of Asia, he was confronted by the urgent task of achieving spiritual unity at Rome itself.

NOTES TO CHAPTER

1. *Quid tibi barbariem, gentesque ab utroque iacentes Oceano numerem? Quodcumque habitabile tellus Sustinet, huius erit.*
2. Florus, II, xiv, 5; Tacitus, *Histories,* I, i.
3. Cicero, *Philippics,* V, xvi, 44: *Ipse princeps exercitus faciendi; ibid.,* III, ii, 3: *Patrimonium suum ecfudit; ibid.,* III, ii, 5: *Tribuenda est auctoritas.* See also *ibid.,* V, xvi, 45; V, xvii, 46–7; V, xviii, 49.
4. Cicero, *De Officiis,* I, xxii, 76: *privatus Tiberium Gracchum interemit.*
5. *Res Gestae,* I, 1: *privato consilio et privata impensa.*

THE IDEA OF THE CITY IN ROMAN THOUGHT

6. Cicero, *Letters to Atticus*, XVI, xi, 5; XVI, xvii, 11; XVI, xv, 3.
7. Cicero, *Philippics*, III, xiii, 32: *Italia tota ad libertatem recuperandam excitata*. See also Augustus, *Res Gestae*, XXV, 4: *Iuravit in mea verba tota Italia*.
8. See R. Macmullen, *Enemies of Roman Order*, London, Cambridge, Massachusetts 1966 – a book which appeared while the first edition of the present work was with the printers. The disruptive factors listed by the author constitute a threat to the existence of the state rather than an alternative ideological system. His list of enemies of Roman order, in fact, includes the guardians of Republican tradition, such as Cato, Brutus, Seneca and Lucan, besides philosophers, mystics, astrologers, prophets, and outlaws.
9. Augustus, *Res Gestae*, XVI, 1: *Pecuniam pro agris . . . quod adsignavi militibus, solvi municipis;* XXVIII, 1: *Colonias in Africa Sicilia Macedonia utraque Hispania Achaia Asia Syria Gallia Narbonensi Pisidia deduxi. Italiam autem XXVIII colonias . . . deductas habet;* VIII, 1: *Patriciorum numerum auxi.*
10. Vergil, *Aeneid*, I, 531: *Terra antiqua, potens armis atque ubere glebae.*
11. Vergil, *Aeneid*, III, 522–4: *Cum procul obscuros colles humilemque videmus Italiam: Italiam! primus conclamat Achates Italiam laeto socii clamore salutant.*
12. Vergil, *Georgics*, II, 136–8.
13. Horace, *Odes*, IV, xv, 12: *et veteres revocavit artes;* IV, xiv, 43: *O tutela praesens Italiae.*
14. Vergil, *Eclogues*, I, 6–7: *O Meliboee, deus nobis haec otia fecit. Namque erit ille mihi semper deus.*
15. *Res Gestae*, XXXIV, 3: *Pro merito meo Senatus consulto Augustus appellatus sum.*
16. *Res Gestae*, III, 3: *Victorque omnibus veniam petentibus civibus peperci. Externas gentes, quibus tuto ignosci potuit, conservare quam excidere malui.*
17. *Res Gestae*, XXVII, 2: *Armeniam Maiorem, interfecto rege eius . . . cum possem facere provinciam, malui, maiorum nostrorum exemplo, regnum id Tigrani . . . tradere. Ibid.,* 4: *Et eandem gentem postea desciscentem et rebellantem domitam per Gaium filium meum regi Ariobarzani . . . regendam tradidi.*
18. See the treatment of this subject on the bowl from the treasure of Boscoreale, now in the Louvre; and on the Gemma Augustea in the Bibliothèque Nationale, Paris. See J. P. V. D. Balsdon, *Gaius and the Grand Cameo of Paris*, in *J.R.S.*, XXVI, 1936, pp. 152 ff. See also the Cameo of Vienna, Kunsthistorischesmuseum, Vienna. See J. Charbonneaux, *L'art au siècle d'Auguste*, Paris 1948.
19. See Plutarch, *On the Fortune of Alexander*, I, 8, B and C.
20. Suetonius, *Augustus*, XXIV, 2 and XXXI, 4; Augustus, *Res Gestae*, XX, 8–13; Cornelius Nepos, *Atticus*, XX.
21. Dionysius of Halicarnassus, II, 19.
22. Vergil, *Aeneid*, I, 282: *Romanos rerum dominos gentemque togatam.*
23. Livy, VIII, xi, 1. See S. Mazzarino, *Il pensiero storico classico*, Bari 1966, p. 41: 'Livy was, with Vergil, the chief exponent of Augustan spirituality.'

24. M. Hammond, *Hellenistic Influences on the Structure of the Augustan Principate*, in *Mem. Am. Ac. R.*, XVII, 1940; P. Grimal, *Auguste et Athénodore*, in *Rev. Et. Anc.*, XLVII, 1945, pp. 261 ff.; G. Pugliese Carretelli, *Auctoritas Augusti*, in *La Parola del Passato*, IV, 1949, pp. 29 ff.; G. W. Bowersock, *Augustus and the Greek World*, Oxford 1965. See also Appian, *Civil War*, III, iii, 13: 'Octavian turned to his mother as if she were Thetis, and repeating the words of Achilles (*Iliad*, XVIII, 98), he said: "O that I might die at once, since I could not save my friend who has been slain!" '

25. Cicero, *Letters to Atticus*, VII, xi, 3; *Letters to Friends*, XVI, xii, 1; *Letters to Atticus*, VIII, ii, 2.

IX

The Idea of Rome Gains Precision

1

Roman Reaction to Greek Disparagement

THE CLASH between the worlds of Rome and of Greece arose primarily from the Latin sense of inferiority. Augustus was the first to appreciate its importance, and realised that the only way to overcome it was to exploit the potential of the national character.

Roman writers alternated between the ambition to equal the masterpieces of Greek literature and the tedious imitation of their detail. The literary world was partly dominated by a Hellenising tendency, detested by the nationalists. The 'new' poets translated or plagiarised Hellenistic models, or at least drew their inspiration from them. In terms of art, this school of writers refined the taste and enriched the vocabulary of Rome; but in terms of ideas their odes, epics, plays and histories brought in characters, events and habits of thought which were alien to the spirit of Rome, and obscured her own deeds and her own myths.

While mystical forces of Jewish, Persian or Egyptian origin were at work among the plebeians, uprooting their attachment to the old pagan religion, the Greek-inspired historians, orators, philosophers, and poets were an equally serious and insidious threat to the educated classes. They considered the Romans to be brutal robbers, and the power of Rome to be a mere transitory episode, attributable to chance.

These ideas were brought in by authors who were favourably welcomed by the conservative aristocracy, and carefully read by the opposition. They imperceptibly undermined the essential foundation of the Empire – the underlying consensus of its citizens. Their irony and elegant scepticism had a far more penetrating effect than the moral resistance of the few surviving republicans, who faded out of the political scene or took refuge in contemptuous isolation.

The effectiveness of the systematic denigration of Roman culture by the Hellenising authors[1] can be appreciated, not so much from their own surviving works, as from the effort which the Augustan authors put into the counterattack. Livy accuses the writers who dared to put the achievements of Rome on the same plane as those of other peoples, or to speculate that her citizens would have yielded to Alexander if he had led his forces into Italy, of superficiality and folly.[2] The embarrassment of Greek 'collaborators', on the other hand, can be detected in the energetic attempt of Dionysius of Halicarnassus (I, iv, 2–3) to reassess the value of the past history of Rome, in opposition to Greek efforts to belittle it, by providing a conciliatory version of events which supposed Rome herself to have Greek origins. The resentment of Roman nationalists can be clearly seen in the works of the Latin poets. Disgusted with Greek self-satisfaction, Tacitus accuses Greek historians of ignoring the deeds of contemporaries such as Arminius, a great man although a barbarian. Tacitus himself pays the German the homage due to an unfortunate hero, 'ignored by the Greek historians, who admire only their own achievements.'[3]

As the Romans recognised the merits of their own moral constitution, with all its faults, in comparison with that of the Greeks, they became more and more aware of the strength of their own case. What if they were still beginners in art, in literature, and in astronomy? Very different tasks had been allotted to them by history – to impose the rules of civilised coexistence on the world, to codify the dealings of man with man, to pacify the whole earth. The Latin poets admit that the Greeks are

143

more famous for eloquence, and the Gauls for physical strength – but in Rome a handful of virtuous men has sufficed to create an Empire.[4]

The whole basic thought of Livy's History asserts that Rome rules the world by virtue of a moral right.[5] In the time of Augustus, when the Empire was threatened more by disruptive ideologies than by hostile armies, Roman thinkers tried to support it by reference to the example of the rustic heroes who had built it up with humble, patient dedication, contrasting them with the smooth talkers, the versifiers, the orators and the artists.

Certain historical characters emerge as exemplary models of the orthodox way of thinking. Livy's Cato (XXXIV, iv, 4) pronounces an authoritative reproof against those who let themselves be led astray by the love of beauty and refinement. Plutarch's Fabricius exemplifies the rough honesty of Roman ethics, in contrast to those of Greece (*Pyrrhus,* 20). Livy never lets slip a chance of humbling the pride of the Greeks. 'They have preserved only the arrogance of their ancient greatness,' he says. And again: 'They fight with books and with words, the only things in which they excel.'[6]

The balance of cultural trade, in fact, was heavily over-weighted on the side of imports; but the Republic threw into the other scale its traditional piety, the discipline of the legions, the sanctity of the family, the respect for law, the parsimony of the magistrates – just as Brennus had once thrown his sword into the scales to outweigh the gold. But as the territory of the Empire increased and wealth poured into it, corruption had gradually become widespread, and the old assumption of moral superiority, as the legitimising force for Roman rule, had ebbed away. There had been an impoverishment of the inner vitality which enabled the Romans to oppose their principles to the influence of Greek and Asiatic thought. To escape defeat in the crowning moment of the struggle with the East, Augustan Rome searched for her strongest claims to pre-eminence, and found them in the deeds of the earliest builders of her power. The myths of *Romanitas* were thus firmly based in the past, and the past was to provide the Empire with a confirmation for its policy, and the opposition with its intellectual motivation.

Augustus taught the Romans to admit their own failings and to make them a source of pride – in other words, to reject the accusations of the Greeks and make it a point of honour to be different from them. 'The words of the Romans come from their hearts,' said Marcus Porcius Cato, 'while those of the Greeks come from their lips (Plutarch, *Cato the Censor,* 12). Popular dislike of the Greeks was so strong that those who sought the favour of the plebeians had always ostentatiously avoided Hellenic ways. When in Athens, Marcus Porcius Cato had always made use of an interpreter, and had complacently remarked on the number of words the Greeks needed to translate a concise Latin sentence (Plutarch, *loc. cit.*). In 155 B.C., when the Athenians sent the philosopher Carneades to Rome as their ambassador, Cato succeeded in having him sent away from Rome, because 'when he spoke, no one could tell where the truth lay' (Pliny, *Natural History,* VII, xxx, 112), and, on the same occasion, he had all the Greeks expelled from Italy.

Marius, that archetypal defender of the City, was always averse to the pleasures of culture, and refused to learn Greek.[7] He boasted that he had learned the trade of arms in the ranks, and not out of Greek text-books, like the patricians.[8] All that Augustus looked for in Hellenic thought and Hellenic literature were maxims conducive to the good behaviour of the individual, both as a private man and as a citizen. He always wrote in Latin; and Tiberius[9] followed his example in this, though he loved Greek poetry.

Augustus may have been pandering to Italian public opinion in this; or he may have been expressing his own real inner feelings. He certainly showed remarkable insight into one side of the ideological requirements of the period. As the national characteristics of the Romans were revalued, the positive aspects of their nature were emphasised. When an embassy returned from abroad, the senators would deplore the subtleties of which their diplomats boasted, maintaining that deceit and cunning

K

were the province of the Greeks, not of the Romans. The word 'Roman' meant straight, manly, sparing of words, and frugal. Camillus rejected the proposal of the schoolmaster from Falerii, who offered to hand over the boys in his charge as hostages to the Romans, and was indignant at the sight of such baseness. A Roman must win with Roman weapons; in other words, with courage and with skill (Livy, V, xxvii, 8). The Roman ambassadors to Alexandria refused the presents that were offered to them, since abstinence was part of their character. Titus Manlius Torquatus opposed the payment of ransom for the Roman prisoners captured at Cannae, despite the appeals of their families, despite the shortage of troops which might compel the Senate to enlist slaves into the army. They ought, he said, to have earned their homecoming on the field of battle: they should have returned to Rome 'while Rome was still their country, while they were still its citizens' (Livy, XXII, lx, 15). The title of citizen, it will be noted, is here reserved for those who deserve it, not for those who descend from Roman ancestors.

The Greek domination of Roman culture had been so overpowering that a reaction was inevitable – the resurgence of the solid Latin qualities against an alien mentality that was so nimble and versatile that it produced dispersion and disruption. According to the Augustan historians, the Greeks are to blame for everything. It was to a Greek that the Romans owed the introduction of the Bacchanalia, those corrupting rites which the Senate wisely banned (Livy, XXXIX, xiv, 6–8). It was from the Greeks that the deceiver Sinon, who persuaded the Trojans to admit the Wooden Horse within their walls, learnt the arts of treachery (Vergil, *Aeneid,* II, 152). It was a Greek who suggested to Fabricius the idea of poisoning Pyrrhus. Another Greek was Ulysses, the 'inventor of infamy' – and we may be sure that the words of Laocoon, 'I fear the Greeks, even when they bring presents', won the applause of Roman readers.[10]

Aware of the resentment of the Latin-speaking population,

Octavian adopted it as his own. He realised that, if Rome were to grow into the role of world-capital and fatherland of many diverse peoples, she must stress her own special characteristics, and not dilute them. Was it not possible that the dismemberment and dissolution of Alexander's empire had been caused by the king's own choice of adapting himself to the customs of the defeated, rather than setting a distinctively Macedonian stamp on the lands that he annexed?

This attitude on the part of Augustus responded to a tendency already visible in the thinking of the Romans, and gave it the prestige of official backing. Some Romans had already tried to win acclaim for the clean concision of Latin, as against the verbosity of Greek. There was Sallust, with his deliberately archaic prose, and Caesar, with the stripped and concentrated brevity of his *Commentaries*. The visual arts expressed the same two tendencies. Some bas-reliefs represent noble, draped figures drawn from classical Greek models; others show us humble artisans, the features of the common man, with crude realism, aiming at the exact observation of reality which is characteristic of Etruscan and Roman portraiture.

Octavian's opposition to everything of Greek origin became more marked during his years of conflict with Antony. Whether because of his natural inclinations or because of the long periods he spent in Greece and Egypt, Antony tried to make himself the interpreter of the needs expressed by the peoples of those lands. He gave up the idea of appealing to the good-will of his own fellow-citizens, and relied on the support of those who were hostile to the power of Rome, tried to discredit her glory, and cursed her policy of economic oppression. The message that he found himself preaching was therefore more spacious in character than that of his rival. From the time of Philippi, he had shown interest only in his eastern subjects. He had made his home in Athens, and had done everything possible to win the love of the people there. Later, at the time of his first meeting with Cleopatra, in Cilicia (41 B.C.), the splendid ceremony that accompanied that political event invited a mystical analogy: it

147

was as if Aphrodite were celebrating her divine nuptials with Dionysus (Plutarch, *Antony*, 26).

A year later, the treaty of Brundisium was concluded, and sealed by the marriage of Antony to Octavian's sister, Octavia. Antony seemed to be renewing his links with Rome. The newly-married couple settled at Athens, and Antony's behaviour there – his whole-hearted adoption of Athenian ways – again won him the affection of the local population (Plutarch, *Antony*, 33, 34). The hopes he inspired in his Greek subjects burnt even more brightly after the successes won by Ventidius against the Parthians. In the Greek-speaking provinces, Antony played the part of the protector of the Greek element in the population against the Asiatic, just as Alexander had done at the beginning of his career.[11] But if that policy, which won him so much support in Greece, had in fact prevailed, the result would have been not so much the weakening of the Asiatic element, as the replacement of the Roman holders of economic power in the provinces by the local Greek aristocracy.[12]

Dionysus reborn, bridegroom of Athene – such were the titles the servile Athenians showered on Antony;[13] and by accepting them, he imparted a new character to his own political stance, which became more and more alien to that of his native City. He thus let it be seen that he now belonged to another City, which was hostile to his own.[14] He claimed descent from Hercules, and tried to follow in the footsteps of his patron gods, imitating their way of dress, and their generous distributions of largesse.[15]

When he repudiated his Roman wife, it was as if he repudiated Rome at the same time. He presented territories to Cleopatra and her children which the Republic claimed as its own. Seated before the multitude on a throne of gold, by the side of the queen, he declared her, together with her first son, monarch of Egypt, Cyprus, Libya, and Coele-Syria. To one of their two boys he gave the crowns of Armenia, Media, and Parthia, as if they were already his to give; the other received the crowns of Phoenicia, Syria, and Cilicia.

This was the consecration of a truly Graeco-Asiatic empire, set up in opposition to the empire of Rome : the constitutional and legal recognition of forces that had hitherto been at work only on the cultural and religious planes. The state that was beginning to take shape under the Roman-Egyptian dynasty of Antony and Cleopatra would have been based on satellite dynasties, in accordance with the invariable practice of the Romans. But the criteria would have been different. The propaganda originating from Alexandria could, in fact, easily be interpreted as meaning that the subject lands would have more independence than Rome would grant them, and, above all, that the Roman element would play a secondary role, and not monopolise the positions of governmental authority and economic power as they did in the Roman Empire proper. The income arising from the agriculture, taxes and industries of those countries would no longer be diverted to Rome. On the political plane, the dominating influence would be that of Athens or Alexandria rather than Rome, and the ruling classes would be recruited among their leading citizens. The transfer of the seat of power from Rome to Byzantium would thus have taken place four centuries before the reign of Constantine.

As an earnest of his intentions, Antony had arranged a marriage between his son and the daughter of the King of Media, to ensure Egypt the military support of that country during the proposed campaign against Parthia. Caesarion, the supposed son of Julius Caesar, was associated with his mother in the rule of her territories. Antony's twin boys by Cleopatra wore the national costume of the countries allocated to them, which also provided their bodyguards. The very names of the royal children were of fateful meaning, laden with mystical allusions : Alexander Helios and Ptolemy recalled the supposed founder of the Ptolemaic dynasty, and also the sun god. Selene, the princess, bore the name of the Moon. These names were meant to represent the gods who watched over all mankind without discrimination, and spread their benefits over the whole world. The names were intended to presage a theocratic,

149

universal monarchy for these children, who, being the fruit of the union between an Egyptian queen and a Roman, seemed to incarnate and personify the long-hoped for fusion of East and West. The mixture of their blood symbolically achieved the union of the races.

Octavian, on the other hand, never left Italy except for reasons of military necessity. He was convinced that Rome would be able to unify the world only if she made herself more Roman than ever, and if she were careful not to lose the essential values of the Roman spirit, while putting herself at the head of a cosmopolitan society full of diverse beliefs and superstitions.

But at the same time, Octavian realised the impossibility of ruling the East, or even of ruling over the upper classes at Rome, without the support of the Greek world. It was therefore no time to heighten the wall of mutual dislike that seemed to coincide with the natural barrier formed by the Adriatic and Ionian Seas. That was where the links between East and West were under strain, where the Empire threatened to split in two. It was in Greece, as Grimal remarks,[16] 'the clasp, the meeting-point of West and East', that the crucial battles were fought to mend the cracks in the fabric of imperial unity – the battles of Philippi, Pharsalus and Actium. When this fragile, precarious unity finally split asunder into the two empires of Rome and Byzantium under Honorius and Arcadius, it was in the disputed prefecture of Illyricum that the break actually took place.

To impose unity on the vast new territories of Rome, Octavian had to gain the good-will of the Greeks; and the first step was to see that Antony lost it.

In the political struggles of the ancient world, the rivalry between men or between parties often projected itself into the heavens, and became a contest between the gods. So Octavian in his turn decided to enlist divine support. Before the final battle at Actium, Antony declared himself under the protection of Dionysus; and Octavian chose 'Apollo' as his pass-word.

During his flight from Troy, Aeneas had landed at Actium. Just across the bay rose the mountainous island of Leucas, on the peak of which stood a temple dedicated to Apollo. According to Gagé,[17] it was one of Octavian's happiest inspirations to adopt a patron god who was a potential link between Hellas and Rome, in order to draw the Greeks away from the contagion of Asiatic ideas, and also to capture part of the good-will which Antony had acquired in Greece. The god of clarity and reason was brought into play against the bestial divinities of Egypt, and against the oriental gods with their orgiastic rites. The son of Jove and Latona had protected the Teucrians in the Trojan war, and now he looked down with favour on the Romans, who were their descendants and the inheritors of their household gods.

Apollo had guided the band of Trojan exiles towards Italy, and had also determined the subsequent course of events. He had kept watch over the first landing of Aeneas from the same heights, sacred to his own godhead, on which he now stood to aim his bow at the forces of Antony and Cleopatra. Indians, Arabs, Egyptians, Sabaeans, all that is summed up by the propagandists of Augustus in the contemptuous term 'barbarian',[18] including Persian mercenaries and even Parthians, were pierced by the darts of the gods, routed and put to flight.

Apollo was now finally transferred to Rome; this was an 'evocation' with full honours. The writers of a later period suggested that there had been a connection between Apollo and Octavian's mother, while she was worshipping at night in a temple. (Ancient biographers were more concerned with providing their heroes with a divine pedigree than with respecting the chastity of their heroes' mothers. Suetonius, *Augustus,* XCIV, 4.) When a thunderbolt fell on the Palatine, in 28 B.C., Augustus built a temple to Apollo there, which is described for us by Propertius (II, xxxi). The golden reliefs on the doors showed how the Gauls were driven back by the thunderbolts of Apollo from Delphi, where they had made their way after the sack of Rome. These were the very Gauls who had burnt the City; the place where the temple was built recalled venerated names such as

151

Camillus and Manlius; the Gauls themselves were a reminder of Julius Caesar – thus many elements combined to form the political image of the Princeps. Apollo was the god of the new age, destined to put an end to discord. From 37 B.C. onwards, the coinage of Octavian carried the tripod and laurel crown which were the symbols of the god.[19]

The divine newcomer to the Seven Hills had been 'evoked' thither from lands which were politically subject to Rome but spiritually hostile to her; and Greece, for all her contempt for Roman good fortune and Roman culture, came to be associated, willy-nilly, with the destiny of the City through the link provided by Apollo, so that the two peoples became allies in the struggle against barbarism.

2

Roman Reaction to the Religious and Social Demands of the East

The subtle antagonism of Greek culture was accompanied by something vaster and more uncontrollable – the influx of mystical ideas and social unrest from the East.

The counter-offensive on Asia, aimed initially against the infiltration of Hellenistic culture, now back-fired on Rome, since it was to Rome that the task of passing on the values of Greek thought to barbarous peoples and future generations had been entrusted by history.

It was against Rome, and her responsibility for the economic oppression that weighed upon the necks of the subject peoples, that the ineffective anathemas of Israel, the ambitious schemes of Egypt, and the general hopes of change and renewal were all directed.

These stirrings found expression in the preaching of the Jews and in the Asiatic Sibylline books. The Jews were seeking converts to their religion all round the Mediterranean basin – spreading monotheism and an austere moral code, and calling on all the oppressed to hearken to the solemn voices of the prophets. If the moral rigour of their teaching seemed to bring them close to Stoicism, their expressed belief in a vigilant God, swift to intervene and to right the wrongs of his people, carried them far away from such a doctrine. Moreover, the white-hot eloquence of the prophets had an intensity and a dark poetic force with which the rational arguments of the philosophers could not contend.

Justice would be done on earth in the end : perhaps after a series of varied catastrophes, perhaps through the intervention of an infallible saviour, who would be born among the people of Israel, which remains the chosen people despite its oppressed state. This message was addressed to all mankind, and had the certainty of an axiom. Its essential content was shared by other religions, such as those of Mithras and Isis, and was also supported by the Babylonian astrologers.[20]

A great fire or flood, the advent of a just monarch, or the descent of a bloodthirsty barbarian horde, would be the sign of the turning upside down of classes and values, a reversal of fortunes in favour of the oppressed. All this was imminent, according to all the prophecies.

The visions of the Persian Magi contain fantasies based on the idea of a succession of Ages in world history; an idea held by Greek thinkers also. These Ages were periods of equal length, in regular succession like the steps of a staircase, each of which corresponded to a planet and took its name from it. In the end, there would be a cataclysm – a great flood or fire. God would send down a new king from the Sun, or from the starry heavens (*Sibylline Oracles*, III, 286–652). According to other oracles, these cosmic events would be signalled by the reign of a woman – it might be Cleopatra, also known as the Widow because of her identification with Isis (*ibid.*, 75). The end of Rome and the transfer of power to Asia is a common idea in the most ancient apocalyptic works. Solemn, mysterious voices hail the advent of a reconstructed society.

We cannot be sure how widely these hopes of radical upheaval were diffused among the plebeians of Italy. But they must have been disseminated extensively by the immigrants, grouping in compact racial communities in every port and every suburb, or mingling in the various levels of society, as slaves, merchants, mimes, actors or sailors. We may assume that their mysterious messages were accepted with superstition and circulated with rapidity. If we want to find a trace of the mentality of those times which has survived to our own day, we must turn to the faith in miraculous cures and the like which has remained alive in the simple hearts of the populace, though the corresponding religious dogmas have vanished at a higher cultural level.

In the days of Augustus, simple faith took a different form, more suited to the context of the period, and was concentrated on the prospect that East and West would come together in a spirit of peaceful, brotherly egalitarianism – which implied an end to the proud hegemony of Rome. Among the cultivated classes, the same yearning for peace and justice coincided with the certainty, derived from the Neo-Pythagorean and Stoic creeds, that a return to a state of pastoral innocence would follow the end of the Cycle of Ages.

We find this craving to escape from lands contaminated by iron and blood in the *Sixteenth Epode* of Horace: 'Away! wherever our feet lead us, wherever Notus or rough Africus summon us across the waves!'[21]

The poet felt the approach of the final Age of the World; he foresaw with terror that the ashes of Rome would be trodden by barbarian cavalry. 'Away!' he said, 'to the Isles of the Blest, where all the animals are tame, and the earth produces her fruits untilled.' The immediate cause of his desire for flight is thought to be the fresh outbreak of civil war in 31 B.C. that led to the battle of Perusia, or perhaps the threat of Parthian attack in the years from 40 to 30 B.C. It is not certain whether the poem was written before or after Vergil's *Fourth Eclogue*.[22]

In Vergil, we find not so much a gloomy presentiment of doom, as the certainty that a great revival will swiftly follow. The cycle of generations will come to an end, the plurality of existence will be no more, and there will be a return to the One – that is, to God. This is the creed of the Pythagoreans, which, according to Carcopino, inspired Vergil's poem. The doctrine postulates fraternal solidarity between all God's creatures, whether stars, plants or animals, since they are, without exception, particles of the All.

Learned critics have traced the doctrinal influences that worked on Latin writers, and have identified the real individuals who appear under allegorical names in the prophecies. Differences of interpretation – whether to attribute one of the more openly anti-Roman fragments to the time of Mithridates or of Cleopatra,[28] for example – serve to show that the combination of thunderous hostility to Rome with faith in a liberating upheaval remained in the air unchanged for many years.

The real political danger presented by oracular and prophetic books is shown by the fact that one of the first tasks to which Octavian turned, after the battle of Actium, was the collection of all such publications by a house to house search. He insisted that they should be surrendered even by private citizens, and made a bonfire of them (Suetonius, *Augustus,* XXXI, 2). The Senate had, in fact, taken similar measures in 213 B.C. (Livy XXV, i ff.); and his successor Tiberius repeated the operation.

This of course is why we now have only fragments of such works, and why it is difficult to understand the equally veiled allusions contained in the Roman literature produced to counter them. But there is no doubt that that literature was heavily charged with polemical content; and it had the advantage, at the time, of wide circulation in an unmutilated form, while the main theme of Augustan literature is the rebuttal both of Greek contempt for Rome and of the obscure threats contained in the popular mystical publications.

The political and religious propaganda of the East contained a message of brotherhood, which transcended the boundaries of

155

the ancient City. This idea had first been diffused in the western world at the time of Alexander's conquests, in the fourth century B.C., had won prestige in the cultural world of Rome through the preaching of the Stoics, and now returned yet again, as a slogan on the banners of Cleopatra. As the final successor of Alexander, the queen hoped to do to Rome what her ancestor had done to Persia – to destroy its power, and then to achieve a full reconciliation between East and West.

A political programme of such vast scope could never have had a chance of success without a religious and dynastic foundation of equally majestic scale. The fragments of Egyptian literature that have come down to us reveal a sublime conception of the divine and the kingly. In comparison with that universal theocratic vision, the Roman gods seem mere provincial powers, concerned with watching over the interests of a single city. Their activities hardly seem to extend beyond the Capitol; and Cleopatra recklessly planned to subject the Capitol to Canopus.[24]

The political ideas which the royal couple made their own brought back to Egypt dreams of imperial splendour which had been forgotten for centuries, and revived the Pharaonic concept that the divine essence is incarnated in the person of the monarch. While Antony played the role of the reborn Dionysus,[25] Cleopatra was wearing the traditional garb of Isis, and thus claiming a form of worship which embraced not only the religious doctrine of resurrection, but also the political doctrine of theocracy.

Nothing could be more repugnant to the feelings of the Romans. The egalitarian mingling of various elements was alien to their traditions, and they detested the cult of personality and the ceremonial of monarchy. Octavian's propaganda was designed to embitter these aversions, as when Antony was described as 'threatening the Romans with shackles removed from the limbs of abject slaves.'[26]

Octavian thus simultaneously encouraged hatred of Antony on two different grounds. One was connected with the security of the State – the Egyptian threat being presented as truly imminent. The other arose out of the social question, with stress on the egalitarian ferment that was inherent in the Egyptian policy.

The last point is of especial importance, if we are to understand certain of the motives that led the Romans to submit so fully to Octavian. It was not merely a question of cowardice, calculation, or the moral degeneration of a class which had been numerically weakened and unmanned by many years of bloody civil strife. Nor was it only exhaustion, servility, or a longing for order; it was fear of the social upheavals which, it was thought, had been averted by the murder of Julius Caesar, but which might be resurrected if Antony won.

The republican party might well have joined the forces ranged against Octavian[27] – as in the earlier case of Julius Caesar and in the later cases of Caligula and Nero – if Antony had not had behind him the ideological forces, the warships, the troops and the weapons of the East. This meant a threat to the fatherland, and Octavian was ready to defend it. The news of the death of Cleopatra lifted up the hearts of the Romans like the passing away of a nightmare at daybreak. 'Before today,' says Horace, 'it would not have been right to tap the Caecuban wine in our ancestral cellars – while the crazy queen was planning the ruin of the Capitol and the Empire.'[28]

The moral desertion of Antony was exposed to the contempt of the Romans by Octavian. Not content with the forging of temporary alliances, like those of Pompey, with eastern powers, he had openly made himself a part of the Asiatic political scene, and had adopted the universalist conception of monarchy.

The ancient historians pick out the contrast between the two positions, which they sum up in speeches supposed to have been made by the opposing champions. Antony adheres to the line of the international propaganda put out in his name, and promises the foreigners who make up his ranks that they will receive complete equality with the Romans. Octavian promises his men an extension of Roman authority over the strangers, according to Dio Cassius (L, 22, 4). He is speaking to Romans, and therefore invokes the past glories of Roman history, the victories won over the barbarians. He rejects the idea that the descendants of Roman heroes could ever fall under the sway of a foreign woman. He holds Antony's abject submission to Cleopatra up to contempt. He stresses the anti-Roman character of Antony's behaviour, and describes him as a typical renegade : 'He has forgotten the dress of his ancestors, and imitates the garb of the barbarians; he lives as the slave of a harlot' (Dio Cassius, L, 25, 3).

The same judgement emerges from the whole body of Augustan poetry. In epic, Aeneas, the mythical forefather of the race, is celebrated as the perfect model of a Roman hero, true to his duty, ready for self-sacrifice for the sake of the mission entrusted to him by the gods.[29] Unlike Antony, he abandons an African queen, to make his way on towards the land assigned to him by Fate.

It was not difficult to find other, similar analogies. Troy, the city of the Romans' ancestors, fell and perished through the fault of a foreign woman.[30] But New Troy would not undergo the same fate, because there was One who watched over her.

To hold Antony up to scorn as an apostate, a renegade, served the plans of Octavian very well. His struggle with Antony was not to appear under the hateful aspect of fratricidal strife, but rather as a holy war, waged in the joint names of patriotism and religion, in defence of the Roman community against the world of barbarism; a crusade of free citizens against hordes of slaves.

The conflict between Octavian and Antony was converted into a truly national war. Backed by Senate and People, by both household and Capitoline gods, the heir of Caesar leads all Italy into battle. Before Actium, he offers a vow, not merely to the Capitoline Trinity, but to all the divinities of the peninsula;[31] the city precinct now embraces the whole country. His sails are filled by a propitious wind, sent by Jupiter, while Antony's fleet labours under the curse of Quirinus.[32] The democratic, rational, individualist West is on the march against the East, with its monarchs, satraps, loathsome gods and orgiastic rites; against the lands where political doctrines are formed of Utopian dreams rather than logical opinions, where justice is not humbly carried out as a part of the daily round, but is a static metaphysical mirage.

Propertius re-emphasises Roman intolerance of absolute power: 'What was the use of breaking the axes of Tarquin,' he asks, 'if we were fated to fall under the yoke of a woman?'[33]

A Roman consul (says Horace), a triumvir, in fact, has turned his back on the ways of his City to wallow in Pharaonic luxury. 'A Roman soldier – posterity will never credit it! – has enslaved himself to a woman, and humiliated himself to the point of obeying her eunuchs. Among the military standards the disgraceful sight of a curtained palanquin sees the light of day.'[34]

To arouse both Senate and People against his rival, Octavian arranged for reports to be made in the Senate House, by men who had deserted the cause of Antony, about the humiliating details of the consul's enslavement to the fiendish enchantress. Octavian forced the Vestals to surrender the testament which Antony had deposited with them. The Romans deplored this sacrilegious action, but were horrified to hear that Antony had expressed the wish to be buried in Egypt, at the side of Cleopatra, and that he had left all his property to her children. Moreover, he intended to offer her the City of Rome as a gift, as soon as he had conquered it, and to transfer the capital of the Empire to Egypt.[35]

Antony's answers to these accusations have not survived. We must note, however, that such charges were often made, when it was a question of discrediting an individual in the eyes of the Romans. Julius Caesar had been accused of planning to transfer the capital – to Troy, as the source of the myths from which he derived prestige; or to Alexandria, so that he could assure himself of the throne of the Ptolemies by virtue of marriage to Cleopatra and permanent residence in Egypt (Suetonius, *Life of Julius Caesar*, LXXIX, 3). It will be noted that the cities mentioned as possible alternative capitals are always better placed than Rome geographically to dominate an empire so widely extended to the east. The contradictory rumours aroused both terror and imaginative speculation; they always had in them an element of intuitive prophecy, true to the future development of Roman political history, and they had their own instinctive logic. There was always an unexpressed fear in the hearts of the Romans that this transfer might really happen one day – that the East would receive formal and final recognition of the spiritual primacy which it already, in effect, possessed, and which was actively coveted by the ascendant power of Rome. The same accusation was brought against Caligula, soon after his death; and it may be supposed that the conspirators spread the rumour, to give his assassination the appearance of a sacred duty. It was also brought against Nero. There were even rumours that Titus, who had been hailed as Emperor by the legions in Judaea, meant to stay there and found an Asiatic empire in opposition to the power of Rome (Suetonius, *Titus,* V).

These rumours and prophecies give us the measure of the masses' sensitive awareness of future possibilities – of events that would really come to pass, but not so quickly as was feared.

To quieten these apprehensions, the writers entrusted with Octavian's publicity launched a manifesto of national patriotism. To the flattering temptations which the East offered to the mighty, and which had seduced Antony, Augustus might reply: 'Here will be our best place to remain.'[36] This tendentious application of the words attributed to Camillus by Livy, though accepted by Mommsen, may since have been authoritatively confuted. In the light of what we know about the controversy that was torturing the consciences of the Romans at that time, however, it is pleasant to read the affectionate words of Camillus, whom Livy calls the leader chosen by Fate, the father of his country, and the second founder of Rome. (Such titles are never bestowed on an ancient hero, unless with the intention of treating him as the prototype of a modern one.) 'Whenever I am far from home,' says Camillus, 'if I think of my country, these are the sights that rise before my eyes – these fields, this Tiber,

160

the countryside I know so well, and the sky under which I was born and grew up' (Livy, V, liv, 3–4).

Still with the idea of freeing men's minds from the Asiatic nightmare, Vergil makes Juno declare that she is now satisfied, and will stop persecuting the Trojans, provided they abandon the Trojan name and adopt that of the country where their long journey has ended.[37] So they must lose their original language, religion, and national characteristics, and adopt the laws and customs of Rome – just as all the subjects of the City would have to do in the future. The goddess herself is the subject of an evocation carried out according to the ancient ritual; finally placated, she signifies her agreement to the transfer. Horace repeats the same tune in a different key, urging the Romans not to overdo their devotion to their original country, nor to try to rebuild the city of Troy.[38]

Octavian was very well aware of the advantage he could derive from Antony's orientalism. But he was certainly also alive to the danger of appearing personally unimpressive by comparison. It suited him to appear before a Roman audience in the role of an ordinary magistrate, whose powers were strictly constitutional and valid only for a limited period; but to compete with a man who had supernatural arguments on his side, Augustus needed a vast and compelling theme. This could not be provided by the practical, legalistic doctrine of Republicanism. So he had to lend universality to the idea of Rome herself.

Various factors may have encouraged him to follow this path, which he certainly made his own. We may discern certain motives, psychological in character, which have been neglected by historical scholarship. All Romans had a feeling of inferiority toward the East, but this must have been particularly strong in the case of Augustus. The oriental lands boasted of immemorial legends, ancient civilisations, and dynasties of divine origin; whereas the Roman kings, to quote Pompeius Trogus (XXXVIII, v), had been 'aboriginal shepherds, Sabine soothsayers, Corinthian immigrants, slaves or sons of slaves, whose most noble title was "*Superbus*"' – which meant 'arrogant'.

161

The story of Julius Caesar gave Octavian a hint how he could raise himself to the same level as a monarch reigning by divine right. The majestic ghosts of heroes could be raised from the shadowy past of Rome – ancestral spirits, who could bestow a sacred authority even on the constitutional magistrate, if he were descended from a hero who was the son of a goddess.

As for his personal position, he had given his sister in marriage to Antony, and seen her repudiated by him – and now Antony was the husband of a queen descended from Alexander, by whom he had had children who ranked as gods. Antony unleashed a propaganda campaign against Octavian – only a few fragments of the material survive[39] – which was aimed primarily at vilifying him personally, reminding everyone of the lowly trades followed by his ancestors at Veliterna. To counterbalance all this, glorification of the origins of Octavian was necessary, together with glorification of the origins of the City. And so the vaguest and most shapeless fragments of legend became the themes of epic poetry. After the defeat of Antony, the poets wrote works designed not so much to assure the power of the heir of Caesar as to reinforce his prestige. These were the poems of Vergil, Horace, Propertius and Ovid. In 12 B.C., at the death of Lepidus, Octavian took the post of *Pontifex Maximus,* and the Altar of Peace (*Ara Pacis*) was built. It bore portraits of his family, with an aspect of eternal majesty, also eagles, winged victories and priestly insignia. A new mythology, and a new tradition, came into being, which gave the Julian dynasty and the City of Rome a mystical prestige of the same kind which had been the boast of their adversaries. The dignified adjective 'augustus' was converted into a proper name, which could be passed on through all generations. It became a title, almost a consecration, capable of obliterating memories of the previous personality of the man who assumed it. A common pedigree was found for Rome and her rulers – the Romans came from Troy, and their leader came from the line of Ascanius.

With public opinion reassured, and with the hearts of men united in the exultation of victory, Octavian knew that Roman

162

patriotism still had one deeply-felt need which had not been satisfied – Carrhae was unavenged.

During the years which followed the defeat of Crassus, the Parthian problem had been shelved. Caesar had been killed on the eve of a campaign against Parthia; the conservatives had feared that, if it ended in victory, Caesar's dictatorship would be turned into a monarchy. A prophet had in fact declared that the campaign would only be a success if the Roman commander had the title of a king[40] – as though a prophylactic dose of Parthianism were needed.

The Romans' rivalry with the Parthians was not merely a matter of economic competition or military quarrel. Parthia was the source of a current of political and religious thought, and the model of an institutional system, directly contrary to Roman ways. The attitude of the Romans to the Parthians was therefore different from that which they showed to other peoples. Crassus had gone out to attack them without any provocation; and he had been defeated and killed. Ancient grudges, dating from before this sorry episode, were still present and active in the minds of the Romans, besides the desire for revenge for Carrhae. For the Parthians were, without any doubt, the most formidable enemies to be found in the sphere of influence which the Romans considered as their own. They provided an armed fist for the expression of the wide-spread hatred of Rome, which Mithridates had represented at the beginning of the century. He died in 66 B.C., and Pompey entered Jerusalem in 63 B.C.; the Roman defeat at Carrhae in 53 B.C. was just ten years later. During this interval, the motives which had contributed to the Pontic king's campaign of hate continued to operate, and were constantly strengthened by new philosophical arguments.

After the death of the leader of the Asiatic revolt and the fall of the holy city of the Jews, the decade leading up to Carrhae was full of prophecies and anathemas; the crushing victory of eastern arms might therefore well appear as the writing on the wall, rather than as a mere isolated episode.

The Parthian armies were the only forces that could compete

effectively with the disciplined might of Rome, because of their numbers, their inaccessible geographical position, and their disconcerting military tactics. The Romans admitted the special importance of Parthia, with a certain amount of condescension. 'Among all the sovereigns of the East,' says Lucan's Pompey, 'the Parthian is the only one to be admitted to my presence on equal terms.'[41] But the Parthians themselves took quite a different view of the matter. The King of Kings condemned a Parthian ambassador to death for allowing Sulla to sit between him and the King of Armenia on a stool of the same height (Plutarch, *Sulla,* 5).

There is a certain contempt for the East in the works of the Roman authors : 'Syrians, Jews, nations born to serve !' says Cicero in the *De Provinciis Consularibus* (V, 10). Such judgements may merely have echoed the views of classical Greece about the Persians. But they cover all the 'barbarian races of the East', and their bitterness is proportionate to the strength of the anti-Roman elements in the culture of the various countries. According to the Romans, any man who follows the mirage of eastern adventure will inevitably fall into the trap of eastern treachery. Both Cicero and Propertius regard Alexandria as the natural home of deceit.[42]

If all the countries of Asia were supposed to be inhabited by faithless, cruel and uncontrollably lecherous tribes, the Parthians were the supreme, proverbial example of falseness. Crassus was defeated, according to the Roman story, not by the armed might but by the low cunning of the Parthian commander-in-chief, – Surena – a man of great physical beauty enhanced by make-up, a general who set out to war accompanied by thousands of slaves and concubines.

By a pretended retreat, by false offers of peace, Surena had lured the aged proconsul, broken by fatigue and by the death of his son, into the ambush where he lost his life. When the Parthian returned to Seleucia, he organised a parody of a traditional Roman triumph, with a procession of harlots following a prisoner with a crown on his head, who represented Crassus. Severed

Roman heads dangled from the axes of the guards (Plutarch, *Crassus*, 32).

He sent the head of Crassus as a present to Artavasdes, who received it while he was seated at a banquet, watching the *Bacchae* of Euripides. The performance had reached the scene where a mother has killed her son without recognising him, in a paroxysm of mystical ecstasy, and brandishes his severed head. The actor seized the head of Crassus, and recited the speech with horrid realism. This is a highly symbolical anecdote, which might have been invented to show the contrast between the aberrations of the East and the Roman way of life – the Roman patient endurance of suffering, and pious regard for the dead.

When Caesar had died, and his plan for a campaign against the Parthians, the outcome of which was so dreaded by the Romans, had consequently been abandoned, the Parthians took the initiative. In 40 B.C., they thrust their way as far as Judaea, led not only by the Crown Prince, Pacorus, but also by a Roman officer, Labienus (Plutarch, *Antony*, 30). He had been sent by Cassius to ask the help of the Parthians, and, after the battle of Philippi, he had stayed with the King of Kings, forgetting the gods of his fatherland. He had advanced into Syria, and incited the Roman garrisons there to desertion (*Dio Cassius*, XLVIII, 25, 2). He had also struck his own coinage, with the title of 'Parthicus'[43] on it. Then the Parthians, as a challenge to Roman authority, put a new king on the throne of Judaea, who belonged to the nationalist movement – Antigonus, the descendant of the Asmonaeans.

Antony was responsible for defending the eastern provinces. Sosius, one of his lieutenants, was despatched to Judaea, and succeeded in removing Antigonus.[44] But Antony decided to lead the main campaign against the Parthians himself – as if to complete the task left unfinished by Julius Caesar, or to repeat the fabulous expedition of Alexander, and the heroic deeds of the fifth-century Greeks. In sympathy with the deep desires of Roman patriotism, he demanded the return of the prisoners of war and the standards taken at Carrhae. The demand was

165

addressed to Phraates, the new King of Parthia, during the siege of Phraaspa. But instead of obtaining satisfaction for his request, he came near to suffering the fate of Crassus, and was forced into a disastrous retreat (36 B.C.).

Augustus was left no alternative by the treachery of Labienus and the failure of Antony. It would now be his task to make a conspicuous demonstration of the primacy of Rome in the uncertain, treacherous regions between the Euphrates and the Jordan. The original sources[45] show us a continuous relationship between Parthia and Judaea, suggesting that the Parthians, besides opposing Rome with a rival imperialism and the force of arms, knew very well how to bring the religious nationalism of the Jews into play against her as well.

The punishment of the Parthians was one of the principal objectives of Octavian's policy, not so much for reasons of national security, as because the Universal City could not come into being while there were rivals to be seen on the ideological plane. The task was a legacy from Julius Caesar. Antony had failed to carry it out, and public opinion insisted on its completion. The Parthian Peril had been in everyone's mind for years.[46]

All this is clear from the many hints in the official literature, not to mention the proud assertions of the Ancyran inscription.[47] The patriots of Rome wanted to wipe out the shameful memory of the unavenged murder of a proconsul, of Roman prisoners getting married to barbarian women and forgetting the religion and the glory of Rome.[48] 'Avenge the dead of Carrhae' wrote Propertius, 'go forth, and provide for the needs of Roman history.'[49]

In 20 B.C., the restoration of the standards was finally achieved by Tiberius (Suetonius, *Tiberius*, IX, 1). This success was so magnified in verse, in sculpture and on coins,[50] that it made an indelible imprint on the Roman consciousness. It was only after the return of the standards that the Senate granted Octavian the honour of using the name of 'Augustus'.[51]

The artists took possession of the image of the suppliant dressed

166

in Parthian garb, and used it again and again for successive emperors. It reappears also in the earliest works of Christian art: for the three kings, with their gold and frankincense and myrrh, prostrate in adoration of the Redeemer, repeat the portrayal of the Parthians.

Augustus chose to carry a representation of the return of the standards on his person, right in the middle of his breast-plate[52] – as if he had imposed the humiliating restitution on the defeated enemy, instead of getting them back by skilful diplomatic negotiation, as had really been the case; as if, in fact, this were the crowning glory of his career. 'At the knees of Caesar, Phraates receives the Law, receives authority.'[53] The 'cruel and insolent Parthian' had long been the Romans' nightmare. Like the destruction of Carthage, the destruction of Parthia became a refrain, which the Roman nationalists constantly repeated to their rulers.[54]

Even if the standards had never been returned, there would be little change, from the point of view of posterity, in the value of Octavian's life-work. The vast plan for the rectification and strengthening of the Rhine and Danube boundaries, the pacification of the eastern provinces, the annexation of Egypt, the monumental administrative, juridical and defensive machine, are enough to make his name immortal.

But the same was not true for the public opinion of Octavian's own time, which was open to other appeals. Carrhae had shed a harsh light on the question of unlimited expansion toward the East; Teutoburgum had had a similar message for those who regarded the Germans, just across the Rhine, as dangerous neighbours. In the life-time of Augustus, the official poets expressed the people's hopes and fears in matters of foreign policy. They addressed to Augustus the same message that had been addressed to Philip of Macedon by Isocrates. And the subject was the same, too: namely the barbarians of Asia – tyrants to their own people, and rivals to the imperialism of the West. 'If you can make the barbarians slaves of the Greeks,' says Isocrates, 'and impose obedience on the monarch called the

167

Great King, it will only be left for you to become a god.' 'If
he can add the Britons and the irksome Persians to the Empire,'
says Horace, 'Augustus will be held to be a god.'[55]

And again 'They threaten Latium itself; when shall we see
them finally tamed, and dragged through the streets in a just
triumph?'[56]

Abhorrence of fratricidal strife causes frequent appeals for
internal harmony. They are invariably accompanied by the
warning: never forget the Parthian peril! If the Romans tear
each other to pieces, the Parthians will profit by it.

It may well be that the Parthians were a long way from
'threatening Latium', in the words of Horace.[57] Authoritative
historians[58] consider that the menace was not really so serious,
and that Augustus exaggerated the military provocation
involved, in order to enhance his success. 'I compelled the
Parthians to return the standards and the booty,' he says, in
Res Gestae, paragraph XXIX. His poets celebrate the act of
restitution as a triumph for his arms – the hands of the Parthians
trembled as they surrendered the eagles, says Ovid.[59]

Visual representations of the scene were spread over the entire
area of the Roman sphere of influence by a long series of issues
of coinage. The success had, in fact, been achieved by Tiberius,
but in theory it had been willed by Augustus. His had been
the prophetic zeal – symbolised by the augur's wand on the
coinage – and his was the credit.[60]

This now becomes the favourite theme of the literature of the
Empire. 'The cities of Asia are tamed, the forces of Armenia
thrust back; now even the Parthian puts his sole trust in flight.'
The monarchs of the lands around the Caspian Sea had been
waiting for centuries, in fear and trembling, for the advent of
Augustus, foreseen by their prophets. Rome gives her laws to
the Medes, and strikes terror into the hearts of tyrants.[61]

The persistence of these boasts, which do not correspond to
any conspicuous military success, shows a psychological need for
reassurance, for conviction that the flood of subversive ideologies from the East has been stemmed for ever. The same

anxieties reappear in the warnings of Lucan to Nero, which express the views of the group, centred around Caius Piso, to which the poet belonged. The young emperor had freed himself from the influence of Seneca, and had laid aside the apparent respect for the constitution which had characterised the beginning of his reign. Like Antony and like Caligula, he was now following the stream of theocratic absolutism. This was a doctrine which drew its inspiration, and even its visual imagery, from the precedent of Alexander. It implied a universalist tendency, which was most unwelcome to the class that exercised responsibility and authority in the imperial City. The ideological leanings of those emperors towards the East can be seen in the surviving anecdotes about them – some, perhaps, pure invention. When Nero died, it was feared for many years that he would come again, at the head of a Parthian army.[62]

NOTES TO CHAPTER

1. One of these authors was the Greek Timagenes, who lived at Rome, as the guest of Asinius Pollio, in opposition circles – see Seneca, *On Anger*, III, xxiii, 4, and *Letters* XCI, xiii. In Latin, we have the *Epitome* of the Narbonese historian Pompeius Trogus. See P. Treves, *Il mito d'Alessandro e la Roma di Augusto,* Milan 1953.
2. Livy calls them *levissimi ex Graecis* – IX, xviii, 6.
3. Tacitus, *Annals*, II, lxxxviii. See Aulus Gellius, III, vii, 19; Macrobius *Saturnalia*, I, xxiv, 4: *Graeci omnia sua in immensum tollunt.*
4. Ovid, *Fasti*, III, 101; Vergil, *Aeneid*, VI, 851; Horace, *Art of Poetry*, 323–5.
5. M. A. Levi, *T. Livio e gli ideali augustei*, in *La Parola del Passato*, IV, 1949, pp. 15 ff.
6. Livy, XXXI, xiv, 6 and xliv, 9. See also Aulus Gellius, XIII, xxiv, 1; III, vii, 19.
7. Cicero, *Pro Archia*, IX, 20; Sallust, *Jugurthine War*, LXIII, 3; Plutarch, *Marius*, 2.
8. Horace, *Satires*, II, ii, 10: *vel si Romana fatigat   Militia adsuetum graecari.*
9. Suetonius, *Augustus*, LXXXIX, 1; also *Tiberius*, LXXI, 1.
10. Vergil, *Aeneid*, II, 164: *Scelerumque inventor Ulixes;* also II, 49: *Timeo Danaos et dona ferentes.*

11. For the imperialism of Cleopatra and the pro-Greek and pro-Asiatic leanings of Antony, see a careful examination of the sources in M. A. Levi, *Ottaviano capoparte*, Florence 1933, Vol. II, pp. 223 ff. This interpretation was probably accentuated by the propaganda of Augustus, which reaffirmed the Roman tradition; later it was taken up and passed on by subsequent elaborators.

12. M. A. Levi, *Il tempo di Augusto*, Florence 1951, p. 128.

13. For the coins, see Lily Ross Taylor, *The Divinity of the Roman Emperor*, Middletown, Connecticut 1931, pp. 267 ff.; also p. 122, no. 15. See also H. Mattingly – E. A. Sydenham, *The Roman Imperial Coinage*, London 1926, Vol. I, nos. 1189, 1197–8. See also Dio Cassius, XLVIII, 39, 2.

14. Appian, *Civil War*, III, ii, 16. Plutarch, *Antony*, 4, 36, 60.

15. Plutarch, *Antony*, 60. H. Jeanmaire, *La politique religieuse d'Antoine et Cléopâtre*, in *Rev. Arch.*, XIX, 1924, pp. 241 ff.; *Dionysus*, Paris 1951, pp. 465 ff.; M. Charlesworth, *Some Fragments of the Propaganda of Antony*, in *Cl. Quart.*, 1933, pp. 172 ff.; K. Scott, *The Political Propaganda of 44–30 B.C.*, in *Mem. Am. Ac. R.*, XI, 1933, pp. 7 ff.

16. P. Grimal, *Le siècle d'Auguste*, Paris 1961, p. 68.

17. J. Gagé, *Apollon Romain*, Paris 1955, pp. 229 and 515. *Bibl. des Ecoles Franc. d'Athènes et de Rome*, Vol. 182. Coinage shown on p. 529, plate IV B. And see R. Syme, *Roman Revolution*, Oxford 1956, p. 448.

18. Vergil, *Aeneid*, VIII, 685–8: *Hinc ope barbarica variisque Antonius armis Victor ab aurorae populis et litore rubro Aegyptum viresque orientis et ultima secum Bactra vehit.* See also W. W. Tarn, *Antony's Legions*, in *Cl. Quart.*, XXVI, 1935, pp. 75 ff.; and Propertius, IV, vi, 25–7.

19. Lily Ross Taylor, *op. cit.*, plate 14, p. 120.

20. Josephus, *Jewish War*, VI, 312; Tacitus, *Histories*, V, xiii; Suetonius, *Vespasian*, IV, 5. See also J. Bidez and F. Cumont, *Les Mages hellénisés*, Paris 1938; F. Cumont, *La fin du monde selon les Mages occidentales*, in *Rev. Hist. Rel.*, CIII, 1931, pp. 29 ff. Also, in the same volume, A. Lods, *Recherches sur le prophétisme israélite*, pp. 279 ff.

21. *Epodes*, XVI, 21–2: *Ire, pedes quocumque ferent, quocumque per undas Notus vocabit, aut protervus Africus.*

22. P. Grimal, *A propos de la XVI épode*, in *Latomus*, XX, 1961, pp. 721 ff.; J. Carcopino, *Virgile et le mystère de la IV églogue*, Paris 1930; E. Barker, *From Alexander to Constantine*, Oxford 1956, p. 214.

23. In support of the first hypothesis, see A. Peretti, *La sibilla babilonese*, Florence 1942, p. 17 note 2, and pp. 339–40. In support of the second, W. W. Tarn, *Alexander Helios*, in *J.R.S.*, XXII, 1932, p. 135 ff.

24. Ovid, *Metamorphoses*, IV, 827–8: *Illa minata Servitura suo Capitolia nostra Canopo.*

25. Plutarch, *Antony*, 24. See H. Jeanmaire, *Le règne de la femme des derniers jours*, in *Mélanges Cumont*, IV, Brussels 1936, pp. 297 ff.; *La Sibylle et le retour de l'âge d'or*, Paris 1939. See also M. Levi, *op. cit.*, p. 107, note 10.

26. Horace, *Epodes*, IX, 9–10: *minatus Urbi vincla, quae detraxerat Servis amicus perfidis.*

27. Suetonius, *Augustus*, LXIV – LXVI.

28. Horace, *Odes*, I, xxxvii, 5–8: *Antehac nefas depromere Caecubum Cellis avitis dum Capitolio Regina dementis ruinas Funus et imperio parabat.*
29. H. Jeanmaire, *La politique religieuse d'Antoine et Cléopâtre*, in *Rev. Arch.*, XIX, 1924, pp. 241 ff.
30. *Mulier peregrina vertit*, in the words of Horace – *Odes*, III, iii, 20.
31. *Hinc Augustus agens Italos in proelia Caesar . . . Dis Italis votum immortale sacrabat.*– Vergil, *Aeneid*, VIII, 678 and 715.
32. Propertius, IV, vi, 21 and 23: *Altera classis erat Teucro damnata Quirino . . . Hinc Augusta ratis plenis Iovis omine velis.*
33. Propertius, III, xi, 47–8: *Quid nunc Tarquinii fractas iuvat esse secures Si mulier patienda fuit?*
34. Horace, *Epodes*, IX, 11–16: *Romanus, eheu, posteri negabitis Emancipatus foeminae Fert vallum et arma miles et spadonibus Servire rugosis potest Interque signa turpe militaria Sol adspicit conopium.* The survival of the Roman prejudice against the softness of the East may be noted even in the fourth century A.D. – see *Panegyric* IX, xxiv, composed in A.D. 313 and Claudian's satire *Against Eutropius*, I, 414–16 and 428; II, 112–13 and 136 – written in A.D. 399.
35. Plutarch, *Antony*, 55, 58, 60, 66; Suetonius, *Augustus*, XVII, 2.
36. *Hic manebimus optime* – Livy, V, lv, 1.
37. Vergil, *Aeneid*, XII, 826–8: *Sit Latium, sint albani per saecula reges, Sit romana potens itala virtute propago: Occidit, occideritque sinas cum nomine Troia.*
38. Horace, *Odes*, III, iii, 57–60: *Sed bellicosis fata Quiritibus Hac lege dico: ne nimium pii, Rebusque fidentes avitae Tecta velint reparare Troiae.*
39. Suetonius, *Augustus*, II, IV, VII, X, XVI. See also H. Jeanmaire, *op. cit.*; M. Charlesworth, *op. cit.*; K. Scott, *op. cit.*
40. Dio Cassius, XLIV, 15, 3; Suetonius, *Life of Julius Caesar*, LXXIX, 3; Plutarch, *Life of Julius Caesar*, 60; Appian, *Civil War*, II, xvi, 110.
41. Lucan, *Pharsalia*, VIII, 230–1: *Solusque e numero regum telluris Eoae Ex aequo me Parthus adit.*
42. Cicero, *Pro Rabirio*, XII, 34; Propertius, III, xi, 33: *Noxia Alexandria, dolis aptissima tellus.*
43. M. A. Levi, *Il tempo di Augusto*, Florence 1951, points out on p. 110 that the title precedes the name on coins; had they been reversed, the meaning would have been 'The general of the Parthians'.
44. T. Reinach, *Jewish Coins*, London 1883, plate III, no. 5.
45. Josephus, *Jewish Antiquities*, XVIII, 310; XV, 3, 1; Philo of Alexandria, *Legation to Gaius*, 282.
46. Cicero, *Letters to Friends*, II, xvii, 1.
47. Augustus, *Res Gestae*, XXIX, 3: *Parthos trium exercituum Romanorum spolia et signa reddere mihi supplicesque amicitiam populi Romani petere coegi. Ibid.*, XXXII, 1: *Ad me supplices confugerunt reges Parthorum Tiridates et postea Phraates, regis Phraatis filius.*
48. Ovid, *Tristia*, II, 227; Vergil, *Aeneid*, VII, 606; VI, 799–810; VIII, 724–731; *Georgics*, III, 30; Horace, *Odes*, I, ii, 21; I, xii, 53–4; II, ix, 20–24; III, v, 4–12; *Epistles*, I, xii, 27.

49. Propertius, III, iv, 9–10: *Crassos clademque piate, Ite et Romanae consulite historiae.*
50. H. Mattingly – E. A. Sydenham, *op. cit.*, I; nos. 17, 37 (triumphal arch erected at Rome in honour of Augustus); no. 16 (temple of Mars Ultor, 20 B.C.).
51. Augustus, *Res Gestae*, XXXIV, 3: *Pro merito meo Senatus consulto Augustus appellatus sum.* See the coins with the inscription *Signis Receptis* in E. A. Sydenham, *Historical References on Roman Coins*, London 1917, p. 19, nos. 18, 19; the triumphal chariot which transported the standards, *ibid.*, nos. 20, 21.
52. J. Charbonneaux, *L'art au siècle d'Auguste*, Paris 1948, plates 50 and 51; p. 31, no. 4.
53. Horace, *Epistles*, I, xii, 27: *ius imperiumque Phraates Caesaris accepit genibus.*
54. Lucan, *Pharsalia*, VIII, 241–3; 429. See also E. M. Sanford, *The Eastern Question in Lucan's B.C.*, in *Cl. M. St.* in honour of E. R. Rand, New York 1938. See also Sydenham, *op. cit.*, p. 52, no. 79, for coin showing an arch erected in honour of Nero in A.D. 64.
55. Isocrates, *Letter to Philip*, II, 5; Horace, *Odes*, III, v, 2–4: *praesens divus habebitur Augustus adiectis Britannis Imperio gravibusque Persis.*
56. Horace, *Odes*, I, xii, 53–4. *Ille seu Parthos Latio imminentis Egerit iusto domitos triumpho.*
57. Horace, *Odes*, I, ii, 21–22: *Audiet civis acuisse ferrum Quo graves Persae melius perirent.*
58. R. Syme, *Roman Revolution*, Oxford 1956, p. 302.
59. Ovid, *Tristia*, II, 227–8: *Nunc petit Armenius pacem, nunc porrigit arcus Parthus eques timida captaque signa manu.* See the coin relating to the Roman intervention in Armenian politics (19 B.C.) inscribed *Armenia Capta*, in H. Mattingly – E. A. Sydenham, *op. cit.*, Vol. I, nos. 40–41.
60. Augustus, *Res Gestae*, IV, 5: *Ob res a me aut per legatos meos auspiciis meis terra marique prospere gestas*; XXVI, 13: *iussu meo et auspicio*. See also J. Gagé, *La victoire d'Auguste et les auspices de Tibère*, in *Rev. Arch.*, XXXII, 1930, pp. 1 ff.
61. Vergil, *Georgics*, III, 30–1; *Aeneid*, VI, 799–801 and VIII, 724–31; Horace, *Odes*, I, xxxv, 9–12; I, xii, 53; I, xxi, 15–16; I, xxxv, 9, 35, 44; II, ix, 19–24; IV, xiv, 41–52; III, ii, 2–4 and iii, 42–4; *Carmen Saeculare* 53–6; *Epistles*, II, i, 256. See also Propertius, II, x, 15.
62. H. P. L'Orange, *Apotheosis and Ancient Portraiture*, Oslo 1947; Suetonius, *Nero*, LVII, 2; Tacitus, *Annals*, XV, xxxvi; *Histories*, II, viii, ix; *Carmina Sibyllina*, IV, 119 ff. and V, 147; Dio Cassius, LXVI, 19.

X

Rome as the City of Mankind

Other peoples have been allotted a certain
defined portion of the earth; for the Romans,
the boundaries of the City are the boundaries
of the world.

OVID, *Fasti*, II, 683–4[1]

AFTER THE annexation of Egypt and the humbling of the
Parthian empire, the power of Rome seemed to have no limits,
and a paean of imperialistic triumph broke out. Now that she
was conscious of her own strength, the City was caught up in
the current of her own greatness. Reflected glory shone on the
very soil of Rome. The earth on which Rome stood was consecrated ground. 'There is no part of the city,' says Livy, 'that is
not full of holiness, full of the godhead' (V, lii, 2). The Tiber
is blessed above all the rivers of the earth, and the empire of
the world has been promised to it,[2] for on its banks is to rise
the City destined to lord it over all other cities, even the
mightiest. Though once a mere stream, despised even by the
cattle, it is now known and dreaded by all the nations of the
earth.[3]

So the City is born which is destined to satisfy in history the
metaphysical needs of the nations. The earthly city differs little
from the Isles of the Blest. Formerly men had believed that the
violent destruction of the earthly city might be a tragic but
necessary prelude to the coming of the divine City of Justice and
Peace. But now that fear had been dispelled, and it only
remained to rejoice at the realisation of the Utopian dreams of

173

the mystics, the renewal of the earth. The City must now cope with tasks of higher scope and longer duration than her immediate problems – tasks of world-wide rather than national significance. Everything now takes on an aspect of eternity, in which the poets felt themselves to be full participants. 'I have built a monument more lasting than bronze,' says Horace,[4] and Ovid claims that neither the wrath of Jupiter, nor fire, nor steel, nor devouring time will ever destroy his work.[5] From the hostile clash between the rival propaganda machines of East and West emerges the concept of Rome as the City of Mankind, the lighthouse of civilisation, the mother of the nations – the greatest, proudest, most eternal, unconquered, protective, divine of all cities, destined to become, in the words of Dante: 'the holy place Where sits the rightful heir of mighty Peter.'

Looking down from heaven over the whole world, Jupiter can see nothing that is not Roman. Evander's mother announces to Vesta that a day will come when a single ruler will hold sway over the holy inheritance of Troy, and over the whole earth; the fateful hills, that stand beside the Tiber, are destined to enclose the spot that will be the source of law for all the universe.[6]

Splendid walls would arise around the City, as Jupiter had promised to Venus, who was concerned about the fate of her son Aeneas.[7] But the City would not remain bounded by the extent of the walls, which were designed to accommodate the vast population of the future. The god Terminus, the vigilant guardian of boundaries, would not yield possession of the Capitol even to Jupiter without a struggle; but he gave way to the Romans. Other nations have received territories of limited extent from him; but the space assigned to the Romans is the whole world.[8] Jupiter remains in charge of heaven, but mortals on earth are subject to Augustus, their father and supreme ruler.[9]

The arts of the Augustan period help in the work of sanctifying the eternal City. The *Aeneid* sets out to show how its greatness was foreordained in heaven. Livy's history celebrates the

174

valour of the makers of Rome, and narrates the gradual rise of the City in a style which blends mysticism with fatalism. Ovid's *Fasti* are meant to give dignity to the ancient rites, rustic in origin, which have now fallen into disuse, and to form the basis of a religious calendar, that would bring the hearts of men, led astray by outlandish festivals, back to the ancient highway of traditional doctrine.

Various prodigies had announced the opening of a new era at the time when Sulla seized power, and again at the crossing of the Rubicon, and at the death of Julius Caesar; now they served to proclaim the rise of an Empire which is beyond the reach of human fate. To bring this about, some power had saved Aeneas from the flames of Troy, and guided him to the shores of Latium. So that he might be informed of the future glories of his own descendants, he was permitted to go down into the lower regions and return alive into the upper world. Vergil's *Aeneid*, the work of his maturity (composed between 29 and 19 B.C.), was designed to provide mythological backing not only for the Julian family's right to rule, but also for the City of Rome's right to supremacy, which heaven had been preparing for hundreds of years. Greece herself was to accept the posthumous triumph of the defeated power of Troy, since Rome was the pre-ordained result of a migration which had taken place in the dawn of history; and soothsayers had long seen in her the future capital of the world (Ovid, *Metamorphoses*, 434–5).

Right at the beginning, there had been a reconciliation between the Greeks and the Trojans. When Aeneas landed on the banks of the Tiber, he met Evander, an exile from Arcadia, who greeted him warmly; and they made a joint sacrifice to Hercules.[10] At this early stage, the Greek and Trojan fugitives reached an agreement based on the concepts personified by the god. It was an alliance of the spirits of reason and liberty against barbarism. In the name of those principles, the City that was later to arise four-square on the site of that sacrifice would extend its walls, metaphorically speaking, to include all civilised

175

men, leaving the barbarians to howl outside. In view of these theoretical suppositions, the City may be regarded as having been planned as a moral concept even before its foundation by Romulus.

With the literature of the Augustan period, a teleological view of history comes into being, some time before the adoption of a similar concept by the Christians. From Aeneas through Romulus and Camillus to Augustus, an unbroken chain of intimately linked events performed the function of preparing Rome to be first the capital of the Empire, and then the seat of the Papacy; to be the Great City that would tower unshaken above the others, as the cypress stands above the pliant reeds;[11] giving her laws[12] to the whole world, predestined to rule over the subject peoples,[13] boundless and enduring for all eternity.[14]

Romulus himself, after his mysterious disappearance from this world, reappears briefly to announce to the living the future greatness of their race. 'Go,' he says, according to Livy (I, xvi, 7), 'go, and tell the Romans that it is the will of Heaven that my City of Rome should become the capital of the world. Let them attend to the arts of war; and let them know – and pass the knowledge on to their descendants – that no human force will ever be able to resist the Roman arms.'

Associated with Romulus, the heroic eponymous founder, was the name of Camillus (Livy, V, xlix, 7). Octavian did not underestimate the awe inspired by the name of his remote ancestor; in fact he made his permanent home in a house on the Palatine which was said to have been formerly inhabited by Romulus. Suggestions were also made that Octavian should adopt his name.

But he preferred the name of Augustus – an adjective of religious, indeed magical overtones, going back to the happy omens which attended the foundation of the City.[15] He preferred, in fact, the peaceful, beneficent, paternal aspects of power, the side of it linked most deeply with the City and with its holy walls. Divine status often implies duality of function, and Augustus chose to be Quirinus rather than Romulus – the two

176

names are synonyms, yet at the same time deeply opposed to each other.[16] There is an analogy here with the way in which Augustus continued the life-work of Julius Caesar, yet at the same time represented the very opposite of his personality.

Caesar had been the heroic warrior, who brought home the splendid trophies of victory, and then ascended into heaven. After him came the pacifier, the laying down of arms, the years of calm. Quirinus would give the Law to his people; the doors of the temple of Janus would be closed, and the impious fury of war would be chained up inside it.[17] Augustus emphasised the beneficent aspect of power. His birth itself was a sign of the benevolence of the gods, and he was destined to be the best possible guardian of the people of Romulus.[18]

Horace repeats and repeats the adjective *bonus*. The gods who gave Augustus to the world are good; his guardianship of his people is superbly good; his military campaigns – a harsh and temporary necessity – are also good; the sweetness of the home that awaits the warrior, the peace of grazing cattle, the fertile fields, the calm sea busy with ships, the home life unsullied by adultery, freed from the fear of barbarian attack – all these are good too, and make up the myth of the ideal City, which the poet now seeks not in far-off, imaginary islands, as in the poems of his stormier years, but here at home, in his own country.[19]

Why should this prosperity, this safety, not be extended to all mankind? Even more lively and frequent than the expressions of gratitude for what Augustus has already done are the suggestions that he should go further. 'The divine Caesar meditates an armed attack on the wealthy Indians,' says Propertius,[20] 'a journey across the ocean, rich in gems, with his fleet. The reward, O citizens, is great; and the furthest of lands offers new triumphs.'

Horace implores Jupiter to protect Augustus, the champion of civilisation against barbarism, who will one day drag the Chinese and the Indians in triumph at his chariot wheels.[21] Juno herself sets the successors of Augustus the task of extending

177

M

the laws of the Capitol to the furthest shores of the earth.[22] The term *terra* is found more and more frequently to indicate the area of Roman power,[23] and the word *orae* to indicate vague, far-off territories. 'The race of Aeneas shall rule over every shore,' says Horace – in other words, the Roman name will be known and feared to the ends of the earth.[24] The invincible Caesar will annex those unknown shores, will keep far away from the hills of Rome the threat of tribes whose names are listed with the more pride because their geographic location is uncertain.[25] To the British (who were in fact known to those who had accompanied Julius Caesar across the Channel) are added the names of the Gangarides, who lived at the mouth of the Ganges; the Egyptians, Armenians, Parthians, Scythians, Getae, Sicambrians, Arabs and Hyrcanians; the Indians, of course, and the inhabitants of the fabulous city of Bactria; finally, the Sabaeans, Numidians and Africans.[26]

Official policy did not set out any idea of unlimited expansion at all. It was the poets who spread it abroad, with a political vision as wide as the earth itself. Scipio, Pompey and Julius Caesar had been its forerunners in the West; in the East, besides Pompey, the figure of Alexander loomed against the background of Oriental legend. The official propaganda of the Empire aimed at replacing that image by another. Octavian's victory over the peoples of the East set the seal of divine approval on his new authority: 'I sang the tilling of the soil,' says Vergil, 'the raising of flocks, the woods, while mighty Caesar blasted the deep Euphrates with the force of arms, passed victoriously among the tribes ready to obey, who willingly accepted the law, opening himself a way to Olympus.'[27]

This was the very delirium of imperialism, which was not destined to be realised in the facts of history. It is aimed primarily towards the East. 'I will add the conquered cities of Asia,' says Vergil (*Georgics,* III, 30). It comes into the dreams of the philosophers, too.[28]

What was to be done with the gods of all those countries? Rome would annex them too. Dionysus, who had been so closely linked with Antony, was represented as abandoning him in defeat: on the night before his death, according to Plutarch, 'when the whole city was in a deep silence and general sadness, expecting the event of the next day, on a sudden was heard the sound of all sorts of instruments, and voices singing in tune, and the cry of a crowd of people shouting and dancing, like a troop of bacchanals on its way. This tumultuous procession seemed to take its course right through the middle of the city to the gate nearest the enemy; here it became the loudest, and suddenly passed out. People who reflected considered this to signify that Dionysus, the god whom Antony had always made it his study to copy and imitate, had now forsaken him' (*Life of Antony*, 75).

The god had abandoned Antony to his fate; but all the mysticism, all the pacific universality of his cult, had now penetrated into the Roman world, despite the ideological barriers erected by Augustus, and had been fully absorbed.

There was an ancient ritual whereby not only the population, but the gods of conquered towns could be invited to join the City of the victor. The process of ideological transfer, which took place in the time of Augustus, reproduced the military ritual of 'evocation', though on a much vaster scale and in a much subtler form. Although the strangers' rites might be forbidden or stamped out, their moral and religious ideas and sentiments were transferred within the walls of the City by what amounted to an 'evocation'; and at the same time they were enlarged to suit the ends of Roman policy, adjusted to the sensibilities of Rome. The spiritual forces which Augustus had proposed to destroy were annexed, tamed and put to work for the benefit of the City. But this time it was not a matter of a single god, patron of a single city whose walls had been ritually erected in his name. A whole new pantheon was being annexed, a new spiritual world, which nevertheless became part of Rome as soon as it penetrated within the walls.

Though Octavian had always claimed to be the restorer of republican tradition, the pious guardian of the ancient City, and though he had always refused unconstitutional powers, he nevertheless introduced the ideas of Divine Right and of world-wide empire to Rome, and thus to the whole Western world. His true genius lay in the way that he Romanised these concepts.

As so often, conquest did not mean the annihilation of the enemy and the ideas he represented, but the adoption and assimilation of the essential features of his message:

> 'As if they both had been of burning wax,
>   Each melted into other, mingling hues,
>   That which was either now was seen no more.'
>
> (Dante, Inferno, XXV, 61–63)

NOTES TO CHAPTER

1. *Gentibus est aliis tellus data limite certo, Romanae spatium est Urbis et orbis idem.*
2. Ovid, *Metamorphoses*, II, 259; Vergil, *Aeneid*, VIII, 64, 65, 72.
3. Ovid, *Fasti*, V, 641: *et quem nunc Tiberim noruntque timentque.*
4. Horace, *Odes*, III, xxx, 1: *Exegi monumentum aere perennius.*
5. Ovid, *Metamorphoses*, XV, 871–2: '*Opus exegi, quod nec Jovis ira nec ignis   Nec poterit ferrum nec edax abolere vetustas.*' E. Maynal, *La Dea Roma à Rome*, in *Mélanges Cagnat*, Paris 1912, pp. 101 ff.; J. Perret, *Pour une étude de l'idée de Rome*, in *Rev. Et. Lat.*, X, 1938, pp. 50 ff.
6. Ovid, *Fasti*, I, 85–6: *Iuppiter arce sua totum cum spectat in orbem   Nil nisi Romanum, quod tueatur, habet. Ibid.*, I, 515–16, 528–30.
7. Vergil, *Aeneid*, I, 258–60.
8. Ovid, *Fasti*, II, 683–4; see note 1 above.
9. Ovid, *Metamorphoses*, XV, 858–60.
10. Vergil, *Aeneid*, VIII, 102 ff. See also P. Grimal, *Enée à Rome et le triomphe d'Auguste*, in *Rev. Et. Anc.*, LIII, 1951, pp. 51 ff.
11. Vergil, *Eclogues*, I, 25.
12. Vergil, *Aeneid*, I, 292; *Georgics*, IV, 562; Horace, *Odes*, II, i, 23, and III, iii, 43; Propertius, IV, iv, 11; Ovid, *Fasti*, I, 516.
13. Tibullus, II, v, 57: *Roma, tuum nomen terris fatale regendis.*
14. Ovid, *Fasti*, I, 85–6; Vergil, *Aeneid*, I, 255; Tibullus, II, v, 23.
15. '*Augusto augurio postquam inclita condita Roma est.*' Ovid, *Fasti*, I, 609. The word 'Augustus' has a common root with words indicating success or growth – *augere, augur, auctoritas*. See G. Nocera, article '*Auctoritas*', in *Enciclopedia del Diritto*, Milan 1959. J. Gagé, *Romulus-Augustus*, in *Mél. Arch. Hist.*, XLVII, 1930, pp. 138 ff.

16. G. Dumézil, *Jupiter, Mars, Quirinus*, Turin, 1955, pp. 58 ff.
17. Vergil, *Aeneid*, I, 293–4; VII, 621; Horace, *Satires*, I, iv, 60–61; *Odes*, IV, xv, 9; Augustus, *Res Gestae*, XXXIV, 2. See also K. Scott, *The Identification of Augustus with Romulus-Quirinus*, in *Trans. Proc. Am. Phil. Ass.*, LVI, 1925, pp. 82 ff.
18. Horace, *Odes*, IV, v, 1: *Divis orte bonis, optume romulae   Custos gentis.*
19. Horace, *Epode*, XVI.
20. Propertius, III, iv, 1–3: *Arma deus Caesar dites meditatur ad Indos   Et freta gemmiferi findere classe maris.   Magna, viri, merces: parat ultima terra triumphos.*
21. Horace, *Odes*, I, xii, 55–6: *sive subjectos orientis orae Seras et Indos.*
22. Horace, *Odes*, III, iii, 42 ff.
23. Vergil, *Aeneid*, VI, 782; Horace, *Odes*, II, i, 23; Tibullus, II, v, 57; Propertius, IV, iv, 11 and III, iv, 3.
24. Vergil, *Georgics*, II, 170–1: *Maxume Caesar   Qui nunc extremis Asiae iam victor in oris; Aeneid*, III, 97: '*Hic domus Aeneae cunctis dominabitur oris.*' And Horace, *Odes*, III, iii, 45.
25. Vergil, *Georgics*, II, 172: *Imbellem avertis romanis arcibus Indum.*
26. Vergil, *Aeneid*, VI, 795; VII, 605; VIII, 685, 722; Propertius, IV, vi, 77 ff.; Ovid, *Consolatio ad Liviam*, 11 ff.; Horace, *Epodes*, XVI, 11 ff.; *Odes*, I, xii, 53 ff.; I, xxix, 1 ff.; I, xxxv, 29 ff.; II, ix, 17 and xi, 1; III, v, 2; III, viii, 18; IV, v, 25 and xiv, 41; IV, xv, 21; *Carmen Saeculare*, 53; Tibullus, *Paneg. ad Messal.*, 107–35; Augustus, *Res Gestae*, XXXI.
27. Vergil, *Georgics*, IV, 559–62: *Haec super arvorum cultu pecorumque canebam   Et super arboribus, Caesar dum magnus ad altum Fulminat Euphraten bello, victorque volentis   Per populos dat iura, viamque adfectat Olympo.*
28. See Seneca, *On Leisure*, IV, 1: *Terminos civitatis nostrae cum sole metimur.*

XI

'The World Made Stable'

If all men have in common reason, moral sense,
and the law, then we are all fellow-citizens, and
the world is as it were a single state.

MARCUS AURELIUS, *Meditations*, IV, 4

SLOWLY, THE walls of the City widen out to embrace the earth.
The cosmopolitan view of the world became universally accepted
as the basic doctrine of imperial policy. Rhetoricians held forth
on the subject of the ideal State, and identified it with Rome,
the City which seemed to bring the dreams of the mystics and
theorists to final realisation in the pages of history.

Improved communications and unified administration had in
fact produced, over very wide areas, a uniformity of habits,
laws, language and institutions, in which the enlightened could
recognise the fulfilment of the Utopian planned society.

In the Augustan age, the conception was still the concern of
poets, who sublimated it by clothing it in lofty artistic forms.
The clemency of Rome toward the conquered, her far-sighted
vigilance, her justice toward all nations, were themes repeated
in the propaganda of poets and artists, in verse and in marble.
These themes were destined to be used and re-used by
rhetoricians and panegyrists, even at times when they did not
correspond to reality.

But beneath the idea of an Olympian monarchy, beneficent
and levelling, lay a second conception, which kept alive the
theme of empire based on racial superiority, and emphasised the

principle, dear to the ruling class of the Republic, that the main function of the emperor is the command of troops in war.

This opinion is more commonly expressed in works of visual art than in literature. To be more precise, the two concepts coexist in visual imagery, but the idea of a paternal monarchy predominates – inspired by the emperors themselves – in the pages of the writers. In the very period when the brotherhood of mankind was becoming the main theme of imperial propaganda, the message of the visual arts was made up of violently contrasting elements – the theme of generous egalitarianism and the theme of brute force. In certain coins of the first and second centuries A.D., we see groups of manacled, abject barbarians, arranged symmetrically on either side of a trophy – one crushed by humiliation, one holding up his shaggy head in insolent revolt. Sometimes they lie, pierced by darts, beneath the hoofs of the emperor's rearing horse, or the horse of some lesser officer. Tombstones carved with such subjects have been found along the Rhine, and even in Britain. Even emperors famed in history for their clemency, like Titus, appear in these scenes of savage oppression – even when the victims are not shaggy savages, but representatives of a centuries-old civilisation, such as the Jews. IUDAEA CAPTA is seen weeping at the foot of a palm tree on the coins of Titus,[1] and the River Jordan appears in a triumphal procession carved on his memorial arch. As evidence of Domitian's victories over the barbarians – non-existent victories, according to the sarcastic testimony of writers who survived him[2] – we can still see his trophies (wrongly attributed to Marius), on the Capitol, and the crude metopes of Adamclissi at the National Museum in Bucharest. Roman legionaries are depicted in the act of dragging off entire families of barbarians into captivity, or carefully picking off with their arrows fugitives who have taken refuge in the branches of trees. This, as Tacitus calmly tells us (*Annals*, II, xvii), was a thing that the Roman archers used to do for sport.

But these scenes of oppressive domination are balanced by

others, of the same period, in which the same emperors give an example of clemency. On some coins, we see Trajan trampling on the fallen enemy. In others he holds out his hand to raise the kneeling figure of Dacia to her feet.[3] The prisoners who are now to be found on the Arch of Constantine are barbarian warriors who preserve their dignity in defeat, and so are the busts in the Nympheum on the Palatine. These are men who might later be welcomed into the brotherhood of Rome. They might be the very heroes and patriots – German or British or Batavian – into whose mouths Tacitus puts severe rebukes and warnings to the exploiting power. Arminius, Caractacus, and Julius Vindex were all heroes cast in the same mould, conscious of their mission to defend the liberty of their countrymen against the armed might and the greedy exactions of Rome – but capable at a later stage of defending Rome, their adopted country, with equal devotion, from the ever-gathering hordes of fresh barbarians on the frontiers of the Empire; also, perhaps, capable of healing the sickness of Rome with their own example. Cicero had hoped that the Italian municipalities would provide some such useful moral examples; but Tacitus found them on the banks of the Rhine, the Danube and the Thames.

Humane good-will toward the conquered is especially apparent in certain works of art, which celebrate the glories of Trajan, but were completed in the reign of Hadrian – the only Roman emperor, except for Julian the Apostate, to have left us no statues or coins that express the idea of oppressive domination. The triumphal spiral relief on Trajan's column suggests that the artist wanted to show his understanding for the sufferings of the beleaguered Dacians; the prisoners, in their picturesque barbarian costumes, are exceptionally handsome. On the arch of Beneventum, the provinces are not depicted in the posture of subjects, but on a footing of equality with the capital City – a theme repeated on all Hadrian's coins. The Germans swear homage, and the god of war presents a barbarian recruit to the Emperor. It might be a deliberate visual representation of the humanitarian concepts included in all laudatory writings of the Antonine period – those of Pliny the Younger, the only author of Italian origin in this group; those of the Asiatic writers Dion of Prusa and Aelius Aristides; and those of the Greek historian Plutarch of Chaeronea. Especially in the case of Hadrian, there is a clear intention on the part of the emperor to show open approval of the levelling ideas of the political philosophers of his day, as preached by the orators in court, by religious speakers at street-corners, and by artists in marble. The few surviving statues from the Hadrianeum in the Field of Mars[4] repeat the themes of the coinage. The provinces are represented not by fettered slave-girls, but by dignified, majestically clothed women, each of whom can be recognised by her special insignia. Africa bears the tusks of an elephant, Britannia has the sea at her feet, and so on. There is no submissiveness about their posture; all of them stand erect. Rome and Italy are not distinguished from the others by any sign of superior rank. The emperor holds out his hand impartially to every one of them. In a complete series, he is shown lifting various prostrate figures to their feet; their position, however, does not denote humility, but the state in which he found them. In every case the emperor has chosen to have a title engraved after his name – the title of Restorer of the province concerned, in token of his good offices towards those countries.[5]

Another form of words, of philosophical inspiration, shows us Hadrian aiming at recognition of a still more ambitious title, that of benefactor of the whole world: RESTITUTOR ORBIS TERRARUM. Yet another proclaims the final result of world-wide pacification: TELLUS STABILITA. 'Thou art a citizen of the world,' wrote Epictetus at about the same time; and again 'The world is one City' (II, x, 3, III, xxiv, 9). Plutarch sees in the sky the only limit to one's native country; here no-one is a foreigner or an exile (*De Exilio,* 600 E, 601 A).

Antoninus Pius evidently wanted to follow the example of his predecessor, and the exhortations of the rhetoricians of the second century A.D. A Bithynian writer, Dion of Prusa, composed four orations in which he listed for Trajan the moral

185

qualities which a ruler should possess. Imperial majesty, he says, should be modelled on the power of Jupiter, and also on the beneficent example of Hercules, 'the god who never sought to exercise command himself, but always to secure the greatest good for the greatest number of men' (Dion of Prusa, *Orations*, I, 65). In keeping with these premisses, the State is identified with the universe, with the harmonious order proceeding from the Divine Mind (*ibid.*, 42). While giving us the details of imaginary conversations between Alexander and his father, Philip, or between Alexander and Diogenes, Dion contrived to express the pleasure with which his fellow-subjects observed that the rule of the Antonine emperors was at last bringing to reality, on this earth, the plan whereby all men might live in peace together, which had been devised as an abstract Utopian concept by the most ancient Greek philosophers. He also compares the power of the monarch with the beneficent action of the Sun (III, 73 ff.), which gives light and warmth to all men impartially, and spreads its rays over the vastness of infinite space. (The cult of the sun-god was later to be used as a means of spiritual unification, by the Severi, in the third century.) Discrimination is a thing of the past; the word 'Roman' is a title of citizenship, and does not indicate birth at Rome, but participation in the human community known by the name of the City.

The ruler also hears from the rhetoricians, from time to time, about the need for respect for the Senate and for democratic institutions. This shows the persistent literary influence of republican models, of celebrated authors such as Cicero and Sallust, even on orators whose language was not Latin. But these references are mere formal evocations of bygone principles, not expressions of the moral and spiritual needs of men used to the exercise of political liberty. To be embedded in a system which reduces the personal initiative – and hence the responsibility – of the individual, does offer a man a feeling of protection. It may even sometimes compensate for the loss of rights which have been forgotten by many citizens, and have never been known to others. In times of war or famine, according to Pliny the Younger, writing during the reign of Trajan, the Princeps will provide for the distribution of grain and the defence of the frontiers. 'If the heavens withhold their bounty, the Princeps will pour forth all the fruits of abundance over the earth' (*Panegyric,* XXXII, 2). A continuous line of walls and fortresses marked the frontier (*limes*), which was entrusted, from the second century onward, to the provincials themselves, as the citizens most interested in the defence of the border-lands.

So Rome lay immobile and secure at the centre of her interminable realm, out of reach of the hordes of any enemy, like a legendary symbol of eternal, invulnerable power. According to Aelius Aristides, the rhetorician of Pergamus, who elaborated the theory of universal monarchy during the reigns of Antoninus Pius and Marcus Aurelius, the fortifications of Rome are not to be found on the City precincts; her walls and her outposts are the provinces themselves.

To give more authority to such doctrines, it was alleged that they were derived from the works of the Pythagoreans and the Sophists.[6] The very same eastern lands which, in the early days of the Roman climb to power, had provided the most biting criticisms, the most skilful denigration of the glories of the Republic, are now the source of the warmest praise for an apparently indestructible empire – especially when defence, administration, and law are the subject of discussion. Superiority in spiritual matters is always reserved by implication for the Greeks. The reality achieved by the unitary government of Rome bore an increasing resemblance to the ideal City, somehow identified with the universe, which had occupied the minds of the political philosophers for centuries. The universe furnished the model for it – the rational organisation of both animate and inanimate nature, with its single substance subdivided into several elements and varieties – ether, water, earth, plants and animals. It was animated by a single spirit, moved by a single force. This is the real City of Justice, and reasonable men will for ever try to set up a city resembling it on earth – even if they can find no example of it in the past, even if their hope of seeing it in the future, except perhaps in Heaven, is in vain. The more men show themselves to be endowed with reason, the more they prove themselves to be men in the full sense of the word, and not mere bipeds; and similarly, the more the City is governed by just laws, the more it will be a City in the full sense of the word, and not a mere conglomeration. Such is the gist of a conversation which Dion of Prusa claims to have held with the Borysthenians – innocent savages of the type which the writers of those days used as examples of pristine simplicity (Dion of Prusa, *Orations*, XXXVI, 20–29; A.D. 95).

So the word 'City', according to the orator, means not just a group of human beings, but a union of rational creatures. The whole globe can be called a city, in so far as it is controlled by a divine Idea. The emperor, as the supreme head of the largest and most rational organisation in history, with princely largesses and honours – not to mention tax concessions – in his gift, is the representative on earth of that divine Idea, and carries out its intentions.

Behind a flowery screen of conventional phrases and exaggerated praise, the orators whose works have survived express the general views of the privileged classes in the eastern provinces of the Empire. In the West, the cult of emperor worship had already taken shape in the time of Augustus, but the emperors made a show of discouraging it, except for Caligula. The *divinitas* of the Princeps was described as a deplorable pretension on the part of Domitian, who loved to surround himself with servile courtiers, in marked contrast with Trajan, who refused to have temples, statues, or priesthoods consecrated in his name (Pliny the Younger, *Panegyric*, XLV, iii).[7] For a parallel to the hosannas sung to the emperors in this period by Asiatic orators we must wait for the works of the Gallic panegyrists at the end of the third century (A.D. 289–389).

The rhetoricians and panegyrists obviously belonged to the élite protected by the emperors. Amid the hymns of praise, however, they inserted vigorous though indirect criticism of the defects of the imperial government – the burden of taxation, the excessive power of officialdom, the secret police. Equally noticeable is the determination of the rhetoricians to induce the emperor to undertake ever wider measures of levelling. Discrimination between peoples, says Aelius Aristides, is a thing of the past; we are judged solely on merit. In the early decades of the second century A.D., Plutarch and Arrian, the biographers of Alexander, attribute similar principles to him, thus using his name to convey a hint to the rulers of their own day.

From the street corners and the schools, these ideas reached the imperial palace. Plato's dream came true – a philosopher was king. 'If all men have in common reason, moral sense and the law,' wrote Marcus Aurelius, 'then we are all fellow-citizens, and the world is as it were a single state (*Meditations,* IV, 4). At about the same time, a Christian author was coming to much the same conclusion: 'You will never be able to govern the State, if you do not know the fatherland of all mankind – the world' (Minucius Felix, *Octavius,* XVII, ii).

The masters of Hellenistic political thinking gave Rome full credit for having modelled her empire on the plan revealed by the Divine Mind in the structure of the Universe. As the spirit animates matter and directs it to higher ends, as the soul of man guides his limbs, so the emperor in Rome directs and rules the immense imperial organism.

This cosmological conception destroys the barriers between nations, cities and races. The walls that used to enclose the world of the Roman citizen, on both the civic and the religious planes, begin to crumble. The civilisation of humanity, which had begun as the typical product of limited communities, now spreads out into an *oikoumene.* The new citizen of the world takes the name of 'cosmopolitan'. Scholars no longer compile treatises merely on the subject of good government, or *politeia,* but turn to plans for a universal monarchy, or *basileia.* The fundamental theme of political writers is no longer love for one's native city, but the joy of belonging to a society which is a model of perfect reason. Political unification is now accompanied by the abolition of local religious feeling. The native gods lurking in the temples of each land are deprived of all their power by the cult of monarchical rule. The figure of the leading citizen, known personally to his people, faithful to the law, the defender of hearth and altar, disappears in favour of the inspired hero, the benefactor of all mankind, guided by mysterious voices, personally unapproachable. The links of family and class become relaxed. The moral forces of the individual are weakened by the absence of competition, and of recognition for personal effort. When ethics lays particular stress on loyalty to a vast collective body, there is a change in the psychological nature of the individual. He comes to feel that it is impossible to excel in so vast a community, that his personal worth is ill-recognised, and is in any case ill-adapted to face the difficulties of an existence increasingly dominated by distant, immeasurable forces.

'Mankind' is an emotive word, but too abstract to give the individual reason to feel himself an active participant in it. Men felt cut off from the solidarity of their race; they felt lost, as if no one were interested in them except a secret network of spies. Traditional morality no longer had any absolute value, even in individual relationships. Men were chained to a definite social class, a specific category of workers, from their birth, controlled by despotic functionaries, fleeced by inexorable tax-gatherers. They finished by putting all their hopes in the far-sighted provisions or the sudden generosity of a remote and inaccessible monarch, equally capable of a sudden increase and of an unexpected remission of taxes. On a more abstract plane, they began to put their hopes in the advent of a divine king, who would lift up the down-trodden, and act as intermediary between the troubled soul of the individual and the threatening powers above.

Utopian hopes of a millennium continued, invariably inspired by deep hostility to Rome. The official literature of imperial Rome was designed to banish such thoughts, as it had been since the time of Augustus. The emperors of Spanish origin who

190

reigned in the second century – Trajan, Hadrian, Antoninus Pius, Marcus Aurelius – were steeped in Greek culture but loyal to Roman traditional feelings. With their advent, the Empire became the instrument of the final revaluation of Roman culture. An ideological counter-offensive was attempted, a return to traditional religion. The virtues of the principate were exultantly proclaimed – the transmission of imperial power by adoption, ensuring a worthy succession; the modest exercise of supreme authority; the use of armed might only to defend the frontiers. It is this republican conception of absolute rule which gives the Antonine era its special brilliance in the eyes of rationalist historians.

Although constantly busy with the defence of the frontiers, the emperors from Nerva to Marcus Aurelius seem intent on erecting barriers against the rising flood of messianic expectation. Mystical dreams and hopes were opposed by the reality of an earthly fatherland of exemplary quality. The demands of a higher justice were met by a real mitigation of the rigours of the laws, largely due to Stoic influence. The timid were assured of effective national defence and guaranteed supplies of food. Waverers were offered an ideology which had no metaphysical vagueness about it, but balanced theoretical idealism with the realities of the Roman Empire. The proselytising of the Jews and the Christians had no effect on those emperors, and its advance was held up for another hundred years. Hadrian suppressed a further revolt of the Jews, as if he wanted to prove yet again that the rule of the proud city of Jerusalem would never become a historical reality. Power belonged to Rome; and the veneration of the nations was also due to Rome, not to the stubborn capital of Israel. The message of the literature of the second century is this: that Rome is the only City of Justice.

Although the visual arts continue to show us scenes of cruel servitude, the writers proclaim with one voice that all distinctions have vanished. 'You have given up the division of nation from nation, of Greek from Barbarians ... you have separated the human race into Romans and non-Romans,' says Aelius

191

Aristides (*To Rome*, 63). And again: 'Rome is to the whole world what an ordinary city is to its suburbs and surrounding countryside' (*ibid*. 61).

Caracalla's decision to grant citizenship to all the subjects of the Empire, in A.D. 212, therefore did nothing more than set the seal on a development for which the political and spiritual preparations were already complete. The new law was the result of the leaning of the Severi, who had little understanding of Roman tradition, towards religious syncretism and racial equality. It may also have been the effect of the young emperor's megalomania, or his wish to imitate Alexander, whom he admired to distraction, according to Dio Cassius (LXXVIII, 7, 4 and 8, 1). Or he may have wished to follow in the steps of Claudius, who had been born at Lyons, like Caracalla himself, and had been the first emperor to open the gates to foreigners. Again, he may have wanted to achieve that religious unification which was the necessary preliminary to the introduction of theocracy, and occupied the minds of all the emperors down to Theodosius. Or his motives may have been purely financial, as Dio Cassius maintains (LXXVIII, 9, 6).

Such are the motives attributed to Caracalla by the experts; but others can be added[8] – the wish to recruit provincials into the regular forces, instead of employing them solely as auxiliaries, or the need to gain the goodwill of the outlying territories at that particular moment. For this was a very difficult time for Caracalla, just after the murder of his brother Geta, a crime which certainly aroused the indignation of the ruling classes at Rome. Also he may have wanted to introduce standardisation of the Empire's administrative and judicial machines – a task of obvious urgency in view of the multiplicity of local regulations in the various cities. A papyrus discovered some time ago[9] contains a whole series of provisions designed to prevent or punish unauthorised social climbing. The document is dated A.D. 149 and is addressed to the inspectors of an Egyptian city; it lays down an interminable scale of fines and confiscations. Now the emperor, by the stroke of a pen, abolished the traditional distinction between classes, the thin-spun yet unbreakable barriers between the steps of a stairway at the top of which sat the Romans in triumph. The administration was simplified, the legal code unified, and racial groups who had recently been beleaguered enemies came under the direct control of the central government, instead of being exposed to the rapacity of local authorities.

True to the traditional methods of ancient historians, Dio Cassius finds room in his narrative for a discourse which can only be described as a political tract for his own times – but he presents it as a speech made by Maecenas to Augustus, many years before.[10] The first part is devoted to a point by point refutation of the speech before, which is supposed to have been made by Agrippa. Then his eloquence takes wing, however, and he begins to offer advice and warning that are perfectly well suited to the political atmosphere of the Severi, but cannot be derived from sources of the Augustan period, for they clearly belong to a later age. 'Appoint senators from other lands besides Italy,' Maecenas is supposed to have said to Augustus, 'from the allied and subject peoples.' They should not be treated as slaves or inferior beings, but invited to participate in government. 'Thus they will live, as it were, in a single city – the one to which we belong – and will consider this to be truly their city, while their present dwelling places will appear to them to be mere villages or hamlets' (Dio Cassius, LII, 19, 6).

The place where a man is born, or the place where he lives, from this point of view, is not his City. The City is that to which he belongs in spirit, that of which all men, even dwellers in the most distant hovels, are now citizens.[11]

The mutilated papyrus of Caracalla's edict may possibly refer only to soldiers. It does in fact refer to the admission to citizenship of those foreigners 'who may be found among my men'. But even in this short fragment we can trace the indefinite mysticism of the time, the desire of Caracalla to show gratitude to the gods – or to placate them – for granting him victory. What victory, is not specified – over the Germans, or over the alleged conspirators led by his brother? But he seeks to please the gods by leading to their altars a long series of conquered peoples.[12] Now the Capitoline gods had had to make room for Egyptian, oriental or other foreign divinities, which had received official welcome.[13] The alien cults had long been banned from Rome,[14] but now they obtained full recognition on a basis of equality with the traditional cults. And at the same time, the Roman gods, who had previously been confined to the Capitols of Italy, Gaul and Spain, migrated to the most distant regions – a highly significant process of exchange.[15]

Another development was the unification of the Law.[16] *Orbis Romanus* was from now on a term which could be used as an exact synonym for the vague geographical term *orbis terrarum*. In the eastern territories it was interchangeable with *oikoumene,* which had the same meaning in terms of living humanity, signifying the inhabited world, or human race. On the Arch of Galerius at Thessalonica, erected in A.D. 303, two female figures accompany Diocletian and Galerius. Their names are inscribed below – *Irene*, or Peace, lays a protective hand on the shoulder of her companion, *Oikoumene*. Such was now the accepted idea of the community to which the subjects of the Empire belonged. The equality of all citizens was becoming an ordinary fact of administrative life. The objections that had been raised to this process for so many centuries by those who looked back nostalgically to the primeval City were lost in oblivion. As the City extended her boundaries to the ends of the earth, she could give the title of citizen to all who lived within those limits. In the first two centuries of the Empire, the ideological process initiated by Augustus reached its fulfilment. To belong to the Roman community now involved a moral consciousness, accompanied by the pride of sharing in a unitary culture. The legend of the City of Justice seemed, to judge by the rhetoric of official literature, to have become a reality. The sacred furrow that had been traced around the narrow confines of the City, in a magical ceremony, now coincided with the fortified *limes,* the heaven-sent system of rivers –

Rhine, Danube, Nile, Euphrates – with which the gods had surrounded the Empire.

But for all its vastness, a City still exists, still enclosed by an outer wall. For though equality and brotherhood have really arrived, they only prevail within the boundaries. 'When you rightly desire the death of a man,' says St Ambrose, referring to the Goths, 'you may rightly demand usury from him; for it is no crime to kill him.'[17]

From the third century on, as the barbarian menace grows more immediate, the barbarian himself ceases to be seen as an innocent, pastoral being, and sinks to the level of an unpleasant phenomenon, ill-omened and ridiculous, but happily impermanent. He is described as cowardly, disloyal, ferocious and even insane.[18] Ammianus Marcellinus, in the closing decades of the fourth century, uses the word *civilis* for the first time in contradistinction to *ferinus*,[19] thus conferring an unquestioned moral superiority on the men of the City – which means members of the community of Rome.

The lunatic barbarians aim at destroying the order which Rome has imposed on mankind; attachment to the rule of law and the principles of civilisation grows ever stronger in the hearts of all citizens. The provincial subjects of Rome are mustered to man the defensive periphery which protects the capital (Aelius Aristides, *To Rome*, 84).

Apart from minor skirmishes on the frontiers, pacification is regarded as both final and universal. 'One day,' says Pliny the Younger, 'the Capitol will give welcome not to false representations of unreal victories, not to chariots drawn from the theatres, but to an emperor who brings with him a genuine, lasting victory, and real peace, and a total submission by our enemies, so that there will be no more foes to overcome.'[20] This is true *Romanitas* in literary form: *Noster orbis* is proudly contrasted with the lands of barbarism.

From Rome the Princeps watches over every part of the Empire, as the soul watches over the body.[21] Plotting against the *Pax Romana* is a crime deserving the harshest punishment;

alongside the works of art which illustrate Roman clemency toward the *subjecti,* we accordingly find others which show (with a significant coarsening of style) the harsh treatment meted out to the *superbi.* Attempts at reassuring propaganda can be seen in the coinage of Septimius Severus and his successors. VICTORIA AUGUSTA – SECURITAS PERPETUA – ROMA AETERNA are the inscriptions most frequently recorded in times of defeat, insecurity, and danger.[22] Arches, columns and coins all help to spread the doctrine of Roman supremacy. But this propaganda is not meant so much to drive home the idea of the racial superiority of the Romans, as to reassure the inhabitants of provinces exposed to invasion – to promise them the protection of Rome, to repeat that Rome is invincible, that the goddess of victory, the Sun, the Guardian Genius, Mars, Hercules and the other gods watch over her emperors and march at their side.

The universality and the eternity of Rome are again emphasised in various administrative decrees: in a proclamation regarding the official prices of foodstuffs issued by Diocletian in A.D. 301, the emperor, who has repulsed the barbarians, says that he wants to preserve forever a well-founded peace within the Empire, and that it is his duty to make provision not for a single city, but for the whole world (*C.I.L.,* III, 2, p. 824).

The literature inspired by the imperial court, in the third and fourth centuries, also bears traces of this theme, which in preceding centuries seemed to find expression only in the visual arts. The Gallic panegyrists of the period from A.D. 289 to 389, living in areas exposed to frequent barbarian raids, speak with inflexible harshness of the enemies of Rome. They denounce their ferocity and their unbridled behaviour, and rejoice at the sight of barbarian prisoners thrown to the beasts in the arena, or at the news of barbarian armies fighting each other.[23]

As for the Christians, they confine themselves to rebutting the pagan accusation that they have brought disaster on the public by their abandonment of the national religion. They raise no objections to the economic and social organisation of the Empire, and have no intention of subverting it. They put forward no schemes of civic reform, no objections to atrociously cruel legal sentences or to the institution of slavery. Their private moral system rejects the professions of the soldier, the actor and the gladiator, but conscientious objectors do not seem to have been a problem for society.[24] Later, when Rome made peace with the Church, in the reign of Constantine, and gave the Christians a momentary illusion that pagan hostility was now a thing of the past, they thought that with the advent of a Christian empire the Kingdom of Heaven had taken on an earthly form, with the emperor as the Vicar of God,[25] inspired by the *Logos,* and destined to guide the universal state in the way it should go.

If there is still a City of God, as the holy books affirm, separate from and standing above the earthly City, it can only be the Church – 'the City of all mankind . . . the faithful Sion, founded on a rock,' fully able to coexist and collaborate with the imperial authority, even, perhaps, to merge with it. The City of Eusebius is the universal City imagined by Plato, and transposed by Philo into the world of Judaeo-Christian thought. The Alexandrian philosopher conceived the universe as a 'Great City', built to a divine plan. Before its appearance in the real world, it had existed in the mind of God. This vast City, the fatherland of all mankind, the world, is but an earthly shadow of the heavenly design, obedient to a unitary code of law, which nature has implanted in the human heart.[26]

The centre of that universal fatherland can only be Rome. Rome was a symbol of supremacy; she was also, on the spiritual plane, disputed territory, fought over by opposed religions right up to the fourth century. Those who wish to deprive Rome of her original political and religious attributes were regarded by the nationalists as 'friends of the barbarians'. This term was applied to the Christians by Symmachus, the *Praefectus Urbi,* in A.D. 384, because they demanded that the Senate

197

should take down the statue of Victory. He went to Milan to implore the young Valentinian II to revoke the anti-pagan laws. He revived arguments typical of the narrow nationalism of republican days, before the coming of the universalist vision of the Empire. 'Everyone has his own habits, his own religious observances. The Divine Mind has given each city its own patron god to protect it. A soul is given to every man when he is born, and every people receives a Genius whose fate is linked to its own.'[27]

Rome herself, in the guise of a venerable, white-haired matron, is introduced to implore that she may be allowed to follow the religious traditions that enabled her to repel the Gauls and the forces of Hannibal from the Capitol.

But the Christians, through their spokesman, Ambrose, the Bishop of Milan, claimed to be better patriots than the pagan magistrate, and more accurate interpreters of the true feelings of the City, ascribing the credit for past victories not to the pagan gods, but to the heroes of Roman history – the valour of Camillus, the austere virtue of Attilius Regulus, the courage of Scipio.[28]

The controversy of A.D. 384 was revived twenty years later by Prudentius, a Spanish poet. It is a debate which has symbolic overtones, both because of its subject and because of the individuals taking part in it. The credit for past victories was due not to the native gods of Rome, but to Christ, who willed and fore-ordained the greatness of the City. Rome herself has received the greatest of all services from Theodosius, the Christian emperor, who has freed her from the dark super-stitions of the pagans. Now a new greatness awaits her. 'God, by Whose will thou dost rule, hath laid at thy feet all that is mortal ... without limit of time or frontier; He teacheth thee to reign without end.'[29]

In the same period, Claudian, the poet who sang the praises of Stilicho, exalts the fame of Rome as the mother of all nations. 'She has given a single name to the human race ... we are all one people.'[30]

NOTES TO CHAPTER

1. H. Mattingly – E. A. Sydenham, *The Roman Imperial Coinage*, Vol. II, nos. 87–9, 128.
2. Pliny, *Panegyric*, XVI, 3.
3. H. Mattingly – E. A. Sydenham, *op. cit.*, Vol. II, nos. 208, 447. See also A. Levi-Calò, *Barbarians on Roman Coins*, New York 1952.
4. Of the surviving statues, three are at the Museo Nazionale in Naples and seven at the Conservatori in Rome. See P. Bienkowski, *De simulacris barbararum gentium apud Romanos*, Cracow 1900.
5. H. Mattingly – E. A. Sydenham, *op. cit.*, Vol. II, nos. 321 ff., 276.
6. L. Delatte, *Les traités de la royauté*, Liége–Paris 1942. After a careful examination of the texts, the author exposes the forgery of certain treatises on monarchy, derived from works of the second and third centuries B.C., but actually written in the time of the emperors. See J. H. Oliver, *The Ruling Power*, in *Transactions and Proceedings of the American Philosophical Society of Philadelphia*, XLIII, 1953; A. Boulanger, *Aelius Aristides et la Sophistique dans la province d'Asie*, in *Bibliothèque d'Athènes et de Rome*, CCVI; E. R. Goodenough, *The Political Philosophy of Hellenistic Kingship*, in *Yale Cl. Stud.*, I, 1928, pp. 55 ff.
7. M. Hammond, *Pliny the Younger's Views on Government*, in *Harvard Studies in Classical Philology*, XLIX, 1938, pp. 115 ff.; K. L. Born, *The Perfect Prince According to the Latin Panegyrists*, in *Am. J. Philol.*, LV, 1934, pp. 20ff.; K. Scott, *The Elder and Younger Pliny on Emperor Worship*, in *Trans. Proc. Am. Philol. Ass.*, LXIII, 1932, pp. 156 ff.
8. V. Capocci, *La Costituzione Antoniniana*, in *Atti della R. Accad. dei Lincei*, CCCXII, 1925, series VI, Vol. I.
9. C. L. Sherman, *The Constitutio Antoniniana in the Light of the Gnomon*, in *Trans. Proc. Am. Philol. Ass.*, LIX, 1928, pp. 33 ff.
10. See M. Hammond, *The Significance of the Speech of Maecenas in Dio Cassius b. LII*, in *Trans. Proc. Am. Philol. Ass.*, LXIII, 1932, pp. 88 ff.
11. *Roma communis nostra patria* – Digest, L, 1, 33. This form of words was not one for solemn occasions only; it appears in the most prosaic sections of the *Digest*, such as XLVIII, 22, 18.
12. The *victae longo ordine gentes* prophesied to Aeneas – *Aeneid*, VIII, 722.
13. *Historia Augusta, Caracalla*, IX, 10–11. See also Aurelius Victor, *De Caesaribus*, XXI, 4.
14. J. Reville, *La religion à Rome sous les Sévères*, Paris 1886.
15. A. Castan, *Les Capitoles provinciaux*, Besançon 1886.
16. This is succinctly defined by Ulpian (*Digest*, I, 5, 17): *In orbe Romano qui sunt ex constitutione imperatoris Antonini cives Romani effecti sunt.*
17. St. Ambrose, *Tobias*, 51, *P.L.*, XIV, 816.

199

18. The commonest adjectives are *lubricus, fallax, levis, ferox*. See *Panegyrics*, II, xi, 15; III, xvi, 5; VII, x, 15; VII, xi, 25; IX, xxii, 20; X, xvi, 10.
19. S. Mazzarino, *Aspetti sociali del IV secolo*, Rome 1951, p. 27.
20. Pliny the Younger, *Panegyric*, XVI, 25.
21. Aelius Aristides, *To Rome*, 29.
22. H. Mattingly – E. A. Sydenham, *op. cit.*, Vol. IV, nos. 1, 2, 3; Vol. V, no. 1.
23. *Panegyrics*, IX, xxiii, 20–5; VII, xii, 20; III, xvi, 4; III, xvii, 25 and xviii, 15.
24. Tertullian, *De Corona, P.L.*, II, 111.
25. Eusebius of Caesarea, *Oratio ad Constantinum, P.G.*, XX, 1315. See N. H. Baynes, *Eusebius and the Christian Empire*, in *Mélanges Bidez*, Brussels 1934, pp. 13 ff.; R. Farina, *L'impero et l'imperatore Cristiano in Eusebio da Cesarea*, Biblioteca Teologica Salesiana, Rome 1967.
26. Philo of Alexandria, *On the Creation*, IV, 17–19; *On Joseph*, VI, 28–30. See also Plato, *Republic*, IX, 591.
27. Symmachus, *Relatio*, III, 10, *M.G.H.A.A.*, ed. Seeck, 1883, VI, 1.
28. St. Ambrose, *Letters*, XVIII, *P.L.*, XVI, 1014.
29. Prudentius, *Contra Symmachum*, I, 427–9: *Hoc Deus ipse Constituit, cuius nutu dominaris et orbi Imperitas et cuncta potens mortalia calcas. Ibid.*, 541–2: *Nec metas statuit nec tempora ponit: Imperium sine fine docet.* See Vergil, *Aeneid*, I, 278.
30. Claudian, *De Consulatu Stilichonis*, III, 151: *Humanumque genus commune nomine fovit;* III, 159, *quod cuncti gens una sumus.* See also Rutilius Namatianus, *De Reditu*, I, 14: 'The Senate does not regard as strangers those whom it accepts as worthy members'– *Nec putat externos quos decet esse suos.* This echoes a thought expressed a hundred years earlier to Constantine by a panegyrist: *Senatus dignitas non nomine quam re esset illustrior cum ex totius orbis flore constaret.*

XII

Social and Economic Disintegration

Every town was filled with tears and complaints, all calling out for the barbarians, and
imploring their assistance.

ZOSIMUS, IV, 32

THE DOCTRINE of *Romanitas*, which for many years provided
the Empire with its ideological basis, was itself based on concepts
of non-Roman origin, on specific factors of a historical or
geographical nature. But *Romanitas* was weakened by the very
vastness of the area it had to cover.

To judge from the surviving evidence, agreement with the
principles of the Empire came from certain privileged classes –
from orators with important government jobs, for example. But
cracks were appearing in the structure of the immense imperial
state, especially round its edges, which gave the lie to the proud
official propaganda. Let us pause for a moment to consider
some indications of the widening gap between the ideal fatherland described by the orators, and the hearts of ordinary citizens.
Even in the second century, when the Empire is described as a
truly providential system, the good deeds for which an exemplary
monarch such as Marcus Aurelius is praised are not so often
positive actions as abstentions from specially oppressive measures.
The emperor, we are told, does *not* demand recruits for the
army, does *not* inflict requisitions or special financial levies on
his people, even in time of war.[1]

These eulogies certainly reflect the anxieties of the *possessores*
of a later time – the period in which the imperial biographies

201

of the Historia Augusta were probably composed.[2] The praise of dead emperors was meant as a veiled warning to the living rulers. There is also plenty of direct evidence of the resentment felt by the underprivileged classes – those who derived from the Empire no social or economic advantage, no protection, and indeed no sort of motive for loyalty.

An inscription in Africa contains the text of a petition sent to Commodus by day-labourers working on government lands.[3] They describe themselves as *alumni* or *vernulae,* which means that they are the children of slave-women.[4] They suffer floggings, torture and forced requisitions to such an intolerable extent that they appeal to the emperor to protect them from his own servants. The end of the petition is ambiguous and threatening. This state of things must cease, they say, or 'we shall flee whither we may live as free men.'

Where were they proposing to go, these desperate peasants? Or those other peasants, in Asia Minor, who wrote to Septimius Severus a few years later, saying that if there were no change for the better, they would find themselves compelled to 'flee from the imperial lands, where they were born and bred'?[5]

Flight could only mean outlawry or exile; or was there perhaps some way of taking refuge with the wandering tribes on the frontier, and giving them useful information for the planning of raids? The growing unrest is not reported in contemporary works of literature, but can be traced in other documents. The vast frontier territories of the Empire seem to fray like a tattered cloth, and soak up the slime of barbarism. Nearer the centre, new plagues were added to the enemy raids, with the coming of social revolts. The Bagaudae – the peasants who took part in them – were described as two-faced monsters by the panegyrist of Maximian. From shepherds, farmers, or day-labourers they have turned themselves into warriors, taking up the sword and 'imitating the barbarians in the destruction of their own fields' (*Panegyrics,* II, iv, 3; A.D. 289).

The populations of the frontier territories spoke dialects full of barbarian words, often incomprehensible to the city-dwellers, whose advantages they did not share. Schools, theatres, baths, arenas were blessings unknown to them. Burdened by taxes, and tied to laborious tasks, to hereditary trades they were not allowed to leave, they were also compelled to pass their lives amid constant threats of disaster. They knew the barbarians primarily as raiders, but also through the exchange of goods, and through direct personal contact. This soon became a source of concern to their rulers. In the Roman scheme of things, the defence works on the ground ought to be backed up by an equally strong moral barrier. Controls were established over the relationship between those who lived on the inner side of the frontier and those who wandered beyond it. Limitations were placed on the use of markets open to both sides and permission to enter Roman territory was rarely granted. These measures reveal the fear that over-friendly relations might be established between the barbarians and their provincial neighbours, who might not have forgotten the blood-bond that linked them to the enemies of Rome.

This fear was strengthened by the knowledge that the treatment of the subjects of the Empire was extremely harsh. In the list of possible disasters, a visit from the tax-gatherer ranks alongside a barbarian raid. Bureaucratic officialdom grew more and more numerous and intrusive with the centralised state system of the Severi. In the third century, which was bedevilled by invasions, dynastic crises and famines, a final break took place between the ancient world, with the moral, social and political values on which it was based, and the new world which was emerging in a virtually medieval form. After this break there was complete separation between the distant City and her subjects, whom she now exploited without offering them any sort of ideal objective in return.

The generals whom the soldiers placed on the throne were now not only non-Italian, but non-European. Septimius Severus and Clodius Albinus were Africans, Philip was an Arab, Alexander Severus a Syrian, Maximian a Thracian – perhaps of Gothic descent. Often they rose to power from humble origins,

203

and were therefore more inclined to feel solidarity with the provincials than with the haughty families of Rome, who still had an anachronistic conviction that it was their right to give guidance to the emperor, to preserve their ancient privileges, and to insist on respect for their religion and their economic leadership from the provincials.

All the traditional ideas linked with the original conception of the City went into decline. Most of the seats in the Senate were now occupied by provincials from the East, who had been the last to be admitted to membership.[6] Barbarian attacks rolled back the most inviolable frontiers. In A.D. 238, the Goths crossed the Danube, and later forced their way on to Thessalonica. The Alemanni reached Milan. The emperors now lived and died on the battlefield. Philip the Arab fell at Verona, Decius and his son in Moesia; Valerian died as a prisoner of war in Persia. The conception of *Romanitas* as membership of an ideal fatherland slowly crumbled. When a separate Gallic state, tolerated by Rome, was set up under Posthumus, for reasons of defence, a local, provincial patriotism arose – or perhaps we should say revived. It went back to the view that a man's fatherland is the country where he was born, with its well-known boundaries at no great distance.

The Illyrian emperors made an attempt to regain the ground lost by these profoundly disruptive movements. But they put forward no new ideological formula, no political programme which could attract those who had lost heart. They could only try to find means of defending a disintegrating state, to find answers to the most urgent problems – the barbarian threat, the devaluation of the coinage, the chaotic state of the administration, the economic crisis. They did not offer a rebirth of the Roman ideal, nor a satisfying answer to the general agonised self-questioning. The most significant and symbolical event of those years was Aurelian's decision to surround Rome – now a capital city only in a metaphorical sense – with a new defensive wall. The threat was coming closer.

When Diocletian became emperor, the situation of the provincials was intolerable. We may suspect Lactantius of prejudice against a monarch who persecuted his fellow-Christians;[7] but there can be no doubt about the significance of the eulogies addressed to Constantine by the Gallic panegyrist a few years later, in A.D. 312. The emperor is thanked for remitting arrears of tribute, and for reducing taxes, in terms which suggest that such mercies were totally unexpected.

The panegyrists give a detailed description of the situation in the Gallic provinces – the insecurity of the *limes*, the social disorders, the piracy along the coasts, the destruction of the towns, the abandonment of the countryside. 'Fields never repay the cost of cultivation, and are abandoned; the farmers are crippled by debts and cannot provide for the drainage of the soil, or the clearance of the land from brambles; and so the fertile countryside is converted to a barren swamp' (*Panegyrics*, VIII, vi; A.D. 312). Vineyards overdue for replanting and unirrigated fields are also recorded. 'Everywhere we see abandoned farmland, full of weeds, bleak, deserted fields ... even the military roads are impassable' (*ibid.*, vii).

These pictures of Gaul can be paralleled by Cyprian's description of Africa, or the account of Bithynia left by Lactantius. All hope has gone of ever bringing back to life the active, harmonious society recorded in the fables of ancient authors. In their description of the horrors of their times, the Christians introduce a note of apocalyptic pessimism. 'The name of Rome, in virtue of which the world is governed today – I tremble to say it, but I must, for it will come to pass! – the name of Rome will be cancelled from the earth. Nor should we wonder that so solidly-based an Empire should one day crumble ... for all the works of mortal man are destined to perish.'[8]

Dismay reaches such a point that there are those who feel a desire for the coming of the barbarians;[9] this feeling is quite often openly expressed. It has also been noted that invasions invariably take place, with suspicious regularity, at times when written sources report a further harshening or deterioration in the administration. Either the defenders lost heart, or can it be that someone was inviting the enemy to invade, pointing out the gap in the walls, or the weak point of the fortifications? It is a legitimate inference, even if there is no positive evidence for it. We even find a panegyrist who expresses himself as follows (referring, in the usual way, to the disgraceful behaviour of the ruling class under the *previous* emperor): 'No one was safe from injustice and oppression, unless he had placated the ferocity of those rapacious villains with presents of gold. Men had reached the stage of wishing for the coming of the barbarians' (Mamertinus addressing Julian in *Panegyrics,* XI, iv, 5–10, in A.D. 362).

Ammianus Marcellinus reports various cases of defection and espionage on the part of citizens who had been driven by excessive taxation to regard themselves as enemies of their country.[10] Zosimus, the Byzantine historian of the following century, went even further when describing this period. Crushed by poverty and by the abuses of the officials, he says, 'every town was filled with tears and complaints, all calling out for the barbarians, and imploring their assistance' (IV, 32).

From time to time, revolts broke out, but were always savagely repressed. The inhabitants of Antioch rose in rebellion in A.D. 387, in fury over the imposition of an extraordinary tax. They overturned the statues of the emperors, which was an act of lèse-majesté that carried the death penalty. From the words of the Bishop of Antioch, who went to Constantinople to beg Theodosius to show mercy, we can see the compassionate understanding of the Church for the sufferings of the people. 'Neither the youth of the accused, nor the universal nature of the uprising, with the whole people joining in the revolt, nor their own promise never to offend again, had any effect. Without any possibility of escape, they were dragged to the place of execution. ... Their mothers followed far behind, gazing helplessly at their sons as they were dragged away, not daring even to weep.'[11]

The historical sources of this period show us a despotic regime, a greedy and inhumane bureaucracy, a mental climate of espionage, cruelty and superstition. Such is the society depicted by Ammianus Marcellinus. This author professes a formal reverence for the traditional ideology of the Republic; but he has no faith, no constructive ideals for the future, no sense of belonging to a community bound by moral obligations. The City is now nothing more than the home of useless, cruel amusements, abject corruption, ignorance, and frivolity. She still inspires respect because of her glorious past, but is no longer the cultural or political centre of the Empire, no longer the true capital of the world. For many years, in fact, the emperors had preferred to reside at Milan, at Trier (Treves), at Thessalonica, or at Constantinople, rather than at Rome, which had lost both its geographical significance as the centre of Empire and its spiritual ascendancy over other cities.

Ammianus Marcellinus paints a deplorable picture of the behaviour of the officials, aristocrats, and even plebeians. Many important centres in Germany are in the hands of the barbarians, he says (*Roman History,* XVI, 2, 12). Defence is hampered by desertions, by the decay of the fortifications, by under-manning of garrisons, by the close links between the population inside the frontiers and the barbarians without, and, finally, by a collapse in morale, which is never explicitly mentioned but is apparent on every page. Little significance can be attached to his literary nostalgia for the civic virtues of the ancient Romans,[12] or his conventional and insincere profession of faith that Rome will endure for ever.[13] These affirmations, like the ostentatious respect he shows to the Senate, are belied by the facts narrated in his history.

We become aware of facts never openly mentioned: that people exist who secretly collaborate with the barbarian invaders of the provinces; that ex-barbarian officers often desert, that the fortresses are being abandoned.[14]

The state of misgovernment is often betrayed by involuntary witnesses. The orator Themistius[15] expresses his joy that the new emperor, Theodosius, is a provincial, of humble origin.

For this at least means that he has shared the sufferings of his people and known their wrongs.

For this dramatic crisis, this spiritual void, the writers of the time can offer no remedy except literary moralising and nostalgia for the past.

The exchequer was supplied by a fiscal policy the abuses of which are denounced with one voice by authors of otherwise opposed views. Favouritism and extortion were common complaints. The legal code was meant to prevent both these abuses.[16]

The administration of each community was not so much entrusted to the municipal officials, *curiales,* as imposed on them. They were forced into office. Formerly, these posts had been elective, and there had been competition for them, in the old days when the municipalities were truly self-governing. But now everything was controlled from the centre, and office came automatically to everyone who possessed eight acres of land. It carried with it the duty of providing for the needs of the community – the execution and maintenance of public works, and the care of the fortifications. It also involved the very onerous obligation of satisfying the demands of the central government. The collection of taxes, and of food for the government pool; the recruitment of soldiers; the imposition of forced loans – all this weighed on the shoulders of these officials, condemned by birth to become instruments of the imperial tyranny, compelled to be cruel in defence of their own lives. The state in which they lived is sufficiently indicated by the terms of a law which was supposed to improve their lot : insolvent *curiales,* whether bankrupt in their private capacity or through the execution of their duties, were graciously exempted from torture by imperial decree.[17]

In these circumstances, it is easy to see why cadres of officials, ready to regard the service of their country as an honour, no longer existed. When Julian visited Ancyra, he was surrounded by citizens with petitions; some had been robbed, and some had been given the rank of *curialis* without good cause.[18] When

208

Valentinian was confronted with a serious short-fall in the yield of the taxes, and ordered that three *curiales* should be put to death in each town, doubt was expressed whether so many could be found.[19]

The *Codex* records about 200 edicts, from A.D. 313 onwards, which deal with every possible method of evasion that could be devised by the *curiales* to escape from the duties attached to their position (*Codex*, XII, i, 1–192). Attempts to join the imperial service, or to enlist in the legions, are foreseen, and even attempts to enter the Church. There are also measures to prevent them trying to escape by 'insolently assuming the mantle of a philosopher.'[20] The sons of a *curialis* must inherit the duties of their father, renouncing all personal ambition.[21] Those who desert may be taken back to their place of duty by force; though sometimes all that can be done is to brand them *in absentia* with the name of 'fugitive traitor'.[22]

Similarly, the soldier's sons are predestined to follow their father's profession. If they are naturally unfit, or have mutilated themselves to gain exemption, they are made to join the municipal service.[23] The penalties for desertion become harsher every year. In the end, the death penalty is decreed for hiding a deserter, while those who cut off a thumb to evade military service are to be burnt at the stake.[24] Recruitment of new troops, apart from soldiers' sons, meets with no less opposition. It was treated as a levy on family fortunes, rather than as an obligation on the class from which soldiers were drawn. As labour grew scarcer, landed proprietors clubbed together to furnish a single recruit between them, or to pay a joint fine in lieu.[25]

The service of one's country, whether as an official or as a soldier, had become something very like a forced loan. And every trade was now regimented into guilds, whose members were bound by the hereditary chain, and could not change their occupation or place of residence for any reason, nor stop work. They were not even allowed to marry outside their own category. All the trades which, in free societies, belong to the

O

artisan lower middle classes and reflect their spirit, their tendencies, their social conditions, were now regarded as forms of state service, to be strictly regulated. Farmer-settlers, dyers, miners, charcoal-burners, bakers, sailors on the grain run from Africa, were not treated as exercising a trade, but as carrying out a form of military service. If they ran away, they would be brought back to their duties by force, 'even if old and unfit,' according to the *Codex of Theodosius* (VIII, 5, 58). For certain categories of workers, such as those employed in arms factories, 'branding on the arm, as for military recruits', is prescribed by the *Codex of Theodosius* (X, 22, 4; law of A.D. 398).

Under this all-absorbing, oppressive system of state control, it is hard to see what forms of employment differ materially from slavery. Any break in a man's service, however temporary, was regarded as equivalent to desertion, and consequently deserving the punishment appropriate for crimes against the state. It is also hard to see who had any interest in the defence of a state which now offered neither protection nor economic security, and was becoming less and less of a cohesive element, less and less of an effective symbol of moral and ideological values.

Supplies of essential foodstuffs – grain, lard, and oil – were distributed free, on presentation of a personal identity token. But their arrival was becoming more and more uncertain, to judge by the security controls exercised by the state over shipping, and the harsh repression of banditry. 'The countryside is infested with bandits,' wrote Symmachus, the *Praefectus Urbi*, in A.D. 382.[26] An edict of the years A.D. 397 and 399 forbids men trained in the gladiators' schools to enter private service (*Codex of Theodosius*, XV, 12, 3). This indicates that many citizens had already started to form private armies on a small scale, for their own protection, as was a common practice in the Middle Ages.

In the fourth century, the countryside in many parts of Italy, even if still free from barbarian attack, already had the ruined appearance that characterised the Italian landscape in the following centuries. A law of 395 exempted large areas of Campania from taxation, because they were abandoned and uninhabited.[27] Later, rural depopulation was such that the government had recourse to the rarest of provisions, a general lightening of the tax burden.[28] The payment of imposts, the forced collections for the government pool, the duty of finding equipment for army recruits, the imposition of administrative duties on small land-owners, the debts caused by these obligations, the dangers of an isolated life in times of banditry and enemy raids, are all factors which help to explain why the less wealthy citizens were often prepared to renounce their property and their personal liberty and enter the service of the great landed proprietors. Valentinian I, who was always a prompt and vigilant legislator, was not slow to check this development, by imposing progressively harsher penalties. The series of laws entitled *De Patrociniis Vicorum*[29] runs from A.D. 360 to 415, and is designed to prevent farmer-settlers, merchants and small-holders from voluntarily ceding their land to their neighbours, in return for their general protection, thus evading the obligation associated with the ownership of real estate. 'The poor,' says Salvianus, borrowing a military term, 'surrender unconditionally to the rich.'[30]

What did the Empire offer, as compensation for forced loans and crippling taxation? Responsibility for defence had been handed over to the individual cities. Everyone, without any distinction of class, was compelled to contribute both money and labour toward the construction and maintenance of walls, fortresses, bridges and roads.[31] The subjects of the Empire were squeezed dry and left undefended. They were also exposed to a most grievous oppression in the most intimate matters of conscience, relating to their religious faith.

The need for religious unity was deeply felt by the emperors, because they were believers in the universal religion of the Supreme Being, and also because religious unity was an indispensable instrument of imperial government. (The adjective 'Catholica', applied to the Christian religion, may have had an influence on the conversion of Constantine.) Consequently they were even harder on heretics, schismatics, or dissidents than on pagans.[32] The reign of Theodosius was particularly marked by religious intolerance. Some of his laws had retrospective effect, which was against the principles of Roman legislation.[33] They encouraged officials and magistrates to constant vigilance, and admitted the use of informers.[34] The penalties were extremely harsh. The recalcitrant were not only forbidden to practise their religion in a different form from that approved by the emperor, but were deprived of the right to hold meetings, to make wills or to inherit property, to conclude contracts, to buy or to sell, or to live in towns. They were excluded from all public office. The stigma of heresy was inflicted on those who deviated from the orthodox doctrine in even the slightest details.[35] Books containing the teachings of the heretics were to be burnt, and anyone who preserved them from the flames was to be condemned for witchcraft.[36]

The owner of the house or land where a forbidden meeting took place was threatened with expropriation, fines or other penalties, which demonstrate the keen interest that the legislator took in breaking up potential nuclei of social revolt. From the very first appearance of the Arian heresy, its followers were designated as outlaws.[37] For Theodosius, the validity of the Nicaean Creed is part of the constitution.[38]

His objective was the same as Constantine's – to establish a uniform religion, that could provide the community with an ideological basis, when civic patriotism faded away. The final product was no less of a state religion than the pagan cult had been; the Church structure was imposed by the government, and guarded by the provisions of the *Codex*. Dissidents were treated as guilty of high treason. Official intransigence takes on a blood-chilling solemnity in a law of 407: 'We announce, in the first place, that heresy is hereby declared to be a violation of public law; for every offence against religion results in damage to the common weal.'[39]

The spirit of schism, in fact, sometimes merged into the spirit

212

of local independence, as in the case of the Donatists of Africa, whose rebellion against Rome lasted more than a century. Though a religious conflict on the surface, this revolt demonstrated, in a disguised form, the social and economic needs, the demand of moral renewal, the stirring of nationalism, which were beginning to find expression, more or less explicitly, in all the provinces.[40]

As if to emphasise the element of social unrest in religious revolt, bands of fanatics, called Circumcellians, began to prowl through the vast estates of Africa, intervening in the defence of slaves, tax-ruined farmers, and bankrupt victims of forced contributions. The importance of the part played in this schism by economic and nationalist factors is proved by the fact that the Donatists – although even more intransigent than the Italian Catholics – had not hesitated, in their zeal to find allies against Rome, to take advantage of the protection of Julian the Apostate, who was a pagan. 'When Julian, out of hatred for the peace of Christ, restored your basilicas to you,' writes St Augustine, apostrophising the Donatists, 'what massacres you committed! At that moment his devils rejoiced with you, from the open doors of your temples.'[41]

The Donatist bishop was stigmatised with the name of 'Gildonian' by St Augustine, because his hatred for Rome had led him to make common cause with the ferocious bands of Moorish rebels commanded by Gildo.[42]

Even in Rome itself, pagans rejoiced at successful invasions of the Empire. In A.D. 405, when Radagaisus the Goth thrust his way as far south as Florence, some Romans hoped that he would take the City, and restore freedom of religion. Years later St Augustine remembered the story of that invasion: how it might have led to the capture of Rome if Stilicho had not checked it; how, unlike the sack of the City by the Visigoths five years later, it might also have led to the revival of the suppressed religion. The saint was grieved by the attitude taken up by the Romans on the first occasion; but this is no longer a reason for surprise to Salvianus, a few years later: 'Are we to

213

wonder if the Goths are not driven back, when the Romans prefer to live with them rather than with us?'[43]

Desire for religious freedom and impatience with their economic burdens led most of the population to see the barbarians as something very different from the arrogant, frenzied savages of official imperial literature. They could, on the contrary, be regarded as liberators. So imperial defence is no longer merely a matter of fortifications – which the cities themselves were in any case left to maintain. It involved a vigilant watch on the personal relationships between barbarians and provincials. Valentinian issued decrees prohibiting commercial exchanges, loans,[44] and, of course, intermarriage.[45] The law entitled *Postliminium* provides for the recovery of property by returned prisoners of the barbarians; but it makes a distinction between those who were dragged off by force and those who 'went with the barbarians of their own free will.'[46] The legislator is aware of the number of voluntary expatriates, and denies repossession of property to those who can be described as refugees rather than prisoners.[47]

Valentinian put all his energies into the reinforcement of existing fortifications, the construction of new towers and forts at shorter intervals than before, to create an unbroken defensive line along the frontiers of all the most exposed territories. Acutely aware of the danger, he incorporated his officers' attendants into the fighting forces, recruited barbarians, and devised harsher punishments for self-inflicted wounds.[48]

Reverting to the traditional themes of ancient rhetoric, Symmachus, the pagan *Praefectus Urbi,* addressed an oration to the emperor, in which he pretended to believe that his concentration on military matters was aimed at the conquest of new territories, rather than caused by a far-sighted recognition of coming disaster. 'I will bid the Senate and People of Rome to send forth the *fasces* into the new provinces,' he says, 'and to select new magistrates to post to the lands beyond the Rhine,'[49] as if the days of colonial expansion were not past.

In February, A.D. 378, the Alemanni crossed the frozen

Rhine on foot. Valentinian's youthful successor Gratian managed to halt them in Alsace. It was the last Roman victory in that war-torn territory.

NOTES TO CHAPTER

1. *Historia Augusta, Life of Marcus Aurelius,* XVIII, XXI.
2. I refrain from quoting the participants in the long and complicated controversy about the exact dates and the precise degree of tendentiousness of the biographies collected under the name of the *Historia Augusta.* The resulting bibliography would be endless. It is enough to indicate that the view is now almost universally held that these biographies of the emperors were compiled by writers other than their supposed authors, at times subsequent to their supposed dates of composition, and that they are coloured by the religious, political and economic prejudices of the senatorial class.
3. *C.I.L.,* VIII, 10570, 14464. See M. Rostovtzeff, *Social and Economic History of the Roman Empire,* Oxford 1926, p. 349.
4. S. Gsell, *Les esclaves ruraux dans l'Afrique romaine,* Mélanges Glotz, Paris 1932, I, pp. 397 ff.
5. M. Rostovtzeff, *op. cit.,* p. 357.
6. C. S. Walton, *Oriental Senators in the Service of Rome,* in *J.R.S.,* XIX, 1929, pp. 38 ff.
7. Lactantius, *The Deaths of the Persecutors,* VII, xxi, *P.L.,* VII, pp. 204 ff.: (here the reference is to the persecution carried out by Maximian in A.D. 243). See also *Panegyrics,* VIII, xi, 15–20: *desperatio perferendi debiti etiam id quod dari poterat inhibebat.*
8. Lactantius, *Divine Institutes,* VII, 15, *P.L.,* VI, 787. See also Cyprian, *Ad Demetrianum,* V, *P.L.,* IV, 564.
9. Ammianus Marcellinus omits to mention that among the bands of Moorish rebels schismatic subjects of Rome were also to be found (*Roman History,* XXIX, 5, 10 ff.). But this is mentioned by St. Augustine, *Against the Letter of Parmenianus,* I, 10, 16, *P.L.,* XLIII, 46. See J. W. Mackail, *Ammianus Marcellinus,* in *J.R.S.,* X, 1920, p. 103.
10. Ammianus Marcellinus, XIV, 10, 7 (A.D. 354); XVIII, 5, 3 (A.D. 359); XXVII, 9, 6 (A.D. 368); XXXI, 6, 5 (A.D. 376).
11. St. John Chrysostom, *On the Statues,* III, a homily pronounced by Bishop Flavian before Theodosius, *P.G.,* XLIX, 56.
12. *Vetus illa virtus et sobria,* as he calls it in his *Roman History,* XV, 4, 3.
13. *Victura dum erunt homines Roma* – *Roman History,* XIV, 6, 3.

14. Ammianus Marcellinus, *Roman History*, XXIX, 5, 10; XIV, 10, 7; XV, 5, 5. This thesis is developed by E. A. Thompson in *Christianity and the Northern Barbarians*, in the volume by A. Momigliano, *The Conflict Between Paganism and Christianity in the Fourth Century*, Oxford 1963, p. 65. See also J. W. Mackail, *Ammianus Marcellinus, loc. cit.* in note 9 above; E. A. Thompson, *The Historical Work of Ammianus Marcellinus*, Cambridge 1947; C. Dubois, *Observations sur l'état et le nombre des populations germaniques dans la II moitié du IV siècle, d'après Ammien Marcellinus*, in Mélanges Cagnat, Paris 1912.
15. Themistius, *Oration VIII*. V. Valdenberg, *Les discours de Thémiste*, in *Byzantion*, I, 1924, pp. 557 ff.
16. *Codex of Theodosius*, VIII, 15, 6.
17. *Ibid.*, IX, 35, 6 (A.D. 399).
18. Ammianus Marcellinus, XXII, 9, 8 (A.D. 362).
19. *Ibid.*, XXVII, 7, 7 (A.D. 365).
20. *Codex of Theodosius*, XIII, 3, 7 (A.D. 369).
21. *Ibid.*, XII, 1, 7 (A.D. 329).
22. *Ibid.*, XII, 1, 119 (A.D. 388).
23. *Ibid.*, VII, 1, 5 (A.D. 364).
24. *Ibid.*, VII, 18, 1 ff. See also Ammianus Marcellinus, XV, 12, 13.
25. During each tax-farming period of five years, the emperor conceded exemption from the *capitatio* to all soldiers and their families. There was accordingly a preference for the enlistment of unregistered citizens. *Codex of Theodosius*, VII, 13, 7. See also S. Mazzarino, *Aspetti sociali del IV secolo*, Rome 1951, pp. 288 ff., 333 ff., and *La fine del mondo antico*, Milan 1959; and A. H. M. Jones, *The Decline of the Ancient World*, London 1966, pp. 64 ff.
26. *Letters*, II, xxii, *M.G.H.A.A.*, Vol. VI, 1, p. 49.
27. *Codex of Theodosius*, XI, 28, 2 (A.D. 395).
28. *Nov. Valent.*, I, 2 (A.D. 440–41).
29. *Codex of Theodosius*, XI, 24, 1.
30. *Dediticios se divitum faciunt* – Salvianus of Marseilles, *De Gubernatione Dei*, IV, viii, 34, *P.L.*, LIII, 102. S. Mazzarino, in *Aspetti sociali del IV secolo*, Rome 1951, pp. 258, 312, ascribes to the term *dediticius*, as employed by Salvianus, a medieval meaning of Celtic origin: that of 'vassal'.
31. *Codex of Theodosius*, VII, 5, 2 (A.D. 404) mentions the obligation to provide *buccellatum* (biscuit) for the troops. *Ibid.*, VII, 15, 1 (A.D. 409) mentions the obligation to cooperate in defence and in the maintenance of fortifications.
32. *Ibid.*, XVI, 5, 1–66.
33. *Ibid.*, XVI, 5, 7 (A.D. 381).
34. *Ibid.*, XVI, 5, 9 (A.D. 382).
35. *Ibid.*, XVI, 5, 28 (A.D. 395).
36. *Ibid.*, XVI, 5, 34 (A.D. 398).
37. Socrates, *Ecclesiastical History*, I, vi, 7. 'Recently,' writes the Bishop of Alexandria, 'there appeared in our diocese certain lawless men ...'

38. Council of Constantinople in A.D. 381; *Codex of Theodosius*, XVI, 5, 6.
39. *Codex of Theodosius*, XVI, 5, 40; *Sirmondianae Constitutiones*, 12 (A.D. 408).
40. See P. Monceaux, *L'église donatiste*, in *Rev. Hist. Rel.*, LX, 1909, pp. 1 ff.; LXI, 1910, pp. 20 ff.; LXIII, 1911, pp. 148 ff.; LXIV, 1911, pp. 21 ff. Also F. Martroye, *Une tentative de révolution sociale en Afrique*, in *Rev. Quest. Hist.*, LXXVI, 1904, pp. 353 ff., and LXXVII, 1905, pp. 5 ff. And see W. H. C. Frend, *The Donatist Church*, Oxford 1952.
41. St. Augustine, *Against the Letters of Petilianus*, II, lxxxiii, *P.L.*, XLIII, 316.
42. St. Augustine, *Against the Letter of Parmenianus*, II, ii, iv, and XV, *P.L.* XLIII, 51, 56, 76.
43. Salvianus of Marseilles, *De Gubernatione Dei*, V, viii, 104, *P.L.*, LIII, 102.
44. *Codex of Justinian*, IV, 63, 2; IV, 41.
45. *Codex of Theodosius*, III, 14, 1.
46. *Codex of Theodosius*, V, 7, 1; *Digest*, 49, 15, 20, 26; *Institutions*, VI.
47. *Digest*, 49, 15, 19.
48. *Codex of Theodosius*, XV, 1, 13; VII, 13, 4, 5 (A.D. 367). See also *Ammianus Marcellinus*, XXIX, 6, 2; XXX, 7, 6; Zosimus, IV, 12.
49. Symmachus, *Oration*, II, 31, *M.G.H.A.A.*, VI, 1, p. 329.

217

XIII

Spiritual Factors in the Crisis

One day the blow that thou hast deserved, O
proud-necked Rome, shall fall on thee from
Heaven.

Sibylline Oracles, VIII, 37

As THE territorial extent of the Empire increased, and as its
defences and administration were unified, an attempt had been
made to create a patriotism wide enough to embrace the whole
world. 'What allies can you hope to find?' King Agrippa asked
the Jews, when urging them to abandon their resistance. 'Will
you search for them in the depths of the wilderness? In the
inhabitable world, you will find no one who is not a Roman.'[1]

But this concept could act as a binding force only at the
social level of a culture transcending national differences. Among
the lower classes, an ideal could be inspiriting only if it offered
the prospect of a better future. In the complete absence of the
element of hope, a gloomy certainty crept into the hearts of
men – the certainty that this world did not offer a country to
which a man could belong. The idea of a society of equals came
to seem an empty fraud. It was replaced more and more by
the feeling of belonging to a spiritual country, sometimes identified with Israel and sometimes with the heavenly abode of the
Divine Father. In accordance with the two views just mentioned,
it could be put forward either as a place of refuge with a
definite geographical location, or as the final goal of man's
earthly pilgrimage.

Thus certain unseen forces again came into play – the same

218

religious forces which, in the days of Julius Caesar and Augustus, had made the Romans fear the propaganda of Mithridates and, later, of Cleopatra; the same which had made them detest the proselytising tendencies of the Jews and, later, of the Christians. Mysterious exhortations forbade the faithful to despair: 'The God of Heaven,' in the words of Daniel, 'will set up a kingdom that shall never be destroyed.'[2]

The message of Judaism continued to spread, and with it the certainty that the empire of Rome, like all empires founded on violence and injustice, would come to an end. For centuries the prophets of Israel had encouraged the people not to despair. The God of Israel may indeed from time to time inflict punishments on the faithful – but the very names of their successive oppressors among the nations shall perish from the earth. 'The swords of the enemy have failed unto the end: and their cities thou hast destroyed.'[3] Those believers who remain true to the laws of their God will be rewarded; but the Lord will sweep away their enemies 'like dust before the wind, like the dirt in the streets', while the chosen will be carried away to a safe haven, to 'a place of pasture and waters of refreshment'.[4]

The books of the Bible continually speak of heavenly abodes, where those who are humiliated today will see justice done and will be comforted. The description of those tranquil retreats is very realistic, in the vivid language of the prophets. Many may well have thought that the regions portrayed really existed, and that events would prove the truth of the prophecy that 'evildoers shall be cut off; but they that wait upon the Lord, they shall inherit the land.'[5]

A holy mountain, with tabernacles rising on its summit, is the dominating image in the minds of the faithful, and their wavering steps are directed towards it. War, disease, persecution and natural catastrophe have no terrors for the chosen, because the horrors of this life are counterbalanced by a vision of peace: 'The stream of the river maketh the city of God joyful. . . . Nations were troubled, and kingdoms were bowed down. . . . We will not fear, when the earth shall be troubled,

219

and the mountains shall be removed into the heart of the sea.'[6]
On high, seated on this throne, the Lord reigns 'in the city of our
God, in his holy mountain.'[7] The kings of the earth will be
confounded, and the triumph of the just will be shared by all
who have believed in 'the city of the Lord of hosts, the city of
our God. God hath founded it for ever. . . . Surround Sion,
and encompass her: tell ye in her towers. Set your hearts on
her strength, and count her palaces, that ye may relate it in
another generation. For this is God, our God.'[8]

There is an increasing urgency, a growing precision, about
the descriptions of the country which is not of this world: 'The
foundations thereof are in the holy mountains. . . . Glorious
things are said of thee, O city of God.'[9]

The ancient hatred of East for West, together with the
certainty that Jerusalem will triumph over the nations of the
earth, resounds in the words of such prophecies. The ways in
which they were understood by those who heard them varied
between the universal sense, acceptable to anyone with a longing
for justice, and a narrowly nationalistic interpretation. The
main theme of the Sibylline writings produced in Asia is always
purification by catastrophe – a catastrophe from which the
world will emerge free of imperfection and injustice. But once
political power – and its natural consequence, economic oppression – were associated with the name of Rome, Rome became
almost the sole target for all these anathemas.[10]

The series of anathemas continues through several historical
periods. Some range from the time of Mithridates to that of
the Second Triumvirate; others belong to the period of the
Jewish revolt against Nero, or in the time of Titus or Hadrian.
The theme is always the same: 'A Blessed One shall descend
from the clouds of Heaven, sceptre in hand, and shall destroy
the cities with fire' (*Sibylline Oracles*, V, 415).

The curse of God shall fall on the city of vice and oppression,
the new Babylon: 'One day the blow that thou hast deserved,
O proud-necked Rome, shall fall on thee from Heaven'
(*Sibylline Oracles*, VIII, 37). 'No more shall the Greek, the

Barbarian or the Syrian bow his neck beneath thy yoke; thou shalt be utterly destroyed.'

In its turn, the language of the Gospels – which, when first heard, was only one voice in the chorus of popular mystical literature – drives home the certainty of the early coming of a kingdom based on moral principles contrary to those prevailing in this world. 'You shall not pass through all the cities of Israel, before the Son of Man comes. This generation shall not pass, until all these things be done.'[11]

From the dark ecstasy of the imagination of Israel arises the vision of the Apocalypse. The woman clad in purple and scarlet, laden with gold, precious stones and pearls, Babylon, mother of fornication and abomination, drunk with the blood of the martyrs, is none other than Rome. Her power is based on the forces of evil, and all the people of the world obey her. But the time will come when all the plagues will fall upon her in the space of a single day – death, and mourning, and famine.[12] From the most distant countries the smoke of the fires shall be seen; she shall be consumed by fire.[13] The seer rejoices at her ineluctable punishment, and predicts in detail the appearance of the City after the passing of her glory: the grinding of corn shall be heard no more, nor the sound of harps and lutes, nor shall any craftsman of any art whatsoever be found, nor shall the voice of the bridegroom and the bride be heard any more.[14]

But after the destruction and the flames, Heaven and earth will pass away, and calm will follow. The prophet sees the Heavenly City, the New Jerusalem shining in the newly-purified sky; she is free from mourning and from tears. Her walls shine like jasper, and she is bathed in unceasing, unchanging light.[15]

This personal vision coincides with the ideas of stubborn racial patriotism held by the Jews. In the midst of the Empire, the little groups of Jews regarded themselves as no more than guests of the Roman cities – though they claimed the full rights of residents. They always sent their annual tribute of an obol to Jerusalem, which they still considered their capital. The Jews, says Philo of Alexandria in the first half of the first century, are present in great numbers in all the Roman cities; but for them 'the Holy City, where the temple of the Most High God stands, is their mother' (*Against Flaccus,* VII, 46).

The temple of Jerusalem had been profaned by Pompey, and robbed by Crassus; and yet, when revolt broke out, in the reign of Nero, it was still the centre of spiritual resistance. 'The most obstinate rebels gathered there,' says Tacitus (*Histories,* V, xii). When Vespasian was sent to put down the rebellion, he saw at once that it was no mere local episode. 'The Jews had summoned many warriors to battle . . . some of them from neighbouring countries. Their co-religionaries dwelt not only within the Empire, but also beyond the Euphrates' (Dio Cassius, LXV, 4, 3).

Many Jews made their way home, when the revolt came. It seemed as if reality were about to be given to the vision of vengeance for the oppressed, which the Psalmist had so often sung. Those who accepted the creed of Israel accepted a universal call to justice and revenge. But Judaism, unlike the sects of the philosophers, was intolerant of other patriotisms and of other cults:[16] it insists on contempt for national religions. This is why even men of conscience like Tacitus approved the persecution of the Christians under Nero. ('Criminals who deserved extreme and exemplary punishment,' the historian calls them – *Annals,* XV, xliv.)

Christians and Jews differed from the other subjects of the Empire. They were reserved, chaste, unwilling to participate in civic affairs. Military successes and the glory of Rome were no concern of theirs. Their eyes were on a future revelation which often seemed imminent; their hearts thirsted for a City of Justice, different from the cities of this world. They were vigorous proselytisers, and this activity spread an atmosphere of expectation, which gave almost any happening the quality of a portent. The great fire of Rome might appear the sign for which the messianic hopes of Jews and Christians were waiting; they expected a purifying holocaust.[17] The years in which the new faith began to spread were years of widening emotional excitement. Under Nero and Vespasian,[18] prodigies and prophecies multiplied in every province of the Empire. Centres of aggressive local nationalism sprang up here and there in every region, accompanied by outbreaks of religious fervour. Sacred writings and prophetic priestesses foretold coming disasters, and spoke of the future triumphs of unknown heroes, the product of unrest among the multitudes.[19] In Britain, 'Women excited to frenzy prophesied impending destruction' (Tacitus, *Annals,* XIV, xxxii); in Gaul, the Druids[20] foretold the triumph of revolution (Tacitus, *Histories,* IV, liv). Even Spain, the province which had been the first to submit to Rome, and was generally the least turbulent of her territories, had prophetic books full of nationalist ambitions hidden away in the depth of her temples, according to Suetonius (*Life of Galba,* IX, 2).

The whole Empire was shaken by tremors of revolt, 'And indeed the civil war, which beginning in Gaul and Spain, and afterwards, drawing into the struggle first Germany and then Illyricum, had traversed Egypt, Judaea, and Syria . . . now that the whole earth was, as it were, purged from guilt, seemed to have reached its close (Tacitus, *Histories,* IV, iii).

The rebellions sprang from the intolerable burden of tribute, or from the brutality and maladministration of the imperial officials. But there were marked differences between one province and another.

The western rebels made specific demands and had a realistic vision of the political and military situation of the Roman world. The Batavians finally gave up resistance, realising that 'the servitude of the whole world cannot be averted by a single nation . . . if we meant to challenge to battle the Roman people, then what a mere fraction of the human race are the Batavi!' (Tacitus, *Histories,* V, xxv).

But there was no such realism in Israel. Her revolt was inspired by books of great antiquity, which promised an early general uprising, to be unfailingly accompanied by the transfer

223

of earthly power to the Holy City. Josephus, a Jew who collaborated with the Romans, condemns the fanaticism of the Zealot extremists, and puts a speech in the mouth of Agrippa II, the Roman-protected king, which is full of counsels of prudence, of advice to submit. How many countries have already submitted to the Romans, though defended by natural barriers, endowed with vast wealth, or strong in the possession of innumerable hordes of warriors! Wise words indeed, but not calculated to persuade those who are convinced that God is on their side, who regard their enemies as damned and their own capital as a Holy City, destined to emerge intact from the ruins of the world.

The enmity of the Jews was based on religion. Their God intervened incessantly to modify the course of events. History, for them, consisted of a series of linked happenings, governed by the divine will, and destined to end in the inevitable triumph of the elect.

There was a very ancient prophecy which foretold that, in the struggle between the power of Rome and the power of Asia, a 'man out of Judaea' would have the upper hand.[21] The Romans regarded the prophecy as fulfilled when they saw imperial power conferred on Vespasian and Titus, the generals who had in turn won victory in Judaea. But the Jews, unshakable in their certainty, continued to find support for the spirit of resistance in it. While the Jews were closely besieged, a miracle took place which often recurs in the pages of ancient historians. 'The doors of the inner shrine were suddenly thrown open, and a voice of more than mortal tone was heard to cry that the gods were departing. At the same instant there was a mighty stir, as of departure' (Tacitus, *Histories*, V, xiii).

It was traditional for the local gods to abandon a country which was about to disappear as a national entity, and for those gods to be absorbed by the victors. But in the case of the God of Israel, the conquerors did not so much place him in their own pantheon to be assimilated as a newcomer, but rather themselves slowly passed beneath his yoke. When Titus became emperor, he had to give up Berenice; his attachment to her, and his troops' devotion to him, were responsible for the rumour that he intended to found a new empire in Asia, to rival the Empire of Rome (Suetonius, *Titus*, V, 2, 3). But a fear remained latent in the hearts of the Romans, and came to fresh life every so often – the fear of seeing a second capital arise in the East, to deprive Rome of her supremacy. 'I *have* returned!' said Titus again and again to his father (*ibid.*), when he came back from Judaea, as if to reassert his loyalty to the City of the Tiber and her heritage of political and religious ideas. His words were really addressed to the wider audience of the Roman people, who had perhaps been afraid that the heir to the Empire would settle in Judaea as Antony had settled in Egypt – trapped, to outward appearance, by his passion for a woman, but probably lured even more deeply by the flattering hope of a power founded on a non-Roman ideology.

The keen awareness shown by Titus of the dislikes of traditional circles at Rome can also be seen in his abandonment of the ancient custom whereby the conqueror assumed the name of the conquered country. Coriolanus, Africanus, Germanicus, Britannicus were titles which symbolised for the heroes of the past the glory of conquests and annexations. But on the coins of Titus we find only the words IUDAEA CAPTA.[22] And on the arch erected in his honour the title IUDAICUS is missing, because it would have meant 'the convert to Judaism' rather than 'the conqueror of the Jews'.

The law is the chief manifestation of a social entity incorporated in a City. To give another law priority over one's own is to confess that one belongs to another country, and to show that one has a different scale of moral principles. Roman hostility to the Jews was caused precisely by their tenacious attachment to their own law. 'They have no respect for the Roman laws, but learn and hold in awe the code which has been handed down in a mysterious volume by Moses,' says Juvenal.[23]

With the spread of Christianity, the converts recognised the

225

authority of the Decalogue of Moses, and neglected the law of Rome, in the certainty that its day was almost past. 'The laws of Caesar are different from the laws of Christ,' announces St Jerome, at the end of the fourth century, 'and Papinian prescribes one thing, while our beloved Paul prescribes another.'[24]

The Jews were superbly confident of their own superiority, and their laws were neither drawn up by specially appointed citizen-legislators, nor adapted by stages to match the changing fortunes of their City. They were never discussed, approved or rejected, in keeping with the varying success of opposed economic and social forces; never modified by the pressures of an ever-widening drive towards improvement. Their laws had been dictated by the Almighty once and for all on Mount Sinai. Moses had transmitted to his own people and to all men the Commandments which sprang from the Divine Mind, and are not transitory nor subject to emendation, but eternal. For they are directed to the human spirit in its universal aspect, the same for all peoples. They are not meant for one particular political community, but for the supreme City, of which all men are citizens. These laws have nothing to do with history; it would have been too lowly a task for the prophet of Israel to write the story of a City built by human hands. And so the Bible begins with the Genesis of the universe, which is the Great City, and the laws of Israel portray the statutes of the world.[25]

Jerusalem, then, stands for the heavenly City, reduced to human scale. To belong to her is to accept the Divine Order. Jesusalem is the Holy City because the Temple is there, but she is also significant in other ways. 'The City of God in one sense is the world; but in another sense it is the wise man's soul,' says Philo of Alexandria, echoing Plato (*On Dreams*, II, xxxvii, 248). Hers is the only genuine law; for it is eternal, rational and universal. All the just surrender to it willingly; for it proceeds directly from the mind of God, and strikes root in every heart.

When it spread beyond the borders of Palestine, this faith

found acceptance in the hearts of men already prepared for a universal message by the thinkers of Greece, whose philosophy of history they adopted, together with the hope of being able to migrate some day to the capital of the spirit.

The call of the ideal becomes louder and clearer as conditions of life deteriorate throughout the Empire, the much-vaunted 'fatherland of all mankind'. The City of the Spirit becomes remote both from the Roman capital and from the Great City of the philosophers. This is no longer the City of all men, governed by a unitary code of law, inhabited by citizens with the same rights, and the same faith; the City of whose coming Cicero and Seneca had dreamed many years earlier, and on whose achievement the emperors had congratulated themselves when they set up the Roman *oikoumene*. All this is transcended by the City of the Soul, which comes closer to realisation as its links weaken with the earthly City, cursed with so many misfortunes. Whether it is seen as the immaterial home of the blest in heaven, or as the spiritual brotherhood of all those who believe in righteousness on earth, the new City does supply what the rationalist system lacked – a tincture of emotion, a thrill of hope.

The experience of the Essenes and the teaching of Christ led men to lay up their treasure within. In the *Epistle to the Hebrews*, Paul speaks of the faith of Abraham, who felt himself to be a stranger on this earth. 'For he looked for a city that hath foundations; whose builder and maker is God' (*Hebrews*, XI, 10). The apostle exhorts his readers to leave their camp – their temporary uncertain abode, since that is what this life is – and 'go forth therefore to Him without the camp. . . . For we have not here a lasting city, but we seek one that is to come' (*ibid.*, XIII, 13–14).

In the *Epistle of Barnabas* – a work of unknown authorship, written between A.D. 120 and 130 – the formalism of the Jews and their external observances are attacked, in the name of a philosophical revaluation of their religion. The City and the Temple lose their material substance, their historical meaning,

227

and take on a symbolical significance. They are no longer buildings of stone, but dwellings of the spirit. When God gave men the gift of prayer, he opened their lips, and the lips of man are the doors of the Temple of God. When he taught man repentance, 'he introduced him into His incorruptible Temple' (*Epistle to Barnabas,* 16).

These earliest Christian writings are not yet free from the bonds of Semitic tradition, from the oriental cast of mind. They admonish their readers not to be amazed : all their sufferings had been foretold by God. In the last days before the coming of the end, says Barnabas, 'God will abandon to destruction the sheep of his flock and their sheep-fold. Then seek we to see whether the Temple of God still exists ... it does, it does ! in the place where he has sworn to build it, in our hearts' (*ibid.,* 16).

The *Shepherd of Hermas,* the work of a Jew who had been taken to Rome as a slave, is a long, rambling, mystical divagation. This visionary also speaks of 'imminent tribulations', foretold by prophetic dreams. 'This world,' he says, 'is fated to perish in fire and blood.'[26] He emphasises the concept of the heavenly fatherland, invites his readers to desert the City of this world. 'As servants of God, you know that you are dwellers in a foreign land; your own country, in fact, is far from here. If therefore you know about your own City, where one day you will go to dwell, why do you buy land, or expensive furniture, palaces or sumptuous habitations here below? They who make purchases in this City, do not intend to return to their true country. ... The master of this land would have a right to say to you : "Keep my laws, or leave my country." And then what will you do, being a follower of another law, the law of your City? ... You live in a foreign land, so do not buy anything which is not strictly necessary to satisfy your real needs; and be always ready. Thus on the day when the lord of this City wishes to expel you for disobedience of his laws, you will leave his domain without loss, light of heart, and make your way to your own land and abide there in accordance with your own law.'[27]

These ideas were current in the thinking of the Stoics during the same period – Marcus Aurelius and Epictetus,[28] for example. A few years later, Plotinus was to make them his own. 'Let us therefore flee towards our beloved fatherland . . .' he writes, 'but how shall we flee? What path shall we take? . . . Our fatherland is there from whence we came, there where our Father is . . . and neither our own feet . . . nor any carriage can help us on the journey.'[29]

The more impermanent earthly things seem to be, the more men turn to a purely internal vision for their scale of values. We are not a foreign people like the Jews, say the Christians, not a racial bloc anchored to its land of origin. The citizenship of Christianity is a spiritual thing, and any man can form part of its community. 'Any man can be admitted to the law of God,' says Tertullian.[30] Men brought up on the idea of the Roman *oikoumene* could feel how incompatible the divine message is with the narrow strictness of the Jewish creed; they abjured every form of racialism. 'There is neither Gentile nor Jew, circumcision nor uncircumcision, Barbarian nor Scythian, bond nor free.'[31] This is the humanity that unites all hearts, the spontaneous, unconscious fellow-feeling which the Stoics had recognised long before in the universal compliance with the laws of Nature. 'The nature of man,' says Tertullian, 'is the same in all peoples. Names and languages vary, but the soul is always the same.'[32] It is the brotherhood of all souls, bound together by the common citizenship of the faith – with a perceptible tinge of Stoic cosmopolitanism : 'We recognise a single republic – the republic of all mankind, the world.'[33]

Despite an occasional hint of loyalty to the emperor,[34] this universalist attitude betrays a withdrawal of man's inward being from a political entity which is known to be doomed to perish. Persecutions grew harsher and invasions grew fiercer during the anarchic third century, ravaged by plague and famine; and the most venerable institutions were in decline. And so pro-

229

vincial Christian literature took on a more and more specifically anti-Roman character, observing the misfortunes of the Empire with something not unlike satisfaction, as undoubted signs of the imminent rebirth of the world. Men waited, in growing expectation, the coming of the kingdom promised by Christ. 'The Lord will not come,' they said, 'until the Empire has fallen.' Its fall was inevitable, heralded by the decadence of all creation. Do you not see, writes Cyprian, how the fertility of the fields has decreased, together with the productivity of the fruit trees – how the ore in our mines, the marble in our quarries, is declining? It is not the Christians' fault, if the world itself has grown old, and lost its vigour, showing, by the deterioration in its material products, that its end is at hand. As the end of time approaches, disasters multiply, unprecedented catastrophes take place. On the eve of the Judgement, the wrath of God grows fiercer, as He smites humanity with plague after plague.[35]

In that tragic third century, the imminent end of Rome was announced by prophetic voices everywhere, but especially in the African provinces. Nothing, however sacred it had been in earlier days, could resist that fiery eloquence. Cobwebs began to cover the gods, who would soon crash from their pedestals of marble. Even the laws, which in those very decades were beginning to take on their final, universal form, were described as unjust and impermanent, because they served to condemn the innocent. The terms used in ancient Semitic literature reappear as the Christian writers rally together against Rome – as in the famous 'Great Babylon' of the Apocalypse (*Revelations*, XVIII, 2).

The texts of the Jewish 'Oracles of the Persian Sibyl' begin to circulate again, and the Christians revive the prophecies of Israel, with the message that the proud domination of the oppressors will collapse. The purifying catastrophe is near at hand.

Commodian, an African or Syrian[36] writer of the middle of the third century, whose Latin already shows signs of decadence, expresses the fervent expectation of the oppressed. The citizens of Rome mistakenly think that they are safe, distant as they are from the areas afflicted by invasion, protected as they are by a vast natural barrier. (Perhaps Commodian was writing before Aurelian had built the great walls around the capital which betray the well-founded fears of the ruling classes.) The citizens still did not realise that there were men in the distant provinces who hoped for the collapse of the defensive line, and savoured in advance the pleasure of seeing the City herself finally invaded. 'Then the senators will weep in their bonds; they will curse the chains with which the barbarians load them.' Then it will be seen how unreal and fragile was the power of the earthly City, how unfounded her pride. 'She who boasted of being eternal shall weep for all eternity.'[37] There will be an end for ever to the power that is based on bloodshed, and maintained by the exaction of iniquitous tributes. Every day brings a new clarity to the Psalmist's vision of the Holy City, which is set is contrast with the City of Rome. 'The City will descend from Heaven. Rain and frost will not touch her golden mansions. There will be no siege, no sack, such as we see today. Nor will the City need the light of lamps, for she will shine with the light of her Builder.'[38]

Some scholars think that Commodian was a contemporary of Arnobius. In that case, the episodes he describes belong to the ten years which ended with the defeat and death of the persecuting emperor Decius.[39] Invasion, plague and famine rode through the land, and the Christians were inevitably accused of responsibility for these disasters. This led them to adopt a particular mental attitude in relation to history – one of self-justification. They traced a teleological connection in each series of events, and attributed a recondite, heavenly cause to every happening. They minimised the extent of the public calamities, or repeated the argument that all men are fated to suffer, that misfortunes occur everywhere, in every period. This is the message of Arnobius, and also the message repeated a few years later by his pupil Lactantius, who echoes the Jewish and Persian oracles which foretold the coming of a great flood or fire, to mark the

231

end of an historical epoch.[40] The Fathers of the Church give a symbolical interpretation to the stories of the Bible. The flight into Egypt signifies the end of the world, when a small number of the elect will be saved. In the *Book of Daniel* there is an old prophecy, expressed in the interpretation which the prophet put on Nebuchadnezzar's dream (*Daniel*, II, 31–45 and VII, 1–14). The king had seen a statue with a head of gold, a breast of silver, a belly of bronze, and feet of iron. Later, the prophet saw four symbolical beasts, one after another. This was interpreted as referring to four successive reigns, which would be followed by a fifth, which 'would never be destroyed in all eternity.'

The kingdoms were supposed to be those of the Chaldeans, the Medes, the Persians and the Greeks.[41] The fifth reign, according to the ambitious ideas of the Jews, would be the eternal dominion of Israel. This vision is typical of the period in which the nationalist reaction under the leadership of Judas Maccabeus, in the second century B.C., inspired the Jews with fresh hatred against the Western powers of Macedon and Syria. In the version of the Roman period, however, the fifth reign, which was destined to continue for ever, was the reign of Rome herself,[42] following those of the Assyrians, Medes, Persians, and Macedonians. But this theory, by the very fact that it emphasised the changeable nature of human kingdoms, might also help the anti-imperialist movements. In point of fact it did come to fresh life during the Mithridatic wars; and Pompeius Trogus made it the basis of his historical work,[43] which was designed to show that the Roman Empire would come to the same end as its predecessors.

These ideas nourished the pessimism of the apologists. 'It is inevitable,' says Lactantius, 'that all nations – which is to say the whole world – will be scourged with disasters from Heaven, while the just people who worship God will be free.'[44] The dominion of the world will revert to Asia. Nor is this anything to wonder at; for all human things are fated to perish. 'The Sibyls had explicitly foretold that Rome was destined to fall.'[45]

The imminence of the inevitable end casts a melancholy shade over the pages of Arnobius and Cyprian. The world is now grown old.[46]

Even those who, like St Ambrose, see Christianity as the culminating fruit on the tree of humanity, borne in its maturity, still think of it as an autumnal product, coming at the end of harvest time and just before the frosts of winter. Those who notice the coincidence and are saddened by it have no right to blame the Christians. 'Let them rather quarrel with the wine-harvest for coming in the summer; or with the olives, for being the last crop of the year.'[47]

St Jerome regards the civilisation of Rome as corresponding to the fourth and last age, the age of iron, which will be followed by the Kingdom of God. This can be deduced from the observed fact that the Romans started by being the strongest of the peoples of the earth, and are now the weakest, 'since they find the need of barbarian auxiliaries both in their civil and their external wars.'[48]

The history of Orosius, written in A.D. 418, follows an identical general plan. The successive kingdoms may not be the same, but the important thing, for these Christian authors, is that the Romans should be the last of the series.[49] In *The City of God*, which St Augustine was composing in the same period, the Biblical prophecies regarding the 'cities of this world' are re-examined, and the saint notices an extraordinary coincidence in the dates : Babylon fell in the very same year that Rome was founded.[50]

The end of the world and the fall of the Empire were analogous events; for no one could imagine a world which was not Roman. They were also imminent, as could be seen by many portents. Evils multiply, confusion and cruelty reign supreme. Soon, writes Lactantius, there will be a general invasion. 'The rapine will spare neither men of virtue, nor women, nor children. The whole earth will be devasted.' And these tremendous events will be preceded by the most fearsome of portents, the fall of Rome. 'None of these things shall come to

233

pass, while Rome remains unstricken; but when the capital of the world falls, the end of humanity and of the whole universe cannot be far off.'[51]

In his oration on the death of his brother Satyrus (A.D. 379), St Ambrose comforts himself with the thought that the deceased has at least avoided the horrifying sight of the invasions; avoided 'falling into the hands of the barbarians, being present at the massacre of all humanity, the end of the world.'[52]

In his sermons of 386, the Bishop of Milan sees in the wars that are devastating the Empire a sign that the end of the world is at hand. 'No one can bear better witness to the truth of the heavenly word than ourselves, whose fate it is to be present at the end of the world. How many wars are raging at one time! The Huns have risen up against the Alans, the Alans against the Goths, the Goths against the Taifali and the Sarmatians ... famine is everywhere, and pestilence afflicting both man and beast ... diseases are spreading, because Time is nearing its end' (A.D. 386).[53]

From these words it is quite a natural transition to the theme dear to the hearts of the afflicted, the theme of the heavenly fatherland which they hope one day to attain. The Bishop of Milan preached a sermon in 387, at which the young Augustine was probably present, in which he takes up the words of Plotinus and of the Shepherd of Hermas. 'Let us therefore flee towards our fatherland, our most true fatherland. There is the country whence we come, there is the Father who has created us all. There is the Heavenly Jerusalem, the mother of all men. . . . But how shall we flee? Not with our feet, which belong to the body, not with ships, carriages or horses ... but rather with our hearts, with our eyes, with the feet of the mind.'[54]

St Jerome had taken refuge at Bethlehem, towards the end of the fourth century, in the hope of finding himself a peaceful corner in this world, where he could devote himself to Biblical studies and prayer, near the scene of the Passion. But news of the misfortunes of those he loved came to disturb his peace. His solitude became populous with the sorrowing, ghostly figures of those who were suffering the horrors of war. He tried to comfort them; but could find no other solution for the problems of the time than the renunciation of all the values of ordinary life on this earth. 'Without Christ,' he says, 'all that we live through is in vain.'[55]

The misfortunes of individuals assume the character of world-wide, everlasting evils. Aware of the universal historical continuity of the fates of men, thinkers begin to look for causes which are not contingent, but eternal. 'My heart sickens,' says St Jerome, 'when I go over the catastrophes that have happened in our time. For more than twenty years, not a day has gone past between Constantinople and the Julian Alps without the shedding of Roman blood. How many matrons, how many virgins dedicated to God, how many free-born women of noble blood, have fallen into the hands of those wild beasts ... bishops imprisoned, priests slaughtered, churches defiled, horses tethered to the altars ... everywhere mourning, groans and the many faces of death ... the world of Rome is falling to pieces. It is the fruit of our sins that the barbarians are strong, the fruit of our vices that the Roman army is defeated.'[56]

At the time of the great invasion of Italy, in 410, Honorius wrote from Ravenna to the authorities in Britain and told them to make their own arrangements for defending themselves. This absolved the inhabitants of their obligation of loyalty to the Empire (Zosimus, VI, 10).

The Empire was, in fact breaking up. There is no properly documented account, no eyewitness description, of the invasions of those years – only the scanty notes of an occasional chronicler, the heart-broken commentary of a distant observer, and years later, the tortured memories of survivors.

Those who gave leadership in matters of conscience turned away from the spectacle of so much disaster, and toward asceticism. When the wife of one of St Jerome's friends left him to go into a convent in Bethlehem, the saint wrote to him as follows: 'You are a wanderer in your own country – nay, not in your country, for that you have lost.'[57] St Augustine was

235

watching over the souls of his flock in the same period, raising their thoughts to the sure and certain fatherland of the spirit. Nectarius, an eminent pagan of Calama, wrote to Augustine in August 408, appealing to him, as an African rather than as a bishop, to intercede in favour of certain pagans who had been condemned to death for excesses against the Church and the Christians:

'I will not pause to describe the power of a man's love for his country,' he says, 'for you know it well already. It is the only feeling, in fact, which can rightly be set above the love we bear our parents. As our life progresses toward its end, our affection for our own city grows stronger every day, and we desire all the more to leave her safe and prosperous.'[58]

For this African the fatherland meant the town of Calama in Numidia, rather than the much-invaded Roman Empire of those days. But for St Augustine it meant neither Hippo nor Rome. 'That a fervent patriotism should still burn in a body weakened by age,' he replied, 'does not surprise me; in fact I praise you for it. . . . Your life, your actions show that your love for your country has no other limits than those of honesty. But we long to have you enrolled as a citizen in the service of a higher and nobler country. We live in the zeal of that country, dwelling in danger and in want, in the midst of those for whom we do our best to help them to achieve that citizenship one day. . . . You would acquire yet greater merit if you served a higher fatherland, in whose eternal peace you would find endless joy. . . . Until that time comes, you must forgive us if our love for our country, which we hope never to abandon, gives no cause for joy to your country, which you wish to leave prosperous.'[59] Such were the words of the Bishop of Hippo.

In March 409, Nectarius returned to the charge, again imploring Augustine to do what he could to obtain a general pardon, or, failing that, to ensure that only those should be punished whose guilt was proved beyond doubt. Nectarius had been brought up on the classics, and the idea of a spiritual fatherland was not new to him. He understood the distinction

236

between this concept and the Great City of the philosophers; but he was not prepared to regard it as a reason for turning his back on the city of his birth, every aspect of which he knew and loved. 'I received with joy your invitation to the worship and the religion of the supreme God, and I accepted with all my heart your exhortation to me to keep my eyes fixed on the heavenly fatherland. I thought, to tell the truth, that you did not mean to refer to the City that is encircled by a wall of stone, nor yet to the City common to all mankind (and equivalent to the world we live in) of which the philosophers tell us; but rather to that City inhabited by God and the souls of the elect, towards which all laws, in their varying ways and with varying scope, continually tend; which we cannot define in words, but may understand in our hearts. I admit that this City should be sought after and preferred before all others; and yet I cannot wish to abandon the city in which we were born and bred, to which we owe the light of life, our upbringing and our education.'[60]

But the Christian had long ago left behind him both the little city where he lived and the Great City of the philosophers. He recognises the dignity of patriotism, but only for the pagans. 'A Christian,' said St Augustine in a sermon of the same period, 'is a man who feels himself a stranger even in his own house, in his own city; for our fatherland is on high. There we shall not be aliens; but here below everyone feels himself a foreigner, even in his own house.'[61]

The Christian, in fact, *wants* to be a foreigner. In a letter of A.D. 396, St Paulinus of Nola admonishes his correspondent as follows: 'We must put nothing before God – not our affections, not our fatherland, not earthly honours.' And again: 'In the years when the cities were mere heaps of ruins, the heart of the Christian exulted with holy joy.'[62]

In a letter to a young widow who hoped to remarry, St Jerome dwells at length on the situation of the world in those years. 'And if both before and after the deluge the maxim held good: "be fruitful and multiply and replenish the earth", what

237

has that to do with us upon whom the ends of the ages are come, unto whom it is said, "the time is short" (I *Corinthians,* VII, 29), and "now the axe is laid to the root of the tree" that is to say, the forests of marriage and of the law must be cut down.' The young woman had apparently mentioned that she needed a man to run her family estate for her. 'Of what then are we talking?' writes the saint. 'Whilst we talk about the cargo, the vessel itself founders. . . . Savage tribes in countless numbers have overrun all parts of Gaul. The whole country between the Alps and the Pyrenees, between the Rhine and the Ocean, has been laid waste by hordes of Quadi, Vandals, Sarmatians, Alans, Gepids, Herules, Saxons, Burgundians, Alemanni, and – alas for the commonwealth! – even Pannonians. The once noble city of Moguntiacum has been captured and destroyed. In its church many thousands have been massacred. . . . Even the Spains are on the brink of ruin and tremble daily as they recall the invasion of the Cimbri. . . . "If Rome be lost, where shall we look for help?" '[63]

The only narrative account of these disasters is to be found in the brief pages of homely chronicle-writers. In 407, the Vandals crossed the Rhine and ravaged Gaul; in 408, the Saxons invaded Britain and the Suevi invaded Spain; on the Lower Danube, the Huns invaded Thrace.[64]

No historical judgement on this collapse has survived, no indication of its causes. Its history is recorded only in chronicle and sermon. But these catastrophes were put in the shade by an event which had little military significance, but struck the minds of men with a shock that still reverberates today: the sack of Rome. This disaster changed the whole concept of history. It became a symbol of the last act, a foretaste of the end of the world.

NOTES TO CHAPTER

1. Josephus, *Jewish War,* II, 388.
2. *Daniel,* II, 44; VII, 14 and 27. For sources of Biblical quotations, see p. 81, note 19, above.
3. *Psalms,* IX, 7 – RV, IX, 6.
4. *Ibid.,* XVII, 17 and 43–4 – RV, XVII, 16 and 42–3; XXII, 2 and 3 – RV, XXIII, 2.
5. *Ibid.,* XXXVI, 9 – RV, XXXVII, 9.
6. *Ibid.,* XLV, 5, 7 and 3 – RV, XLVI, 4, 6 and 2.
7. *Ibid.,* XLVII, 2 – RV, XLVIII, 1.
8. *Ibid.,* XLVII, 9 and 13–15 – RV, XLVIII, 8 and 12–14.
9. *Ibid.,* LXXXVI, 1 and 3 – RV, LXXXVII, 1 and 3.
10. *Sibylline Oracles,* III, 45–62 (probably 43–41 B.C.); III, 182–95 and 287 (reign of Nero); IV, 115–39 and 120–4 (reign of Titus). Verses 130–5 may be a reference to the disaster which overtook Pompeii. Rome is compared with Babylon, and the fall of Rome is hymned in V, 155–78. See A. Peretti, *La sibilla babilonese,* Florence 1942, pp. 319–61; Lactantius, *Divine Institutes,* VII, xv, *P.L.,* VI, 787; *ibid.,* VII, xvi, xvii, *P.L.,* VI, 794. For the prediction that, as Rome had lasted the full length of the Great Year of 365 ordinary years from her foundation in 755 B.C. to her sack by the Gauls in 390 B.C., so the Church in her turn would last 365 years, from the Crucifixion in A.D. 33 to the expected date of A.D. 398, see J. Hubeaux, *La crise de la 365 année,* in *Antiquité classique,* 1948, pp. 343 ff.; also *St. Augustin et la crise eschatologique de la fin du IV siècle,* in *Acad. Royale de Belgique,* XL, 1954, pp. 658 ff.
11. *Matthew,* X, 23; *Mark,* XIII, 30.
12. *Revelations,* XVII and XVIII.
13. *Ibid.,* XVIII, 8.
14. *Ibid.,* XVIII, 22–3.
15. *Ibid.,* XXI, 1–2, 4, 18–25.
16. *Spretis religionibus patriis,* says Tacitus, *Histories,* V, v.
17. *Deuteronomy,* XXVIII, 22; *Isaiah,* LXV, 5.
18. Tacitus, *Germania,* VIII; *Histories,* I, x and V, xiii. See also Suetonius, *Vespasian,* V, 2, 3 and VII, 2, 3; Josephus, *Jewish War,* III, 399. Also R. Lattimore, *Portents and Prophecies in Connection with the Emperor Vespasian,* in *Class. J.,* XXIX, pp. 441 ff.
19. Tacitus, *Annals,* XIV, xxxii and XV, xlvii; Suetonius, *Nero,* XLVI, 2; *Galba,* XVIII, 2–4; *Vespasian,* V, 6.
20. On the nationalist significance of these political priesthoods, see A. Momigliano, *L'opera dell'imperatore Claudio,* Florence 1932, p. 57.

H. Last, (*Rome and the Druids*, in *J.R.S.*, XXXIX, 1949, pp. 1 ff.), on the other hand, thinks that the bans on their activities pronounced by Augustus, Tiberius and Claudius were motivated by the cruelty of their rituals.

21. Suetonius, *Vespasian*, IV, 5; Tacitus, *Histories*, V, xiii.

22. See p. 199, note 1, above.

23. Juvenal, XIV, 100–3: *Romanas autem soliti contemnere leges Judaicum ediscunt et servant et metuunt ius, Tradidit arcano quodcumque volumine Moyses.*

24. St. Jerome, *Letters*, LXXVII, *P.L.*, XXII, 691.

25. Philo of Alexandria, *Moses*, II, ix, 51.

26. *Shepherd of Hermas*, Fourth Vision.

27. *Shepherd of Hermas*, First Parable.

28. Epictetus, *Encheiridion*, XVI.

29. Plotinus, *Enneads*, I, vi, 8. See also St. Ambrose, *De Isaac et Anima*, VIII, 79, *P.L.*, XIV, 532; W. Jaeger, *Early Christianity and Greek Paideia*, Cambridge, Massachusetts 1965; P. Courcelle, *Ambroise lecteur de Macrobe*, in *Rev. Et. Lat.*, XXXIV, 1956, pp. 232 ff.; St. Augustine, *Enarratio in Ps. CXXVI*, I, *P.L.*, XXXVII, 1667.

30. Tertullian, *Adversus Iudaeos*, I, i, *P.L.*, II, 633.

31. *Colossians*, III, 11.

32. Tertullian, *De Testimonio Animae*, VI, *P.L.*, I, 618.

33. Tertullian, *Apologeticum*, XXXVIII, *P.L.*, I, 528.

34. Tertullian, *Ad Scapulam*, II, *P.L.*, I, 778.

35. St. Cyprian, *Ad Demetrianum*, V, *P.L.*, IV, 565–6.

36. P. Labriolle, *Histoire de la littérature latine chrétienne*, Paris 1943, I, p. 257; J. Dürel, *Commodien*, Paris 1912; P. Monceaux, *Histoire littéraire de l'Afrique chrétienne*, Paris 1923, Vol. III, Chap. II, pp. 451 ff.; H. Grégoire, *Les persécutions dans l'Empire Romain*, Brussels 1964.

37. Commodian, *Apologeticum*, 801, 923, *P.L.*, V, 202 ff.; *Luget in aeternum quae se iactabat aeterna.*

38. Commodian, *Instructiones*, II, iii: *De caelo descendit Civitas . . . Inibi non pluvia, non frigus in aurea castra. Obsidiae nullae, sicut nunc, neque rapinae. Non lucernae lumen desiderat Civitas illa, Ex auctore suo lucet.* See also verses 11–15 of the first book.

39. J. Gagé, *Commodien et le mouvement millénariste du III siècle*, in *Revue d'histoire et de philosophie religieuse*, XLI, 1961, pp. 355 ff. For the opposite view, see P. Courcelle, *Commodien et les invasions du V siècle*, in *Rev. Et. Lat.*, XXIV, 1946, pp. 227 ff. This writer thinks that Commodian lived in the period from the reign of Valens to that of Honorius.

40. Arnobius, *Adversus Nationes*, I, iii–x, *P.L.*, V, 723–32. F. Cumont, *La fin du monde selon les Mages*, in *Rev. Hist. Rel.*, 1931, pp. 29 ff.

41. J. W. Swain, *The Theory of the Four Monarchies*, in *Classical Philology*, XXXV, 1940, pp. 1 ff.

42. Dionysius of Halicarnassus, I, 2; Appian, *Preface*, 9; Claudian, *De Consulatu Stilichonis*, II, 159–66.

43. Pompeius Trogus, XXX, iv, 4; XXXIV, i, 3; XXXIX, v, 15.

44. *Divine Institutes*, VII, xv, *P.L.*, VI, 787.
45. *Ibid.*, 789–90.
46. St. Cyprian, *Ad Demetrianum*, III, *P.L.*, IV, 564: *Senuisse jam mundum.*
47. St. Ambrose, *Letters*, XVIII, *P.L.*, XVI, 1021.
48. St. Jerome, *Commentary on Daniel*, *P.L.*, XXV, 504: *et regnum quartum erat veluti ferrum.*
49. Orosius, *Against the Pagans*, II, i; VII, ii.
50. St. Augustine, *The City of God*, XVIII, xxii, xxvii.
51. Lactantius, *Divine Institutes*, VII, xxv, *P.L.*, VI, 812: *Cum caput ille orbis occiderit . . . quis dubitet venisse iam finem rebus humanis, orbique terrarum . . . Illa, est Civitas quae adhuc sustentat omnia.*
52. *De excessu Satyri*, XXX, *P.L.*, XVI, 1356.
53. *Expositio Evangelii Secundum Lucam*, X, 10, *P.L.*, XV, 1898.
54. *De Isaac et Anima*, VIII, 79, *P.L.*, XIV, 532. See also P. Henry, *Plotin et l'occident*, Louvain 1934; P. Courcelle, *Plotin et St. Ambroise*, in *Revue de philologie*, LXXVI, 1950, pp. 29 ff., and *La postérité chrétienne du songe de Scipion*, in *Rev. Et. Lat.*, XXXVI, 1958, pp. 224 ff.
55. St. Jerome, *Letters*, LX, *P.L.*, XXII, 597 (A.D. 396).
56. *Ibid.*, 600.
57. *Letters*, CXXII, *P.L.*, XXII, 1046 (A.D. 408).
58. *Letter of Nectarius to St. Augustine*, XC, *P.L.*, XXXIII, 313.
59. *Letters*, XCI, *P.L.*, XXXIII, 315.
60. *Ibid.*, CIII, *P.L.*, XXXIII, 386.
61. *Sermons*, CXI, *P.L.*, XXXVIII, 642.
62. *Letters*, XXV, *P.L.*, LXI, 301; *Carmina*, XXVI, 5–7, 22–8, *loc. cit.*, 638–9.
63. St. Jerome, *Letters*, CXXIII, *P.L.*, XXII, 1057.
64. *Chronica Gallica*, IX, pp. 653–4; *Codex of Theodosius*, XI, 17, 4; XV, 1, 49 (A.D. 407).

Q

XIV

The City of God

> After the community or City comes the whole
> earth, wherein is placed the third stage of
> human society, which begins from the house-
> hold, then extends to the city, and finally to
> the world.
>
> ST. AUGUSTINE, *The City of God,* XIX, 7

> Just as a universal Empire, made up of many
> cities, is known as the community of Rome; so
> many nations go to make up the City of which it
> is written: Glorious things are spoken of thee,
> O City of God.
>
> ST. AUGUSTINE, *Cons. Evangelii,* II, xxxv[1]

ST JEROME, in a letter written after the one just quoted, reported
the news from Rome in the following terms: 'A dreadful
rumour came from the West. Rome had been besieged and its
citizens had been forced to buy their lives with gold. Then,
thus despoiled, they had been besieged again so as to lose not
their substance only but their lives. My voice sticks in my throat,
and, as I dictate, sobs choke my utterance. The City which
had taken the whole world was itself taken; nay more—famine
was beforehand with the sword, and but few citizens were left
to be made captives. In their frenzy the starving people had
recourse to hideous food; and tore each other limb from limb
that they might have flesh to eat. Even the mother did not
spare the babe at her breast. "In the night was Moab taken,
in the night did her walls fall down" (*Isaiah,* XV, 1). "O God,
the heathen have come into thine inheritance; thy holy temple

have they defiled; they have made Jerusalem an orchard. The dead bodies of thy servants have they given to be meat unto the fowls of the heaven, the flesh of thy saints unto the beasts of the earth. Their blood have they shed like water ... and there was none to bury them." [2]

Nothing like this had happened since the sack of Rome by the Gauls, exactly eight hundred years before. The damage may have been smaller and the victims less numerous than in certain other sacked cities; but there is no doubt that the disaster was grim enough. This can be inferred from the fact that the chroniclers do not distinguish the fall of Rome from the sack of other cities, while the Christian authors show a suspect keenness to minimise its horrors. The historian Orosius, a collaborator of St Augustine, describes Alaric as 'gentle in the midst of slaughter'. The saint himself makes a similar comment: 'But that which was so unaccustomed, was that the savage nature of the barbarians should put on a new shape and appear so merciful' (*The City of God,* I, vi). This particular divine mercy benefited also certain pagans, who successfully pretended to be Christians (*ibid.* I, i). The Christian reply to the accusations of Roman patriots was naturally an attempt to prove that the wars and invasions of those years were nothing to what had happened before the Empire became Christian.

Like the widening circles made by a stone thrown into a pond, the image of the event took on gigantic proportions as time went by, and as the news spread to distant lands, where it dismayed ex-pupils of Roman schools who had learnt from their earliest days that nothing could ever graze the majesty of Rome.

A few weeks later, the news of the fall of the capital was brought to St Jerome by the refugees who suddenly thronged his retreat.

'Intelligence was suddenly brought to me,' he writes, 'of the death of Pammachius and Marcella, the siege of Rome, and the falling asleep of so many of my brethren and sisters. I was so stupefied and dismayed that day and night I could think of

243

nothing but the welfare of the community; it seemed as though I was sharing the captivity of the saints, and I could not open my lips until I knew something more definite. . . . I was wavering between hope and despair, and was torturing myself with the misfortunes of other people. The brightest light of all lands is put out; the head of the Roman Empire is cut off. To speak more correctly, the whole world perished in one City.'[3]

Having left Rome behind him, Alaric pushed on toward the south. In August A.D., 410, the Visigoths thrust on towards Sicily down the Via Appia, a straight line drawn across the burnt-out landscape. The carts used in their nomadic wanderings now carried the works of art, clothing and jewels captured at Rome. Behind them followed the prisoners, destined to the service or the pleasures of the conquerors. There was little hope of ransom; few indeed still had the money to buy back a son.

The laws of the time were designed to prevent speculation at the expense of those unfortunates. They urged all citizens to welcome the refugees, and to set free after five years' service any slaves they bought from the barbarians.[4]

The Goths marched on toward Africa. Alaric knew that he could not regard himself as the master of Italy, until he had occupied the grain-producing provinces of Africa, whose governor, Heraclian, had remained loyal to Honorius, and had easily repelled a feeble attack mounted by Attalus. The King of the Visigoths had occupied Rome and carried away Galla Placidia, the sister of Honorius and daughter of Theodosius, as a hostage; but all this was not enough. The emperor had to sign a treaty which would assure Alaric a legitimate title, and the Gothic people a permanent home. And above all he had to have grain.

There are no eye-witness accounts as such of the sack of Rome or the Gothic advance down to Calabria. But it is obvious that Alaric intended to transport his armies over to Africa, and that he wanted to use the shortest crossing, since the barbarians had no experience of ship-building. The Gothic historian Jordanes, writing a century after the event, describes the end of Alaric; his grief at seeing his ships wrecked in the straits, his death, his legendary burial under the river-bed of the Busento.[5] The Italians seem to have been struck dumb by the violence they suffered during the repeated passage of the barbarians. The historical facts of those memorable days, the personal feelings of those who lived through them, can only be reconstructed with great difficulty. The sources are incidental remarks in letters, indirect comments, or the texts of new laws designed to arrest the process of moral and material collapse. For the chronicle-writers information is very scanty, and the Christian writings are tendentious.

A girl of patrician family, who had escaped to Africa with her relations, decided to enter a convent. The impact of events on the minds of her contemporaries is revealed by the letters she received from leading Christian thinkers – from St Jerome, St Augustine, and the British monk Pelagius (who was later condemned for heresy). Pelagius paints a magnificent, sinister picture of the Last Judgement; and the first scene that comes to his mind for purposes of simile is the sack of Rome, at which he had probably been present. 'The event is recent, and well known to you,' he says. 'At the blast of the strident trumpet, at the harsh cries of the Goths, Rome the mistress of the world, was oppressed by hideous fears and trembled. Where, at that time, was the distinction between nobles and plebeians? Where the unmistakable signs of aristocracy? Everything was turned upside down, all alike were utterly bewildered. Servants and masters were all the same. The face of death had the same aspect for everyone.... Such being then the strength of our fear of the enemy, what will become of us when the tremendous sound of the last trump begins to blast from the heavens?'[6]

There is a very similar allusion in St Jerome's letter to the same correspondent: 'It is not long since you trembled in the hands of the barbarians and clung to your grandmother and your mother, cowering under their cloaks for safety. You have seen yourself a prisoner and your chastity not in your own power. You have shuddered at the fierce looks of your enemies;

245

you have seen with secret agony the virgins of God ravished. Your city, once the capital of the world, is now the grave of the Roman people.'[7]

An event of such wide repercussions as the fall of Rome inevitably reinflamed the dispute between pagans and Christians; it spread such bewilderment that the formulation of a new doctrine became urgently necessary – a doctrine which could provide a fresh point of orientation for men who had once more lost their way in a slough of uncertainty. When the City that had symbolised so much fell into the hands of enemies, the shock gave a definite form to opinions which had been in the air for decades, and led to their expression in solemn and memorable terms.

'So this was the blessed state promised to the Christians! These were the new glories foretold by Christ! '

Those who were responsible for mens' souls could not let things slide, could not show indulgence toward these murmurers. It was essential to point out to them the sins into which they had fallen, to denounce their transgressions of the Commandments. Refugees from the fallen capital sat among the faithful who listened to St Augustine, as he preached in the echoing vastness of the basilica at Hippo.

The long, close-knit discourse which winds its way through Augustine's sermons, and, later, through the pages of *The City of God,* must have been aimed at specific listeners or readers; but it is difficult to hear their voices across the silence of the centuries. From the earliest days of the preaching of the Gospel, some had wondered at the long delay of the Second Coming. St Paul had already admonished them: 'Be not easily moved' (I *Thessalonians,* V, and II *Thessalonians,* II). Hellenistic thinkers had always been opposed to the Christian version of history, according to which earlier centuries had served only to prepare for the entry of the Godhead into the temporal world (that is, the birth of Christ), while the centuries after the death of the Saviour had no other purpose but to prepare his return.[8]

Now the uncertain and the sceptics were joined by many

others who deplored the fall of the capital, and drew from it the lesson that the invasions were due to the revenge of the gods, who had been neglected too long; and by Christians who were amazed to see that the prophecies had not come true, even after this calamity, and murmured against the Providence that had now failed them. St Augustine is more a polemicist than a theologian in this part of his work, and his arguments are aimed at individuals in his crowded audience, at individual states of mind in the contemporary generation.

In the saint's letters, in the intimate, vibrant oratory of his sermons, and later in the involved, solemn periods of *The City of God,* his arguments presuppose a tumultuous chorus of wrathful and heart-broken voices, which he successively reduces to eternal silence. We cannot hear these voices ourselves, but every sentence evokes a face – just as the bodily shape of those who died at Pompeii, their attitudes, their last moments of terror, can be discovered by pouring plaster of paris into the cavities left in the ashes. The refugees from Rome appear from the shadows one by one to raise a protest, an accusation, a lament. The bishop replies; and they vanish for ever.

Beneath every line of his writings we can trace – as if from a palimpsest – the record of episodes to which there is no other testimony, the feelings of those who lived through these disasters, the rumours that were in circulation, the pathetic observations of human voices that would never be heard again.

We can see that the sack of Rome – exhausted by the siege, stripped of her wealth, deserted by her leaders, abandoned by her emperor and her pope – was a very grim affair, relieved only by some instances of respect for the sanctity of the churches. We can see, above all, that the traumatic effect of the disaster on contemporaries was immeasurable.

The sermon *De urbis excidio,* written before Augustine's confutation of the charges of the pagans, reflects an immediate reaction to the news from Rome.[9] The gravity of what has happened is admitted. 'Tidings of horror are reaching us. There has been a massacre; also great fires, looting, murder, torture.

247

We have indeed heard much, and we have grieved at every word. We have often wept, and have been consoled with difficulty. I do not deny it, I do not deny having learnt of many horrors that have taken place in that city.'[10]

At this moment it is not the voice of the Roman, the philosopher, or the theologian that we hear, but the voice of the shepherd caring for his flock, dismayed by the violence of the reaction to the fall of Rome, striving with all his might to hold back the landslide of collapsing morale. The first complaint of the victims of the disaster is one of injustice. The pagans had posed as Christians in order to win sanctuary in the churches. Why should the benefit of divine mercy have been granted to unbelievers? Why should the good have been horribly tortured to make them reveal where their treasures were hidden? The good, replies the bishop, may *appear* to be good by human standards, but not by those of God.

The scale of merits is turned upside down; truly meritorious actions are not those recognised and rewarded by the civic community. No one is able to see into the secrets of his neighbour's heart, or even to know the truth about himself. For evil is deeply rooted in human nature, and the only hope of salvation lies in the mystery of divine grace.

The words of another of Augustine's sermons suggest that during the first few days it was believed that Rome had been levelled with the dust. It was necessary to watch the effect of such stories, which might have been deliberately exaggerated. 'Do you ask me what scandal has caused my indignation? It is the import of the words and phrases which men now din into our ears: "See to what a pass the times of Christianity have led! ... behold, in the times of Christianity such tremendous disasters have come to pass and the whole world is laid waste." And you reply to them: "But Christ had foretold these things to me before they happened." "Did you then believe what was prophesied unto you, and are you now distressed because it has happened? Some strange storm has blown up in your heart; take care that it does not wreck you. ..." Such are the words we hear from pagans, and, worse still, we hear them repeated by bad Christians.'[11]

In Africa, during the same years, Donatist propaganda had been fiercely active. Augustine wrote to Olympius, the successor of Stilicho, in 408, begging him to intensify repressive measures against heretics and pagans.[12] He hints at heavy calamities, causing great agitation in the Church. 'There are some,' he says, 'who support the ever-harsher attacks of our enemies with exemplary patience, along with us; but we fear for the weakness of the greater number.'

In a letter to Nectarius, written at the same time (November 408), he deplores the fact that the excesses committed by pagans against Christians had been regarded with complete indifference by the authorities; 'no one intervened to stop them', he says.[13] In his following letter, written in 409, Augustine attacks certain Christians who had not scrupled to take part in the looting which followed the burning of the church at Calama, under cover of the general confusion.[14] Luke-warm faith was the trouble, and the confusion of the invasions – the perilous confusion among the Christians observed at Rome by Orosius in 405, when the hordes of Radagaisus were quartered at Fiesole.[15]

In the autumn of 410, when Alaric was driving on toward Sicily, the Africans began to fear invasion. Augustine, who had had to leave his diocese for reasons of health, wrote to his flock to encourage them, to exhort them to find in their danger a new stimulus to thoughts of eternity, and to urge them to undertake works of charity. 'For as men betake themselves in greater haste to a place of greater security when they see in the shaking of their walls the ruin of their house impending, so ought Christians, the more they perceive, from the increasing frequency of their afflictions, that the destruction of this world is at hand, to be the more prompt and active in transferring to the treasury of Heaven the goods they were proposing to store up on earth.'[16]

At the beginning of 411, he wrote to a patrician family that had emigrated from Rome to Africa to express his regret at not having been able to visit them at Tagaste, because of the calls of his ministry: 'The congregation of Hippo, whom the Lord has ordained me to serve, is ... of a constitution so infirm that the pressure of even a light affliction might seriously endanger its well-being. . . . Moreover, when I returned to it recently, I found it offended to a most dangerous degree by my absence ... there are many here who by disparaging us, attempt to excite against us the minds of the others by whom we seem to be loved, in order that they may make room in them for the devil ... those whose salvation is our care are angry with us.'[17]

The wording of Augustine's letters and sermons, in the first few months after the invasion of Italy, contained hints at all the themes which were later to be fully developed in *The City of God*. The impact of the pagans' accusations was evidently upsetting many pious souls. 'To this very day they continue ... praising the time that is past, and accusing the time of Christianity.' ' "Behold," they say, "Rome is perishing in the time of Christianity." But perhaps she is chastised and not destroyed. Rome does not die, unless the Romans die. And they will not perish, as long as they praise God. Of what does Rome consist, if not of the Romans themselves? It is not a matter of stones and beams, of high buildings or of strong walls. All those things are made in such a way that they must fall some day. The whole world has been made perishable by God ... the skies and the earth are impermanent. What wonder, therefore, that a City should pass away?' And again: 'The City is built of citizens, not of walls.'[18]

The fall of Rome was assumed to be inevitable; it had been foreseen for such a long time! The catastrophe had to come, as the logical conclusion of a centuries-old chain of events, as the last stage before the great purification. Augustine clearly shows the traditional certainty of the mystics at this point: 'The time has now come that God had foretold,'[19] he says. Up to the moment in which he is writing, everything that happens fits into the prophetic scheme. Fire and looting are foretold as a punishment for sin. 'Who will dare to claim that he obeys all the

Commandments? No man. It is right that we should all be punished.'[20]

These are the ideas in general circulation at the time. St Jerome was writing much the same thing to his correspondents: 'The world sinks into ruin: yes! but shameful to say our sins still live and flourish. The renowned City, the capital of the Roman Empire, is swallowed up in one tremendous fire; and there is no part of the earth where Romans are not in exile. Churches once held sacred are now but heaps of dust and ashes, and yet we have our minds set on the desire of gain.'[21]

The news of the sack of Rome aroused consternation everywhere in the world; the great cities, even in the most remote lands, were plunged in mourning – even in the East! And yet as soon as they landed in Africa, the refugees from Rome returned to their pleasure-seeking ways, and thronged the theatres and circuses. 'Future generations will hardly believe this, if one day they hear of it,' writes St Augustine in *The City of God* (I xxxii).

The pagans' recriminations against the Christians, meanwhile, grew bolder every day. It was the old story: 'The rains have failed – to the lions with the Christians!' Since the days of the first persecutions, the Christians had been the scapegoat for every public calamity. Quite recently, Symmachus had told St Ambrose that the bad harvest was due to the abandonment of the old religion. Christian apologists had been refuting these accusations for two hundred years. But this time, the dispersed citizens of a decapitated state had good reason to complain of the period in which they lived. A disaster had taken place the like of which had not been seen for eight hundred years – a disaster regarded as so incredible that it seemed like a supernatural portent. And now that Rome had fallen, the Christians were asking why the heavenly City had not materialised and opened its gates to them.

The spectacle of death and destruction falling to the lot of the unjust and the true believer alike made hope of messianic salvation wither away. Men concluded that the setting up of a just and holy commonwealth, which they had expected to follow the fall of Rome, would never happen at all. After the sack of Rome, Christians lost their faith not only in the inviolability of the City and the majesty of the Empire, but also in the early realisation of the Kingdom of Heaven on earth. 'Like the *Republic* of Plato, like the *De Republica* of Cicero, St Augustine's *City of God* springs from an experience of crisis — the crisis of the Athenian Empire, the crisis of the Roman Republic, and the crisis of the Roman Empire respectively.'[22]

Augustine, in his pastoral capacity, at once sees the urgent necessity of clearing away the relics of paganism that persist in Christian society. For they are the root of these doubts, and of these jeremaiads about the 'defeats suffered in the time of Christianity'. But why, after all, should anyone think that belonging to a particular religion is an insurance against disasters? God sends them to test us, in accordance with his own secret ends. Confidence in the protection of a tutelary deity belonging to one's own community was a concept typical of the cities of an earlier period, with their utilitarian cults. But to be a Christian does not mean belonging to any one nation. It means belonging to a brotherhood of the spirit, to an invisible *civitas*, which has indeed an unconscious heritage from classical Rome, but is free from restrictive features such as walls, institutions, and resident gods. 'The City of God is not concerned with differences of custom, law, or institution,' says St Augustine (*The City of God*, XIX, xvii).

So there is an end to the connection between religion and nation which formerly gave the governing classes the power to invoke supernatural penalties. Christianity does not sink or swim with the Empire, and is not wounded by its defeats. The Faith has a life of its own, separate from that of the state. The Church is now herself an empire, widely diffused and invisible, that may work alongside the state, but is not identified with it. Membership of the Church is a spiritual matter, which has nothing to do with nationality. The God of the Christians, unlike the various pagan divinities, has no obligation to protect one population at the expense of the other.

Interwoven with this theme, which ignores the differences between nations and takes little heed of the facts of history, there is a second theme running through the pages of *The City of God,* which seems to contradict the first. One sets out to controvert the ancient assumption that religion is the shield of the fatherland, and that a god will, if correctly propitiated, protect one city, and only one; the other sets out to oppose those who follow the Sceptics, Stoics and Epicureans in regarding the gods as remote and indifferent beings. Horace ridicules the Jew Apella, who firmly believes that God intervenes actively in the course of history to guide, to rescue, and briefly to punish his people.[23] But Augustine follows the Jewish line of thought. He agrees with a view which Philo of Alexandria was the first to express in an historical work, and which was later adopted by the Christian apologists – the view that even the most apparently irreconcilable events are part of a divine plan, and that history is a coherent, intelligible process, with a definite beginning and a transcendental end.

But under cover of this assumption it would be all too easy for the utilitarian principle to re-emerge, according to which religious conformity is a sort of insurance. The Christian belief is not purely materialistic; it does not imply that the divine favour protects from earthly misfortune; it has no racial or geographic bounds. Yet it does contain a touch of exclusivity. How many warriors have adopted war-cries such as 'God with us!' or *'Deus vult!'*?

Primitive Christian art selected from the stories of the Bible those episodes which would furnish believers with edifying examples of the work of divine providence. The Christian version of history also uses such episodes for purposes of apologetics. In mosaics, frescoes and reliefs, we see Isaac saved from the sacrificial knife, Moses rescued from the water, Jonah from the whale, Shadrach, Meshach and Abed-nego from the fiery furnace, Daniel from the lions, Noah from the Flood, Jesus from Herod. In exactly the same way, the gradual increase in the power of Rome came to be seen by Christian

253

thinkers as planned by God in preparation for the coming of Christ. Everything develops to a regular design in accordance with definite objectives. If man cannot see the pattern, it is because the plans of God are inscrutable.

St Augustine is against cyclic theories of history, with successive ages separated by recurrent cataclysms at regular intervals. In Christian thought, history is a one-way process, along a route starting at the Creation and ending at the Last Judgement: linear, plain and unequivocal (*The City of God*, XII, x-xx).

So Rome has been invaded! But consider how long this event has been predicted by soothsayers and sibyls. And honest citizens – priests, even – have been cruelly used, slain, or carried away captive; virgins and chaste matrons have been raped – would they have done better to escape this disgrace by suicide? The examples dear to the moralists of the Republic come to mind – heroes and heroines who preferred death to dishonour, such as Lucretia, Cato, or Virginia, killed by her father. But these case-histories could only be regarded as valid for a community of limited size, committed to a national system of ethics. They are not models for Christians to follow. Those dignified Roman citizens, those inflexibly chaste Roman women died to keep faith with ideals based on transitory values – unwillingness to bear shame and dishonour, pride in their own virtue, human dignity. For the Christian, the judgement of his fellow-citizens does not matter. God sees into our hearts, and knows very well whether violence has been inflicted with or without the secret complicity of the victim.

St Augustine pays ample tribute to the virtues of the pagans. We have something to learn even from them: moral will-power, for example. The pagan Atilius Regulus, for instance, faced prison and torture rather than break his word; if the Romans are proud of this single hero, why do they reject the testimony of the whole Christian community, which is also summoned to offer proof of its love toward the City of the soul? The Christian who doubts his God because of the sufferings he has undergone is compared with the pagan heroes, very much to the latters' advantage (*The City of God,* V, xviii).

So Rome has fallen! And was her fall not predicted by the Christian writers? 'A bare handful will survive to tell the tale,' wrote Commodian. 'The lands of the nations shall be devastated, the whole City will be levelled with the dust.'[24]

Since all this had come to pass in conformity with the visions and predictions of the prophets, the exiles wanted to know whether they could now expect to see the heavenly Jerusalem descend from the skies. The City promised in the *Psalms,* and eagerly awaited by the mystics, is lofty and radiant. Snow and rain never trouble it. Commodian added some extra touches of his own to that vision, which reveal what conditions must have been in the cities of his own time: 'There shall be no sieges, such as we see now, and no plundering.'[25] The artists who depicted the heavenly City, in the mosaics of the apse of Santa Pudenziana, in the fourth century A.D., drew its portrait from the City they had before their eyes. For, though Rome to them was the City of sin, they could not imagine a sublime City that would not resemble her.

St Augustine also felt a yearning toward the fatherland of the soul; he may have derived it from Plato and Plotinus rather than from the *Psalms.* Even in the works he wrote in 386–387, just after his conversion, he uses the word *patria* for the dwelling place of the spirit, the port anxiously sought by souls lost like seafarers in a tempest. He even addresses the Almighty as *patria mea.*[26] In a sermon preached in 391, he describes to his listeners the brilliant vision that is soon to be realised: 'Behold Jerusalem, your heavenly Mother, comes to meet you, joyously calls you by name.'[27]

Meanwhile, a new idea was forming in his mind – the idea that human society on earth is a shadow (*umbra*) of the heavenly kingdom, and that humanity is divided into two groups. There are those who desire only the goods of this world, and those who adore the true God in the annihilation of the Self.[28] In a work written in 396, he described man's love for this

255

world, for things which 'are born and pass away', as worthy of blame.[29] A typical feature of his thought is a yearning toward a timeless, eventless state of calm and stability, and a distaste for the transitory and the changeable, which are blemishes brought into the world by sin. Impermanence came into the world by contagion, like a leprosy. It is this infection, ineradicable since the days of Adam, which gives history its gloomy stamp, its desperate anguish. 'The time of this life is but a race toward death,' he says in *The City of God* (XIII, x). So time inevitably runs out for everything which is material, perishable, contaminated by sin. Humanity is making rapid strides toward destruction (*ibid.,* XIII, xiv). Different by far is the state of the Heavenly City, where 'no one is born, and no one dies'.[30]

In man dwell two citizens, the corruptible and the eternal; in the world dwell two apparently similar sets of human beings, which march on side by side, indistinguishable to human eyes; but one set is bound for the heavenly fatherland and the other is bound for the shadows. 'Thus two Cities, one of the wicked and one of the saints, are carried down from the beginning of the human race even to the end of the world; now united in their bodies, but separated in their wills, but in the day of Judgement destined to be separated in their bodies also. For all men who love pride and temporal rule, with vaingloring and pomp of arrogance, and all spirits who delight in such things, and seek their own glory in the having mankind as their subjects, are all found together in one fellowship. . . . And again, all men and all spirits who humbly seek the glory of God, not their own, and religiously follow Him, belong to one fellowship.'[31]

In this pronouncement some writers have seen traces of two doctrines which had exercised a profound influence on the spiritual development of St Augustine – Manichaeanism and Neo-Platonism.[32] The first can still be detected in the dualistic contrast between two wholly different classes of soul, two Cities with nothing in common; the second in the certainty that Truth proceeds from God, and that wisdom can be attained by the contemplation of Truth.

Gradually the two cities become better defined, and are identified with the symbolical cities of the Bible – Jerusalem and Babylon. Babylon is the city of evil, which cheats men into captivity with false flattery – the city where men carry on the precarious and chaotic activities, such as farming, soldiering, the law and commerce, which Augustine calls 'streams of Babylon' because they flow continually away and sink into the sand. But in Sion 'All things stand fast, and nothing ebbs away'.[33]

The faithful naively asked St Augustine whether his Jerusalem were the City described by David – the Jerusalem whose victory over all nations has always been expected by the Jews. No, said Augustine, it is impious to identify the heavenly City with the capital of the Jews.[34] The Jerusalem which can be seen by mortal eyes is but a shadow of the other. When David sang of the future glories of the City, Jerusalem was still intact, with her Temple unprofaned. David was therefore speaking of a City of the future, the bricks of which would be the souls of the faithful; it would be inhabited by those who live in the fear of God, and the expectation of his presence.[35] The earthly City is but 'a prophetic shadow and image' – a phrase which some authorities regard as openly Platonic.[36]

In view of this shining goal, life on earth is but a pilgrimage, and while it lasts we must make every effort to bring into being the Kingdom of God, to which, at the same time, we desire to ascend. At our side march fellow-travellers who also advance yearningly toward the Divine City, and urge us to make haste. 'Let us run faster,' they say, 'for we approach the dwelling place of God.'[37]

The distinction between the City of this world and the City of the Beyond might have seemed clearer before the sack of Rome; but in certain of the texts quoted above we can already plainly see the contemporary quality, the originality and the constructive force of Augustine's thought. The two Cities are

R

seen as parallel and coexistent, rather than as clashing forces. Both the physical man whose strength is consumed in this world, and the spiritual man who fulfils himself in the next, are called on to live in both Cities at once, not passing from one to the other in time, unaffected by distinctions of race, class or country. The word 'city' no longer means a complex of buildings gathered round a temple, or a racial group living in a particular area with a wall round it; it means a place of refuge for the spirit.

In his ambiguous but deeply suggestive way, with his dynamic, seminal style, Augustine tells us that the two Cities are, 'in this world, interwoven and confused, until the Day of Judgement comes to separate them.'[38] 'The earthly realm, the State, exists today, in the secular world, and the heavenly realm exists here too; both the one and the other give shelter to citizens who are passing through, mingled together.'[39]

Rome has fallen and the Heavenly City has not been seen descending from the clouds. This leaves no alternative but to locate the City on this earth. Augustine uses the word *Civitas* here, not *Urbs* – not so much 'town', but rather '*body of citizens*' – a diffuse community. Its members give reality in this world to the sublime justice that they have long hoped to see imposed from on high. Transcendence and immanence blend and alternate, as one level or the other in turn predominates.

We arrive at a concept of citizens living together in apparent equality, but, like their predecessors in earlier times, spread out across the various provinces of the Empire, and divided into those that have full rights of citizenship and those that have not, the second class being again subdivided according to the different ends pursued by its members and by the different fates that await them. These ideas may have been formulated by St Augustine in the period when the Emperor Theodosius was passing his coercive legislation in favour of Orthodox Christianity. Converts flocked in in such numbers that even the most vigilant priest found it impossible to tell the wheat from the tares. These ideas took on a new clarity at the time of the invasions when the State, its institutions, and the very concept of the fatherland were shattered. The immanence of the Heavenly City became even more obvious when the City of marble had collapsed, the columns of the temples were blackened, the golden statues had vanished, and the citizens of Rome had been dispersed through the world – leaving the problem of re-awakening in the hearts of those refugees a feeling of belonging to a human fellowship, that could offer them the warmth of companionship with men of similar views.

Now their stately sinful City, so often contrasted with the calm City floating amid visionary clouds, is nothing more than a family chapel where the memorials and records of ancestral glory are kept. Many years have passed since Rome housed the Emperor, the supreme army command, or the high officials of the State.

Only her prestige was left, which was largely a literary matter, but still so strong an influence that St Augustine himself, when referring to Heaven as a refuge where offenders may receive the remission of sins, can think of no more appropriate analogy than the asylum which Romulus offered to criminals in order to swell the population of his new city (*The City of God*, V, xvi). Whatever is venerable or august inevitably takes on a Roman image. Even Christ himself and the apostles appear in the mosaics of Santa Pudenziana dressed in togas and sitting on traditional Roman stools, like senators.

The City of God, then, will not be seen coming down from above, like a resplendent piece of painted scenery, as was formerly promised; the faithful must build it in their hearts, by daily effort. It is the tacit brotherhood of every man who believes in righteousness, no matter what his duties or his position may be, or even his religious faith – 'among the enemies of today are sometimes hidden her future citizens,' says Augustine. And again : 'The City of God, as long as she remains in exile on earth, gives refuge to men who are joined to her in the communion of the Sacraments, but will not be joined to her in the eternal home of the blest.'[40]

St Augustine was no stranger to the times he lived in. He had known in his own life all the experiences of his contemporaries, in the fields of personal emotions, of literary culture, and of ideas. He knew the social, political and ideological foundations of his period. When they began to crumble, he purposefully began to carry out a thorough re-examination of them, in order to make sense of recent events for himself and, above all, to help his fellow men to survive. In those years in which everything seemed to be collapsing, he was searching for a way through the ruins, along which he could urge even the last and most reluctant of the brethren into the City of righteousness, taking with him a valuable load of the moral principles which had served to make the earthly City great.

While the other directors of men's consciences guided the faithful toward the renunciation of this world, Augustine saw that the imperative moral necessity was to collaborate with the civilisation of the future. They exaggerated the horrors of the present to persuade men to abandon this vale of sorrows; but Augustine took the opposite course. Blatantly tendentious, he minimised the extent of the current disasters, and cut the celebrated glories of Rome down to size, not without a touch of hostility against the capital. Is a State based on oppression, he asks, really a State at all? (*The City of God,* II, xxi and XIX, xxi).

Reviving the anti-Roman themes of Hellenistic propaganda, he poses the question: what is an empire without justice but a gigantic conspiracy to rob? (*ibid.,* IV, iv). We seem to hear again the judgement pronounced by Carneades, to re-read the anti-imperial Greek historians. In fact, St Augustine does quote Pompeius Trogus, the most anti-Roman of them all. He also includes an anecdote about that eternal symbol of greed, and of hunger for power, the inevitable figure of Alexander. This time a pirate is called on to preach a little sermon to the Macedonian, comparing his own modest breaches of the law with the enormous robberies committed across the world by the conqueror. In every earthly State we find evil – the excesses of a tyrant, or the violences committed by the populace. No nation can claim that it has never strayed from the paths of legality. And what does it matter, in any case, under what regime, what laws, what customs those find themselves who are citizens of the Heavenly City, and are but exiles on this earth? (*ibid.*, XIX, xvii).

But indifference toward the problems of the citizen was not a predominant feature of Augustine's writings. In 412, a friend who wrote on behalf of certain pagans who were on the brink of conversion, explaining their final difficulties, posed certain fundamental questions to Augustine.[41] It is interesting to note that they apparently had no objections to the commandments governing private morality, but could not get over the incompatibility between the precepts of Christianity and the duties of the citizen. Never to render evil for evil, in the words of *Romans*, XII, 17, always to turn the other cheek, were hardly acceptable doctrines to those who were accustomed to consider defence a duty, oppression a right. They were all the less inclined to accept an obligation to forgive and be merciful at a time in which they were subjected to nameless brutalities.

St Augustine's answer to this letter – the valuable contribution of an intellectual toward the solution of the problems of his day – was written fourteen years before the publication of *The City of God*. While for the other Christian thinkers the true believer is an individual wholly bent on the perfecting of his own soul, committed to the struggle against evil habits and instincts, St Augustine does not make asceticism the only objective for the souls of men. He tries to understand the mentality of those patriotic doubters; he is just as concerned for the State as they are.[42]

In a letter written not longer after (414), St Jerome lays stress on the contrast between the two cities, but does not suggest any connection between them. 'The Promised Land is not Judaea,' he says, 'nor the earth which is promised as the inheritance of the meek. For the earth, in its material sense, belongs to the violent, and to those who are ready to lay their hand to the sword. This is the earth where we live – where those who live a holy life can hope to win eternal treasure.' How can anyone believe that God looks down with favour on the cities, which daily go up in flames, or believe that he has bidden us to toil in the fields of this world, to earn our daily bread? No, no; the land where we should toil is the land of the spirit, which produces the bread of truth. For the material earth 'is cursed by God in the Book of Genesis.'[43]

St Augustine, on the other hand, is concerned with the theoretical foundations of the State. He does not hope for an uprising of the nations, nor for the provinces to turn the tables on Rome, nor for social or economic revolts of slaves against masters, workers against capitalists, or taxpayers against the pitiless machine of collection. Nothing of that sort appears in the writings of the period, even when the spectacle of iniquity and injustice is depicted with all the feeling of a man personally affected. St Augustine did not retire to a cave in his youth, nor to a life of study and prayer in a monastery in his old age, like St Jerome. He lived in the society of his time and gave heed to its problems. He saw clearly that the State must one day rise again from the ruins in which it lay, and order itself anew in an unpredictably changed world of men. He saw it as his duty to provide that future society with a set of principles to follow.

The laws of Theodosius were much stricter and more demanding than those of Constantine. They had put the Christian religion in such a favoured position within the State, that it was necessary to create a new balance between Christianity and the Government. The new principles on which the Bishop of Hippo wanted to found the City of the Future are the very opposite of those which had prevailed up to that time. His is an inward City. It is no one's birthplace, has no empire, no proud artistic or cultural heritage to win it acceptance as a fatherland; yet it is a fatherland – the country of all souls harmoniously striving toward better things. To live according to the rules of the Gospel is not inconsistent with the practical

262

obligations of life, and the precepts of Christianity are not hostile to the State. 'They accuse our religion of being the enemy of the State; but what is the State if not the common good; and what is the City but a multitude of men joined together by a bond of harmony?'

The Gospel nowhere forbids us to fight for our country. In Luke we find only the words 'Be content with your pay' addressed to the soldiers (III, 14). Our wish is that men would pay heed to the simplest of the Commandments, which is enough to revolutionise relations between individuals and between States – 'Love your neighbour'. For this Commandment is addressed to collective bodies of men no less than to individuals. The City, indeed, can be founded and can be kept in being only if it is based on principles which ignore temporal disasters, and proposes eternal goals.

If the concept of forgiveness is confusing, turn to the pagan authors. Do they not praise Caesar's clemency above all his other merits? Before condemning Christianity as damaging to the State, let us examine the real motives that led the pagans to make so grave an accusation – they do not want the State to be founded on moral principles, because they claim impunity for their vices. Instead of murmuring against us, let them begin to put our precepts into practice; let them obey the teaching of Christ in their respective positions, as fathers, husbands, sons, masters or servants, judges or soldiers, tax-gatherers or tax-payers, and afterwards let them dare to come and say that the State which will result from their actions is not a desirable one!

Those precepts which seemed to be incompatible with life in a community and with the defence of one's country were given to us primarily for the sanctification of the individual, rather than the satisfaction of the requirements of society. They should be considered as moral restraints, designed to moderate the force which the soldier must use in the defence of his country, the judge must use in the punishment of the guilty, and the educator in the just chastisement (for their own good) of the pupils entrusted to him. The virtues should be taken as means to

263

moderate the impulses of the soul; 'but outwardly we should act as we think best for the attainment of those ends.' If these rules are followed, we shall succeed in setting up a harmonious society 'in the earthly City ... but we shall also attain the divine and heavenly City. . . . By giving fame and power to the Empire of Rome, God showed the value of the civic virtues, even without faith, and taught us that with faith men may become citizens of another City, whose ruler is truth, whose laws are charity, and whose time-span is eternity.'

This letter defines a new and unforeseen kind of human being – the Christian who is also a citizen. To free himself from the past and win fulfilment in the future, he should shake off the burden of pagan ideas and pagan values. St Augustine tries to do it for him, and is ready to answer any question, no matter how childish. He will provide a philosophical solution for thinking men, and also the homely counsel of a parish priest to simple souls. 'I will answer all that they have to say,' concludes the letter just quoted, 'if God grants me length of days, whether by my letters or by my books.'

A year later, in 413, he began work on *The City of God* – that complex work, often confused, long-winded and contradictory, bristling with inconsistencies and repetitions, which of all Augustine's writings is the most immediately motivated by the outer world, showing him as involved in history rather than in theology. At the same time, it provides a fresh answer to the age-old yearning of the human spirit for the establishment of a City of Justice.

Many of his writings are aimed at the confutation of schismatics, heretics, or philosophers of various clearly defined types – Academics, Arians, Donatists, Manichaeans, Pelagians. It may be that the vehemence of Augustine's attack on each group is proportionate to the subtlety with which its thinking has retained a foot-hold in his own mind. *The City of God* is addressed to men and women of every sort – to those who have lost their families, their property, their country, and all the certainties to which they were born. They have seen the City they believed to be eternal sacked and set on fire. Leaving Rome behind them, they have lost all sense of belonging to a civilised society.

Because of its closeness to the events and thoughts of those years, *The City of God* contains polemical passages concerned with ephemeral disputes, left over from earlier works defending the orthodox position. But as they passed through the fire of St Augustine's mind, these incidental elements were transmuted into spiritual values which remained valid for the whole medieval period, and indeed remain so for ever in the ideological heritage of Christianity.

In a letter written in 417[44] St Augustine summarises both the views of his opponents, which he intends to confute, and the content of the work on which he is engaged. Some of its component books, he writes, are already finished – 'the others I hope to write, God willing, amid the press of other business.'

In 424 he replied to Paulinus of Nola, who had asked for his advice, by referring to the opinion he had recorded in *The City of God,* the publication of which, he said, was now imminent. The *Retractations,* which he wrote during the last few years of his life, contain a summary of *The City of God,* which he describes as a final confutation of the arguments of the pagans.[45] Their accusations, at the time of the sack of Rome by the Goths, had become bitterer and more violent than ever before; 'whereat I burned with indignation.'

But it was not only a matter of silencing those who had chosen the moment of invasion to insult Christ more savagely than ever; Augustine had to face the contrast between the pageant of past history and the ruined landscape of the present, and gird up his loins to make a fresh start. Earlier letters already show the working of the stimulus which led him on to success:[46] amid the general bewilderment in the hearts of men, their spiritual father could see the possibility of formulating an ideological system capable of creating a new mentality, which would soothe their sufferings and give them a new set of bearings for the future.

A single idea dominated all that he wrote – often without

265

much logical order – against the pagan cults or the systems of classical philosophy, against fanatic admiration for the glories of Rome, against the characteristic vices of the Romans. This was the primitive idea of freeing the soil completely of every trace of paganism – not in its aspect as a formally professed religion, but in its far more deeply rooted aspect of attachment to the values of the past.

In Augustine's day, the only possible model for a vast collective venture was Rome. His knowledge of that colossal *civitas* provided him with the framework of his book and its terminology, and with a constant standard of comparison. But he is always intent on proving that the City of God is 'incomparably more splendid.'[47] In the first place, Rome was born under the sign of discord – of fratricide, in fact. Cain was the founder of the City of Sin for all mankind, and Romulus for the Romans.[48]

In view of all the talk about the size of the Roman Empire, it is well to state that there is no evidence that mere size was ever beneficial.[49] The pagan authors themselves have several times declared that moral degeneration was the first result of territorial expansion.[50] All mankind has been ravaged by the most typical of Roman vices, the lust to dominate.[51] The history of Rome is one long series of arrogant cruelties and injustices. Even the pagan historians tell a story of outrageous means and dishonest ends, recording for posterity the diseases of their country – the hedonism, lechery, greed and cruelty of their compatriots.[52] St Augustine does not indulge in apocalyptic outbursts against the Second Babylon; for the prophecies of the seers have already come true. Now the survivors must be induced to make the manly admission that the Empire of Rome, like any other empire, has come to an end; that the great *Urbs*, the capital city believed to have been appointed by fate, predestined to rule by Divine plan rather than by her own material power, was just a city like any other. The myth of Rome had been elaborated in the reign of Augustus, when Roman culture had reached awareness of its own moral worth, to combat

266

the propaganda of Hellenistic historians – now the time had come to demonstrate the emptiness of that myth.

All through the work runs a contrast – on the one hand, the material City of earlier days, splendidly enclosed by its walls, coming to full flower in the outward signs of wealth and strength; on the other, the inward City, confined to no one land, secret, present in men's hearts, set up as the final aim of life. We can see the same contrast between the traditional gods and Christ. The old gods dwelt in shrines, from which they were thought to radiate a kindly influence over their faithful citizenry; but in the Heavenly City there are none of these deceiving gods, which are really evil spirits.

So there are two Cities – the past one, rich in territory, slaves and renown, and the future one, immune from upheaval because it is outside time. There are also two Cities in the sense of human communities, two groups of citizens set apart not in time but by the spirit that animates each of them. The earthly City belongs to the workers of evil, and at the same time it is the theatre for the everlasting struggle between right and wrong; the Heavenly City is the kingdom of God, the earthly reign of which has already begun to dawn, and will grow stronger day by day.

The two Cities are called on to live together, to go on side by side, 'intermingled in time, until they are set apart at the Last Judgement' (*The City of God*, I, xxxv). Time is the medium in which a perpetual antagonism develops between the two communities, intertwined for so many centuries. History is in fact the story of this struggle, and the progressive elevation of mankind is its slowly achieved result.

The morality of life must therefore be seen in terms of living in a community rather than in ascetic isolation, or in the harsh daily spiritual exercises of the individual. In this society, compounded of the transitory and the eternal, of evil and good, there is sometimes an interchange of roles. 'Do not let us despair if at times the citizens of the Heavenly kingdom perform the offices of Babylon, and carry out earthly tasks, in the earthly state.' It can happen, in fact, that the citizen of Jerusalem makes himself useful in Babylon: 'He may wear the purple, he may serve as a magistrate, aedile or consul ... provided that his heart is set on Heavenly things.'[53]

So there is nothing impossible about the idea of a State administered in the spirit of Christianity – humanitarian, frugal and just. If kings, common people, princes, judges and all men would but listen to the precepts of our religion and put them into practice, the resulting State would be the pride of the world. In this Utopian vision of the future, there is also room for a semblance of continuity with the Rome of earlier days – the Republic which, according to Sallust, was so excellent a State until the vices of the Romans filled it with evil and discord (*Catilinarian War*, IX, 10). Yet it may be that a shadow of the ancient virtues lives on in the hearts of the citizens; and St Augustine appeals to those virtues, as he calls all righteous men to come into his City: 'O sons of the Scipios, the Reguli, the Fabricii, awake!' he cries, 'the day is at hand!'[54]

Those men were steeped in memories of an idealised past; it was time for them to free themselves from the old ghosts. Regret for the past was a more insidious peril than the brutal force of pagan persecution. The thinkers of antiquity had always tended to place their golden age in the past, and the temptation to do so was all the stronger now that so much had been lost.

The new City makes her appeal to citizens of every nation, crying out in every language to call together a community of diverse peoples.[55] She presents herself without the defects that have made the City of this world so unpleasant: 'Here no one dies ... here reigns perfect felicity ... there shall be no need to respect the common treasury more than the private; truth is all the treasure that lies there.'[56]

In the immense variety of his arguments, St Augustine foresees every possible objection, from the most commonplace to the most subtle. This leads him to pass in review the doctrines of the ancient philosophers, from Thales to Plotinus. Naturally, their efforts to attain truth appear barren and futile to the believer in revelation. Yet Augustine does hold out a hand to them. Those philosophers who believe in a single, incorporeal God, an incorruptible Creator, 'whether they be Platonists or of another school, to whatever nation they belong, if they held thus of God, they held as we do.'[57]

The immediate task had been to deprive the pagans of the best argument they had ever possessed – the contention that Rome had never experienced these disastrous defeats while the gods charged with her defence were still properly worshipped. It was a childish argument to put up against a controversialist accustomed to pitting himself against theologians and philosophers; it had moreover been exhaustively answered by Christian apologists from the third century on. Any school-boy could quote the examples of cities like Troy and Saguntum, which had fallen despite the pagan devotion of their citizens. The subject of the debate was, in fact, much wider than that. The Christian mentality was ranging itself against the traditional culture, with its pagan mythology, its obsession with sensual themes, its dreams of military power, and its rationalist philosophy.

Augustus had strengthened the nationalism of the Romans by encouraging a nationalist mythology, against which Christianity now set its face. The Christians reversed the ethics harking back to traditional morality, which had been the basic theme of Roman ideology. Aware of the spiritual emptiness of the Empire, Augustus had tried to give it a strictly Latin moral stamp by sanctifying ancient customs, rites and traditions. At the moment of proclaiming the doctrine of *Romanitas,* he had sought to improve the scanty spiritual heritage of the Empire by trying to inspire a mystical faith in the eternal destiny of the City, and by claiming that she had become the capital of the world because she had been selected as the second home of the Trojan gods. This idea had already enjoyed a life of four hundred years, and there is plenty of literary evidence that it took on fresh life during the time of the invasions.[58]

St Augustine aims his attack against this whole cultural

heritage, not against individual pagan refugees, or grumblers, or calumniators of Christ. We cannot tell whether a pagan party of significant intellectual or social standing continued to exist at Rome, after the defeat of Eugenius and the death of the patrician notables who had supported him. If so, the proofs are lost. But even if we had written evidence of this kind, it would not help us to understand the inward torment of Roman society; it could only give us the thinking of a limited group, faithful to the outer forms of the ancient world rather than to its spiritual content. *The City of God* was not written for them.

If we are to understand the objects of the work, we must consider to what extent paganism was still an active force in those days. For country folk, it was an attachment to old traditions; for certain intellectuals, a continuation of the revival of Hellenism (expressed mainly by the soulless virtuosity of the rhetoricians) which had reached its peak under Julian. It was no longer a significant political tendency, nor was it a conception of the universe based on a valid philosophy – apart from Neo-Platonism. The teaching of that school did indeed attract mystics, thinkers, and admirers of ancient Greece. But it was excessively abstract, and its comprehension demanded a high level of intelligence. Neo-Platonism was therefore neither a vigorously stimulating nor a rapidly growing faith.

It is in the souls of recent converts to Christianity that we must study the mentality of the pagans – their habits, their psychological attitudes, and the criteria by which they judge the values of life. 'They go now unto plays with them, and by and by unto the church with us.'[59]

The last official pagan ceremonies were celebrated in the reign of the usurper Eugenius, which ended with his death in 394. The last pagan inscriptions are of that period.[60] From then on, the legalised persecution of the pagans by the Christian governing class became general. The recruitment of new converts was intensified, to such a point as to alarm those who were more concerned with quality than quantity. There were still some cases of violence against Christians in those years, but

270

they were isolated incidents, with no ideological significance – the murder of two missionaries and a bishop at Trent and the riots at Calama. We also hear of heathen festivals in outlying places, in celebration of seed-time or harvest.[61] There was no longer any systematic thinking or coherent controversial position behind any of this.

In 403, Prudentius tried to express the rhetorical themes of the Christian apologists in the elevated terms of epic poetry. But his arguments were the same as those used by St Ambrose in 384, in the middle of the pagan reaction. They had been appropriate to the earlier situation, which was a debate before an emperor of uncertain religious views, between two orators of equal prestige – Ambrose, the Bishop of Milan, and Symmachus, the patrician *Praefectus Urbi*. But nearly twenty years had gone by when the Spanish poet began to versify those arguments, and the legislation of Theodosius had already brought about a wave of mass conversions. Prudentius, in fact, boasts about them himself.[62]

The laws of the time certainly indicate that heathen sacrifices and other acts of worship had not ended. The repression of paganism had been put in hand by Constantine in 321, and continued until 435 (*Codex of Theodosius* XVI, 10, 25) or even 438 (*Nov. Theod.*, 3). But during that period of over a century there were sixty-six decrees against heretics and only twenty-six against pagans. These decrees, moreover, were addressed to local governors, in places remote from each other, out in the vast imperial territory. We can often work out whose efforts were at the back of these governmental measures. We see, for example, St Ambrose influencing Gratian, Olympius influencing Honorius and St Augustine influencing Olympius.[63]

From certain of the laws mentioned, it appears the Christians had gone over to the offensive with a violence that alarmed the authorities. The laws of 399, for example, are designed to protect heathen temples from being dismantled or set on fire – evidently a common occurrence. These laws were probably suggested to the young Emperor Honorius by Stilicho, who wanted to follow the victory of Theodosius over the pagan reaction at Rome by a more conciliatory policy, in order to get the conservatives on his side.[64] When Stilicho died, however, the party of orthodox uniformity took over at Ravenna, and the pagan temples were converted into public buildings. A law of 423, when St Augustine was approaching the end of *The City of God,* speaks of rooting out the last survivors of paganism, 'though we trust that none in fact remain' (*Codex of Theodosius,* XVI, 10, 22).

In the same year, another law enjoins the Christians 'not to make wrong use of the authority of religion, not to commit acts of violence against pagans and Jews who are living in peace, and not to offend against public order by illegal or seditious gestures. Anyone who commits acts of violence against those who are living in security, and takes away their property, must replace not only his ill-gotten gains, but also three times their value' (*Codex of Theodosius,* XVI, 10, 24).

From the accession of Theodosius until the middle of the fifth century, a powerful wave of expansion had carried Christianity forward, but not in a direction that made sense with its internal state. This was the very time when the influx of converts from other religions had prompted the theologians to carry out a rigorous definition of their dogmas, which had often been misunderstood. It had also compelled the directors of men's consciences to emphasise the ethical content of the Christian message. And so, in the very years when synods and councils were proclaiming the necessity of a wholly uncritical acceptance of their doctrines, and rejecting any more conciliatory view of the matter, it happened that Christianity took on a mentality very like that shown by the pagans, when paganism had been the State religion. The passage of time had produced an interchange between two positions which had originally been wholly irreconcilable. Christianity moved from the condition of a private, secret religion on to the plane of dogma. From being a persecuted sect, it became an intolerant religion. The last of the anti-pagan laws uses the very language of the earlier persecutors of Christianity, and repeats their ideas. How can a sovereign hold his hand, when he sees that 'the rhythm of the seasons is broken, that the wrath of heaven is aroused, because the obstinacy of the pagans can be seen to upset the balance of Nature?' (*Nov. Theod.*, 3; A.D. 438).

St Augustine played a major role in the reshaping of Christian thought so as to eliminate intrusive theological elements which were still contaminated by ethical and rationalist ideas of pagan origin. His long and bitter polemic against Pelagius is in itself enough to demonstrate this.[65]

In *The City of God,* he does not limit himself to dissertations against a definite doctrinal framework, but attacks paganism for its attachment to the values of this world – even if they take the noblest forms, such as love for one's country. If the paganism of the later Empire concealed lofty spiritual aspirations – at least for a restricted circle – behind the thin veil of symbolical rites and mysteries; if it included the hope of eternal life, the yearning toward monotheism, the elevated moral teachings of Orphism and Mithraism, Augustine pretends not to know about it. He does not mention Mithra at all, though this god was the most serious opponent of Christ. Augustine prefers to mock at the divinities worshipped by the lower classes, or to deplore the obscenity of certain rites which enlightened pagans, in fact, disliked as much as he did.

Augustine himself believed the old gods to be evil spirits.[66] He therefore knew very well that a sincere Christian could still think it unwise to offend the gods which had presided over the fortunes of the City for so many centuries. Some, no doubt, went to church and still believed in soothsaying and astrology; some partook of the holy sacraments and still mechanically kept up certain observances, certain superstitious traditions, which were habits of daily life. The little gods who were concerned with the success of the detailed happenings of family life – weddings, births, the weaning of the child, his first steps, his first words – must have been invoked, like domestic good fairies, by countless Christian mothers.

273

S

The vehemence of Augustine's *The City of God* betrays the fact that, quite apart from rites and observances, paganism had come to fresh life in its aspect of love for the earthly City and her ways, at the very time when the institutions and the social and economic structure on which she was based were melting away. *The City of God* therefore aims not so much at the refutation of precise accusations formulated by a robust and coherent ideological movement, as at overcoming the bewilderment of all those whose only ideal of culture and of civilised living together in a community was represented by Rome.

Augustine bravely denied the values of the past to which Roman patriotism harked back – a past which had lost its power to stimulate, its fruitful vitality. As Marrou remarks, the saint was the first man to see 'the profound decrepitude of the ancient culture.'[67] His attitude was the very opposite to that of Augustus and the writers of his time, who had created the myth of Rome. The saint was however like Augustus in having the rare intellectual gift, found only in a handful of true political geniuses, of a precise understanding of the fundamental needs of his period, an ability to see which of the forces at work were vital and enduring, and which were shallow and ephemeral.

Augustine was a mystic, who referred every human capability, on both the cognitive and the ethical planes, to divine illumination, rather than to Man's own powers. But finding himself immersed in the tumult of secular existence, he came to see that he must attempt a mediation between Christianity and life. *The City of God* does not propose a complete rejection of the City of this world, where indeed the Heavenly City begins to achieve reality, as a preliminary to its fulfilment on high. The one is, in fact, an indispensable step toward the other. There is an antithesis between the two Cities, but also an unbreakable bond of coexistence.

The concept of the Heavenly City, as St Augustine tells us in the Preface to Book XI, is derived from *Psalm* LXXXVI (RV, LXXXVII). The same vision gives rise to frequent references in his Sermons and in his commentaries on the

274

Bible. 'Glorious things of thee are spoken' . . . these words were written, in the first place, about Jerusalem, and had a nationalist, patriotic meaning for the Jews. Later, after their country had been defeated and their people scattered, the vision finally left the material plane of national revenge, and rose to the level of a metaphysical concept.

Rome was another matter. Here the sublimation of the City was a gradual process, and was not immediately regarded by those who fled from the fallen capital as their sole consolation. Cosmopolitanism had been both a theoretical doctrine and a political reality for Rome, and had helped her to rid the Empire of its outdated exclusivity, and also to direct men's minds toward acceptance of an ideal society which made the existing society irrelevant. In earlier days, the conglomerate of human beings, with its buildings laid out according to an organic plan, with its subdivision into classes, with its identity as a political, economic and religious unit, had been a concrete and tangible object, and, at the same time, the blue-print for an idea – it existed simultaneously on the material and the theoretical plane. But the coming of the Empire had transferred the fatherland to the ideal plane, and had given a universal significance to political power.

Meanwhile St Paul was freeing Christianity from the heritage of Judaism, which was deeply impregnated with the spirit of exclusivity, to make way for the universality of Christian love and the everlasting immanence of Divine charity. With the Christian apologists emerged a conception of history as a process dominated by providence and therefore having a unity of its own, a river into which the stories of the individual nations flowed as tributaries.

All these elements contributed to the work of St Augustine – Jewish, Pauline and Roman thought, and of course the ideas of the Greek masters down to Plotinus. The development of the visual arts was from naturalism towards abstraction, and there was a parallel movement towards a more abstract type of political concept, which became less and less closely linked to a specific place, temple or forum.

The walls of Rome had been extended from the perimeter of a City to a line embracing a whole Roman world. But as the ancient world reached the end of its allotted span, those walls yielded before the invaders, and became insignificant in the eyes of the citizens. Universalism on the political plane had been achieved by violence, and had taken the form of a unity brought about by duress, which was not the unity desired by the Christians (*The City of God*, XIX, vii). The ideal City is not the one which the Romans built by conquest and legislation; nor is it the supernatural City, floating in permanent immobility.

The City exists in her citizens, wandering as strangers through the world of time. Plato's idealism and the contemplative vision of the mystics are given new life by the realism of Rome. The City is a spiritual goal, to be attained in eternity, but also an ideal to be striven after day by day. She is given reality every time that just men believe in her and work for her fulfilment. But as the just go on, century by century, endeavouring to advance her creation in the world of time, their hearts are full of a melancholy awareness of the truth:

'In Heaven there is laid up a pattern of it, which he who desires may behold, and beholding, may set his soul in order in the likeness of a perfect City. But whether such a one exists, or ever will exist in fact, is no matter. For he will live after the manner of that City' (Plato, *Republic*, IX, 592 B).

NOTES TO CHAPTER

1. *Post civitatem vel Urbem sequitur orbis terrae, in quo tertium gradum ponunt societatis humanae, incipientis a domo, inde ad urbem, deinde ad orbem progrediendo.*

   Sicut Universum Regnum in tot civitatibus constitutum dicitur Romana Civitas; cumque in tot gentibus constituta Civitas sit de qua scriptum est: Gloriosissima dicta sunt de Te, Civitas Dei.

2. *Letters*, CXXVII, *P.L.*, XXII, 1094. The quotation comes from *Psalms*, LXXVIII, 1–3 – RV, LXXIX, 1–3, which is also quoted by St. Augustine, *The City of God*, I, xii.
3. *Preface to Commentary on Ezekiel*, I, *P.L.*, XXV, 15.
4. *Codex of Theodosius*, V, 7, 2; *Sirmondianae Constitutiones*, 16: Laws of 408 and 409.
5. Jordanes, *Getica*, XXX, 158.
6. *Letter to Demetriades*, XXX, *P.L.*, XXX, 45.
7. *Letters*, CXXX, *P.L.*, XXII, 1109.
8. H. I. Marrou, *L'ambivalence du temps et de l'histoire chez St. Augustin*, Paris 1950; J. Guitton, *Le temps et l'éternité chez Plotin et St. Augustin*, Paris 1933.
9. *P.L.*, XL, 715 – dated 410. (The attribution of this and certain other sermons to St. Augustine is still the subject of learned debate.)
10. *De urbis excidio*, II, 3, *P.L.*, XL, 718.
11. *Sermon*, LXXXI, *P.L.*, XXXVIII, 504.
12. *Letters*, XCVII, *P.L.*, XXXIII, 357 (November 408).
13. *Letters*, XCI, 8, *P.L.*, XXXIII, 317.
14. *Letters*, CIV, *P.L.*, XXXIII, 391.
15. Orosius, *Against the Pagans*, VII, 37.
16. *Letters*, CXXII, *P.L.*, XXXIII, 470.
17. *Letters*, CXXIV, *P.L.*, XXXIII, 473.
18. *De tempore barbarico*, III, 4, *P.L.*, XL, 702; *Sermon*, LXXXI, 9, *P.L.*, XXXVIII, 505; *De urbis excidio*, VI, 6, *P.L.*, XL, 721.
19. *De tempore barbarico*, I, 2, *P.L.*, XL, 700.
20. *Ibid.*
21. *Letters*, CXXVIII, *P.L.*, XXII, 1099 (A.D. 413).
22. D. Pesce, *Città terrena e città celeste nel pensiero antico*, Florence 1957, p. 169.
23. Horace, *Satires*, I, v, 100–4: *Credat Iudaeus Apella Non ego; namque deos didici securum agere aevum Nec, siquid miri faciat natura, deos id Tristis ex alto caeli demittere tecto.*
24. Commodian, *Carmen Apologet.*, II, iii, 997: *Vix remanent pauci, qui referant talia facta. Ibid.*, 1031: *Vastantur patriae, prosternitur Civitas omnis.*
25. *Revelations*, XXI, 11–27; Commodian, *Instructiones*, II, iii, 12–13: *Inibi non pluvia, non frigus in aurea castra. Obsidiae nullae sicut nunc, neque rapinae.*
26. *De quantitate animae*, I, 2, *P.L.*, XXXII, 1035. See also Commodian, *Instructiones*, II, iii, 33: *De caelo descendit Civitas in anastase prima.*
27. *Sermon*, CCXVI, iv, 4, *P.L.*, XXXVIII, 1078.
28. *De vera religione*, 50, *P.L.*, XXXIV, 144 (A.D. 390). See A. Lauras and H. Rondet, *Le thème des deux cités dans l'oeuvre de St. Augustin*, in *Etudes Augustiniennes*, Paris 1953, pp. 99–160.
29. *De agone christiano*, *P.L.*, XL, 299 (A.D. 396).
30. St. Augustine, *On the Book of Psalms*, CV, 34, 5, *P.L.*, XXXVII, 1417.
31. St. Augustine, *On Catechising the Unlearned*, 31, *P.L.*, XL, 333 (A.D. 399). See also *On the Book of Psalms*, LXI, *P.L.*, XXXVI, 733.

THE IDEA OF THE CITY IN ROMAN THOUGHT

32. L. Grandgeorge, *Augustin et le néoplatonisme*, Paris 1896; P. Alfaric, *L'évolution intellectuelle de St. Augustin*, Paris 1918; E. Gilson, *Introduction à l'étude de St. Augustin*, Paris 1949; H. I. Marrou, *St. Augustin et la fin de la culture antique*, Paris 1958.

33. *On the Book of Psalms*, CXXXVI, *P.L.*, XXXVII, 1763.

34. Eusebius of Caesarea, *Commentary on the Psalms*, LXXXVI, *P.G.*, XXIII, 1043. See also St. Jerome, *Letters*, CXXIX, *P.L.*, XXII, 1099.

35. St. Augustine, *On the Book of Psalms*, CXXI, 3, 4, *P.L.*, XXXVII, 1620. See also *ibid.*, LXI, *P.L.*, XXXVI, 733.

36. *Umbra et imago prophetica*. See F. H. Crantz, *De Civitate Dei*, XI, ii, in *Speculum*, 1950, pp. 215 ff.

37. St. Augustine, *On the Book of Psalms*, CXXI, *P.L.*, XXXVII, 1619.

38. *The City of God*, I, xxxv. See also *On the Book of Psalms*, CXXXVI, I, *P.L.*, XXXVII, 1761.

39. St. Augustine, *On the Book of Psalms*, LI, 4, *P.L.*, XXXVI, 602.

40. *Ibid.*, LI, 4, *P.L.*, XXXVI, 605; *ibid.*, LXI, *P.L.*, XXXVI, 733. See also *The City of God*, I, xxxv.

41. *Letters*, CXXXVI, *P.L.*, XXXIII, 514. See also A. Chastagnol, *Le sénateur Volusien et la conversion d'une famille de l'aristocratie romaine au Bas Empire*, in *Rev. Et. Anc.*, LVIII, 1956, pp. 240 ff. S. Cotta opposes the view of *The City of God* as a rejection of the City of this world, in *La città politica di S. Agostino*, Turin 1960. pp. 15–44.

42. *Letters*, CXXXVIII, *P.L.*, XXXIII, 528.

43. *Letters*, CXXIX, *P.L.*, XXII, 1099, *Ad Dardanum*. The final reference is to *Genesis*, III, 18: 'Thorns and thistles shall it bring forth unto thee.'

44. *Letters*, CLXXXIV, *P.L.*, XXXIII, 791.

45. *Retractations*, II, xlii, *P.L.*, XXXII, 647.

46. *Letters*, CXXXVIII, *P.L.*, XXXIII, 525.

47. *The City of God*, II, xxix.

48. *Ibid.*, XV, i, v, xvii.

49. *Ibid.*, IV, iii.

50. *Ibid.*, III, x; he quotes Sallust, *Catilinarian War*, V, and Vergil, *Aeneid*, VIII, 326–7.

51. *Ibid.*, III, xiv.

52. *Ibid.*, IV, iii and V, xix.

53. *On the Book of Psalms*, LI, *P.L.*, XXXVI, 605; *ibid.*, LXI, *P.L.*, XXXVI, 735. See also *The City of God*, I, xxxv.

54. *The City of God*, II, xxix.

55. *Ibid.*, XIX, xvii.

56. *Ibid.*, V, xvi.

57. *Ibid.*, VIII, x.

58. Ammianus Marcellinus, XIV, 6, 5; St. Jerome, *Letters*, CXXI, *P.L.*, XXII, 1037; Claudian, *De Consulatu Stilichonis*, III, 150–9; Prudentius, *Contra Symmachum*, I, 541–2, and *Hymn.*, II, 425–32; Rutilius Namatianus, *De Reditu*, I, 63. See also J. Perret, *Pour une étude de l'idée de Rome*, in *Rev. Et. Lat.*, X, 1932, pp. 50 ff. The persistence of the Roman tradition in Augustine himself – in his concepts and in his vocabulary –

is shown by Donald Earl, *The Moral and Political Tradition of Rome*, London 1967, Chap. VI, pp. 122 ff.

59. *The City of God*, I, xxxv.
60. See inscriptions nos. 846, 504, 512, 1780, of the years from 376 to A.D. 390 in *C.I.L.*, VI. See also A. Alföldi, *A Festival of Isis in Christian Rome*, in *Dissertationes Pannonicae*, London 1937, Series II, Vol. 7; A. Alföldi, *Die Kontorniaten*, Budapest 1943; S. Mazzarino, *La propaganda senatoriale nel tardo impero*, in *Doxa*, 1951, pp. 121 ff.; A. M. Geachy, *Aurelius Symmachus and the Senatorial Aristocracy in the West*, Chicago 1942 (and here see also N. H. Baynes, *J.R.S.*, XXXVI, 1946, pp. 173 ff.); H. Bloch, *A New Document of the Last Pagan Revival in the West*, in *Harv. Th. Rev.*, XXXVIII, 1945, pp. 199 ff.; H. Bloch, *The Pagan Revival*, in A. Momigliano's *The Conflict Between Paganism and Christianity in the Fourth Century*, Oxford 1963, Chap. VIII, pp. 193 ff.
61. Rutilius Namatianus, *De Reditu*, I, 375; Maximus of Turin, *Sermon*, CI, *P.L.*, LVII, 733.
62. St. Ambrose, *Letters*, XVIII, *P.L.*, XVI, 1013; Prudentius, *Contra Symmachum*, I, 544–7.
63. St. Augustine, *Letters*, XCVII (to Olympius), *P.L.*, XXXIII, 358 (A.D. 408): *Accelerandum suggero, peto, obsecro, flagito*.
64. *Codex of Theodosius*, XVI, 10, 15, 18. (N.B. The law XVI, 10, 25 emanates from Constantinople, in 435, and gives instructions to destroy the heathen temples.)
65. G. Plinval, *Pélage, ses écrits, sa vie et sa réforme*, Lausanne 1943.
66. M. D. Madden, *The Pagan Divinities and their Worship as Depicted in the Works of St. Augustine*, Washington 1930.
67. H. I. Marrou, *St. Augustin et la fin de la culture antique*, Paris 1958, p. 356. And see correspondence between St. Augustine and Marcellinus, referred to in Note 42 above; also A. Chastagnol, *op. cit.*

Bibliography

Abbott, F. F., and Johnson, A. C., *Municipal Administration in the Roman Empire*, Princeton, 1926.
Baldry, H. C., *The Unity of Mankind in Greek Thought*, Cambridge, 1965.
Barker, E., *From Alexander to Constantine*, Oxford, 1956.
Bowersock, G. W., *Augustus and the Greek World*, Oxford, 1965.
Carcopino, J., *Les étapes de l'impérialisme romain*, Paris, 1961.
Cavallera, F., *St. Jerome*, Louvain, 1922.
Christ, F., *Die Römische Weltherrschaft in der Antiken Dichtung*, Stuttgart, 1938.
Cochrane, C. N., *Christianity and Classical Culture*, Oxford, 1940.
Courcelle, P., *Histoire littéraire des grandes invasions germaniques*, Paris, 1964.
Cumont, F., *Les religions orientales dans le paganisme romain*, Paris, 1929.
Demougeot, E., *De l'unité à la division de l'empire romain (395–410)*, Paris, 1951.
Dudden, H., *The Life and Times of St. Ambrose*, Oxford, 1935.
Earl, Donald, *The Moral and Political Tradition of Rome*, London, 1967.
Francisci, P. De, *Primordia civitatis*, Rome, 1959.
Gilson, E., *Introduction à l'étude de St. Augustin*, Paris, 1949.
Grimal, P., *Le siècle d'Auguste*, Paris, 1961.
Grimal, P., *Le siècle des Scipions*, Paris, 1953.
Guitton, J., *Le temps et l'éternité chez Plotin et St. Augustin*, Paris, 1933.
Hammond, M., *City-state and World-state in Greek and Roman Political Theory until Augustus*, Princeton, 1951.
Jaeger, W., *Early Christianity and Greek Paideia*, Cambridge, Mass., 1965.
Johnson, A. C., *see under* Abbott, F. F.
Jones, A. H. M., *The Decline of the Ancient World*, London, 1966.
Labriolle, P., *Histoire de la littérature latine chrétienne*, Paris, 1947.
Lot, F., *La fin du monde antique et les débuts du moyen âge*, Paris, 1951.
Macmullen, R., *Enemies of Roman Order*, London, 1966.
Marrou, H. I., *L'ambivalence du temps et de l'histoire chez St. Augustin*, Paris, 1950.
Marrou, H. I., *St. Augustin et la fin de la culture antique*, Paris, 1958.
Mazzarino, S., *Aspetti sociali del IV secolo*, Rome, 1951.
Mazzarino, S., *La fine del mondo antico*, Milan, 1959.
Mazzarino, S., *Il pensiero storico classico*, Bari, 1966.
Mazzarino, S., *Stilicone e la crisi imperiale dopo Teodosio*, Rome, 1942.
Mohrmann, C., *Le latin des chrétiens*, Rome, 1958.
Momigliano, A., (ed.), *The Conflict Between Paganism and Christianity in the Fourth Century*, Oxford, 1963.

281

BIBLIOGRAPHY

Mumford, L., *The City in History*, New York, 1961.
Oost, S. I., *Galla Placidia Augusta*, Chicago, 1968.
Palanque, J. P., *St. Ambroise et l'empire romain*, Paris, 1933.
Paratore, E., *Storia della letteratura latina*, Florence, 1957.
Pettazzoni, R., *La religione della Grecia antica*, Turin, 1954.
Piganiol, A., *L'empire chrétien*, Paris, 1947.
Rostovtzeff, M., *Social and Economic History of the Roman Empire*, Oxford, 1926.
Sherwin White, A. N., *The Roman Citizenship*, Oxford, 1939.
Sinclair, T. A., *A History of Greek Political Thought*, London, 1951.
Sirago, V. A., *Galla Placidia e la trasformazione politica dell'occidente*, Louvain, 1961.
Solari, A., *La crisi dell'impero romano*, Genoa, 1933.
Stevenson, G., *Roman Provincial Administration*, Oxford, 1949.
Syme, R., *Roman Revolution*, Oxford, 1956.
Tarn, W. W., *Alexander the Great and the Unity of Mankind*, London, 1933.
Toutain, J. F., *Les cultes paiens dans l'empire romain*, Paris, 1907.
Treves, P., *Il mito d'Alessandro e la Roma d'Augusto*, Milan, 1953.
Vogt, J., *Il declino di Roma*, A.D. 200–500, Milan, 1965.

Index

Absorption policy, 68
Academics, 264
Aelius Aristides, 185, 187, 189, 191, 195
Aeschylus, 17, 54
Aesculapius, 71
Aggression, Roman, 29, 30, 31, 32, 50, 106, 135
Agrippa, 193
Agrippa, King, 218
Agrippa II, King, 224
Alans, 234, 238
Alaric, 243–5, 249
Alemanni, 204, 214, 238
Alexander the Great, 12, 19, 23, 55, 82–98, 105, 110, 111, 135, 136, 143, 147, 148, 156, 162, 165, 169, 178, 186, 189, 192, 260
Alexander Helios, 149
Alexander Severus, 203
Ambrose, St., 195, 198, 233, 234, 251, 271
Ammianus Marcellinus, 26, 195, 206, 207
Ancus Marcius, 28, 43, 45, 107
Ancyran inscription, the, 128, 129, 130, 166
Annexation, 22, 52, 106
Antigonus, King of Judaea, 165
Antiochus of Bithynia, 50
Antiphon, 53
Antoninus Pius, 88, 185, 187, 191
Antony, Mark, 90, 95, 102, 106, 125, 127–30, 134, 138, 139, 147–51, 156–62, 165, 166, 169, 179, 225
Apollo, 71, 150, 151, 152

Appian, 25, 40, 91, 100
    Civil War, 91, 100
Appius Claudius, 34–5
Apuleius, 68, 75
Arcadius, 150
Archias, 42
Arians, 212, 264
Ariovistus, 30, 111, 114
Aristonicus, 56
Aristotle, 83
Armenians, 178
Arminius, 143, 184
Arnobius, 231, 233
Arrian, 83, 84, 94, 189
    Expedition of Alexander, 84, 94
Asceticism, 26
Assimilation, racial, 21, 22, 23, 34, 38, 42, 43
Atargatis, 74
Ateius, the tribune, 32
Athene, 148
Athenians, 37, 53, 55, 96, 148, 149
Athenodorus, 104
Attalus, 244
Attilius Regulus, 198, 254
Atys, 74
Augustine, St., 15, 16, 78, 213, 233–8, 242–79
    The City of God, 15, 233, 242–79
Augustus, 12, 13, 21, 22, 40, 46, 50, 69, 92, 93, 99, 100, 103, 126, 128–39, 142–7, 154, 160, 161, 166–8, 174, 176, 177, 179, 188, 190, 193, 194, 219, 266, 269, 274, and see Octavian
Aurelian, 204, 231

Babylonian astrologers, 153
Barbarians, 14, 17, 18, 25, 30, 44,
  53, 76, 88, 96, 109, 112, 113,
  128, 130, 135, 151, 152, 154,
  167, 176, 177, 183, 195, 196,
  203, 207, 214, 234, 235
Barnabas, Epistle of, 227, 228
Batavians, 184, 223
Berenice, 225
Blossius, 56
Brennus, 109, 144
British, 117, 168, 178, 184, 235
Brotherhood, human, 17, 19, 20, 23,
  55, 71, 88, 155
Brutus, 128

Caesar, Julius, 13, 30, 31, 39–43,
  63–6, 87, 90–5, 100–22, 125–9,
  132–4, 137, 138, 147, 149, 152,
  157, 159, 162–6, 175, 177, 178,
  219
  African War, 65
  Commentaries, 113, 147
  Gallic War, 30, 111, 113, 114
Caesarion, 149
Caius Piso, 169
Caligula, 79, 95, 157, 160, 169, 188
Camillus, 73, 108, 111, 136, 146,
  152, 160, 176, 198
Canuleius, 37, 38, 45, 46
Caracalla, 93, 192, 193
Caractacus, 184
Carneades, 145, 260
Carthage, 28, 31, 37, 49, 52, 56, 120
Cassius, 165
Catiline, 40
Cato the Censor, 31, 40, 56, 59, 68,
  69, 72, 90, 111, 132, 134, 144,
  145, 254
Cato of Utica, 90, 103, 132
Ceres, 76, 108
Christ, 198, 227, 230, 246, 254, 259,
  265, 267, 273
Christianity, Christians, 14, 15, 46,
  72, 167, 176, 189, 191, 196–8,
  205, 211, 219, 222–41, 242–79
Chrysippus, 55

Cicero, 29, 32, 36, 37, 40–3, 62–6,
  69, 75, 76, 85, 87, 91, 99–105,
  115, 116, 119–22, 127–33, 138,
  139, 164, 184, 186, 227, 252
  Catilinarian Orations, 64, 101
  De Legibus, 62
  De Natura Deorum, 69
  De Officiis, 29, 64, 85, 102, 103
  De Provinciis Consularibus, 164
  De Republica, 62, 63, 66, 85, 102,
    122, 128, 130, 252
  Letters to Atticus, 41, 65–6, 87, 102
  Letters to Friends, 105, 120
  Philippics, 120, 127, 128, 129
  Pro Archia, 42, 64
  Pro Balbo, 43, 119
  Pro Flacco, 76
  Pro Fonteio, 42
  Pro Lege Manilia, 65, 91
  Pro Marcello, 121
  Pro Milone, 64
  Pro Roscio Amerino, 64, 99
  Verrine Orations, 41, 101
Cimbrians, 31, 39, 42, 109, 113, 238
Cincinnatus, 90
Cinna, 39
Circumcellians, 213
Classes, 23, 29, 34, 38, 57, 58, 66,
  72, 102, 105, 111, 126, 132,
  218, 273
Claudian, 198
Claudius, 44–6, 85, 192
Cleomenes, 56
Cleopatra, 94, 95, 106, 147–59, 162,
  219
Clodius Albinus, 203
Commodian, 230, 231, 255
Commodus, 202
Conservatism, Roman, 25–33, 76,
  95, 100, 101, 113, 143
Constantine, 149, 197, 205, 212,
  262, 271
Cosmopolis, 23, 55, 84, 92, 129, 189,
  275
Crassus, 32, 70, 87, 106, 139, 163–6,
  222
Crates of Thebes, 49, 53

Curtius Rufus, 85, 86
Cybele, 73, 84, 119
Cynics, 17, 84
Cyprian, 205, 230, 233
Cyrus, 55

Dacians, 184
Daniel, prophet, 219, 232
Decius, 136, 204, 231
Democritus, 53
Demosthenes, 88–9
Dictatorship, 13, 40, 42, 45, 64, 99, 111, 115
Dio Cassius, 30, 44, 114, 119, 157, 158, 192, 193, 222
Diocletian, 194, 196, 204
Diogenes Laertius, 54
Dion of Prusa, 185, 186, 188
Dionysius of Halicarnassus, 70, 75, 143
Dionysus, 72, 89, 104, 148, 150, 156, 178, 179
Domitian, 183, 188
Donatists, 213, 249, 264
Druids, 223
Drusus, 46, 64

Ecumenism, 20, 22, 23, 49–61, 103, 119
Egyptians, 76, 82, 87, 106, 142, 151, 178
Epictetus, 83, 185, 229
Epicureans, 31, 58, 253
Eratosthenes, 83
Eugenius, 270
Euripides, 17, 18, 165
Eusebius, 197
Exclusivity, Roman, 21, 38, 41, 42, 89, 96
Expansionism, Roman, 25, 27, 32, 50, 58, 59, 109, 116, 118, 130, 178

Fabius Maximus, 35
Fabricius, 90, 144, 146
Florus, 105
Fonteius, 41

Galerius, 194
Gauls, 40, 44–6, 65, 111–19, 151, 152, 198, 243
Germans, 30, 31, 46, 65, 113, 114, 117, 118, 167, 184, 193
Glabrio, Acilius, 50
Goths, 15, 195, 204, 214, 234, 244, 265
Gracchi, the, 56, 57, 58, 109, 112, 128, 132
Gratian, 215, 271
Greeks, 16–21, 23, 32, 36, 40, 42, 49–60, 62–3, 70, 77, 79, 82–98, 102, 103, 130, 132, 142–52, 167, 175, 187, 191, 227, 260, 270

Hadrian, 64, 83, 184, 185, 191, 220
Hannibal, 90, 109, 198
Helvetii, 30, 111, 113
Heraclian, 244
Heraclitus, 11, 52
Hercules, 86, 89, 111, 148, 175, 186, 196
Hippias, 53
Honorius, 150, 235, 244, 271
Horace, 76, 106, 134, 154, 157, 159, 161, 162, 168, 174, 177, 178, 253
Huns, 234, 238

Imperialism, 22, 31, 32, 50, 56, 57, 118, 121, 128, 167, 173, 178, 189, 190
Isis, 74, 75, 76, 153, 156
Isocrates, 18, 88, 167
Isolationism, 22, 66, 89
Italians, 35, 36, 39, 101, 133, 184, 245

Janus, 13, 130, 177
Jerome, St., 226, 233, 234, 235, 237, 242, 243, 245, 251, 261, 262
Jewry, 14, 36, 76, 77–9, 106, 134, 142, 152, 153, 163–6, 183, 191, 197, 218–32, 253, 257, 275
Jordanes, 244

Josephus, 224
Judas Maccabeus, 232
Jugurtha, 108
Julian the Apostate, 184, 206, 208, 213, 270
Julius Florus, 44, 46
Julius Sacrovir, 44, 46
Julius Vindex, 184
Juno, 28, 73, 76, 161, 177
Jupiter, 28, 35, 72, 87, 99, 151, 158, 174, 177, 186
Juvenal, 225

Labienus, 134, 165, 166
Lactantius, 78, 205, 231, 232, 233
Lepidus, Aemilius, 162
Livius Drusus, 35
Livy, 11, 25, 26, 28, 29, 32, 34–9, 43–6, 49, 50, 69, 73, 90, 136, 143, 144, 146, 155, 160–1, 173, 174, 176
Lucan, 64, 65, 86, 100, 138, 164, 169
Lucius Balbus, 42–3
Lucretius, 31, 108
Lucullus, 63
Lycurgus, 55

Macedonians, 81, 84, 85, 89, 91, 111, 120, 232
Macrobius, 73
Maecenas, 193
Magna Mater, 73
Mamertinus, 206
Manichaeanism, 256, 264
Manilius, 122
Marcus Aurelius, 88, 182, 187, 189, 191, 201, 229
Marcus Manlius, 112, 152
Marius, 31, 39, 41, 42, 65, 87, 107, 108, 109, 111, 114, 115, 145, 183
Maximian, emperor, 203
Maximian, panegyrist, 202
Metellus, 89
Minucius Felix, 189
Mithras, 75, 153, 273

Mithridates, 27, 39, 104, 105, 119, 155, 163, 219, 220, 232
Monarchy, 17, 19, 40, 45, 105, 106, 128, 137, 162, 182, 183, 189, 190

Nationalists, 46, 77, 84, 126
Nectarius, 236–7, 249
Neo-Platonism, 256, 270
Neo-Pythagoreanism, 79, 154
Nero, 95, 157, 160, 169, 220, 222, 223
Nerva, 191
Nicomedes, 104
Numa, 38, 45, 69, 93

Octavia, 148
Octavian, 102, 120, 125–31, 134, 136, 138, 147–52, 156–62, 166–9, 176, 178, 179, and see Augustus
Olympius, 249, 271
Orosius, 78, 233, 243, 249
Orphism, 273
Ovid, 70, 99, 121, 122, 125, 162, 168, 173, 174, 175
  Fasti, 70, 99, 121, 122, 173, 175
  Metamorphoses, 125, 175

Pacorus, 165
Paganism, 70, 246–74
Pan-Hellenism, 83
Parthians, 32, 105, 106, 134–9, 148, 151, 154, 163–9, 173, 178
Patricians, 23, 27, 38, 39, 40, 46, 66, 101, 108, 114, 270
Patriotism, 114, 115, 133, 160, 165, 218, 237, 274
Paul, St., 226, 227, 246, 275
Paulinus of Nola, St., 237, 265
Paulus Aemilius, 56
Pelagius, 245, 264, 273
Persians, 13, 18, 54, 82, 84, 142, 151, 153, 164, 168, 232
Philip of Macedon, 19, 88, 167, 186
Philip, emperor, 203, 204

Philo of Alexandria, 36, 37, 77–9, 86, 197, 221–2, 226, 253
Phraates, 166, 167
Plato, 15, 17, 18, 19, 54, 79, 137, 189, 197, 226, 252, 255, 276
The Republic, 19, 252, 276
Plautus, 59
Plebeians, 34–5, 45, 66, 76, 92, 109, 154
Pliny the Elder, 62, 77, 145
Pliny the Younger, 185, 187, 188, 195
Plotinus, 229, 234, 255, 268, 275
Plutarch, 16, 39, 40, 43, 55, 64, 70, 73, 82, 83, 88, 100, 109, 110, 112, 119, 144, 145, 148, 164, 165, 179, 185, 189
Alexander, 88
Antony, 148, 165, 179
Caesar, 110
Camillus, 73, 112
Cato, 40, 145
Crassus, 70, 165
De Exilio, 185
Marius, 39, 109
On the Fortune of Alexander, 16, 55, 82, 83
Pompey, 64, 119
Pyrrhus, 144
Romulus, 43
Sulla, 100, 164
Plutarch of Chaeronea, 185
Polybius, 20, 56, 57, 63, 70, 119
Pompeius Trogus, 32, 85, 105, 161, 232, 260
Pompey, 42, 63, 64, 65, 76, 87, 100–6, 117, 118, 120, 126, 128, 138, 139, 157, 163, 164, 178, 222
Pontifex Maximus, 110, 112, 121, 162
Poseidonius, 20, 104, 121
Posthumus, 204
Priesthood, 30, 34, 35, 46, 66, 69, 70, 94, 110, 112, 121, 162
Propertius, 26, 159, 162, 164, 166, 177

Provinces, 45, 46, 51, 58, 65, 87, 101, 103, 195
Prudentius, 198, 271
Ptolemy XI, 106
Ptolemy, son of Antony and Cleopatra, 149
Pyrrhus, 146
Pythagoreans, 155, 187

Quirinus, 28, 158, 176, 177

Race issue, the, 14, 21, 22, 23, 34–48, 57, 59, 66, 102, 192
Radagaisus, 213, 249
Romulus, 22, 43, 45, 69, 75, 93, 108, 121, 176, 177, 259, 266

Sabines, 38, 43, 45, 46
Sallust, 26, 27, 31, 39, 40, 41, 105, 120, 147, 186, 268
Catilinarian War, 31, 41, 268
Jugurthine War, 120
Letter of Mithridates, 27, 105
Letters, 39, 40
Oratio Lepidi, 120
Salvianus of Marseilles, 211, 213
Sarmatians, 234, 238
Saxons, 238
Sceptics, 253
Scipio Aemilianus, 56
Scipio Africanus, 57, 58, 63, 73, 90, 103, 112, 132, 178, 198
Scipio Nasica, 128
Scythians, 85, 178
Seneca, 16, 31, 36, 37, 86, 169, 227
Septimius Severus, 196, 202, 203
Servius Tullius, 38, 44
Sextus Pompeius, 138
Shepherd of Hermas, The, 228, 234
Sibylline Oracles, the, 77, 153, 218, 220, 232
Silius Italicus, 90
Slavery, 12, 17, 18, 34, 52, 56, 72, 197, 210
Socrates, 17, 53
Sophists, 17, 18, 53, 84, 187
Sophocles, 18

Sosigenes, 121
Sosius, 165
Spartans, 52, 55, 56, 57
Sphaerus, 56
Spurius Carvilius, 35
Statius, 83
Stilicho, 198, 213, 249, 271, 272
Stoics, 17, 31, 55, 56, 62, 83, 85, 102, 131, 134, 137, 153, 154, 156, 191, 229, 253
Suetonius, 40, 94, 107, 121, 136, 151, 155, 159, 160, 166, 223, 225
  Augustus, 136, 151, 155
  Galba, 223
  Julius Caesar, 40, 94, 107, 159
  Tiberius, 166
  Titus, 160, 225
Sulla, 40, 63, 64, 87, 92, 99, 100, 107, 108, 119, 120, 126, 132, 164, 175
Sulpicius, 39
Surena, 164
Symmachus, 197, 210, 214, 251, 271

Tacitus, 11, 26, 44, 45, 143, 183, 184, 222, 223, 224
  Annals, 11, 44, 183, 222, 223
  Histories, 222, 223, 224
Tarquin, King, 38, 45, 128, 159
Tertullian, 78, 229
Teutons, 31, 39, 42, 109, 113
Thales, 268
Themistius, 207
Theodosius, 192, 198, 206, 207, 212, 244, 258, 262, 271, 272
  Codex, 70, 209, 210, 212, 271, 272, 273
Theophanes, 104
Thucydides, 16
Tiberius, 44, 46, 145, 155, 166, 168
Tigranes, 119

Titus, 183, 220, 224, 225
Titus Manlius Torquatus, 146
Trajan, 13, 26, 184, 185, 187, 188, 191
Trojans, the, 72, 107, 108, 134, 151, 158, 161, 162, 174, 175, 269
Twelve Tables, The, 16, 26, 29, 72

Unity of human race, universalism, 12, 21, 36, 54, 55, 59, 62, 63, 78, 79, 93, 97, 104, 169, 179, 189
Utopian ideas, 11, 13, 21, 51, 59, 63, 159, 173, 182, 186, 190, 268

Valentinian I, 209, 211, 214, 215
Valentinian II, 198
Valerian, 204
Vandals, 238
Velleius Paterculus, 44, 109, 117
Ventidius, 148
Venus, 31, 107, 108, 110, 127, 174
Vercingetorix, 44
Vergil, 122, 134, 146, 154, 155, 161, 162, 175, 178
  Aeneid, 134, 146, 174, 175
  Eclogues, 122, 154
  Georgics, 133, 178
Verres, 41
Vespasian, 222, 223, 224
Vesta, 72, 119, 136, 174
Visigoths, 14, 213, 244

World state, 37, 50, 53, 54, 55, 63, 173, 185

Xenophon, 17, 55

Zeno, 55, 83
Zosimus, 201, 206, 235